abbe

(Mathieu) Orsini, Patrick Power

Life of the Blessed Virgin Mary, Mother of God

abbe

(Mathieu) Orsini, Patrick Power

Life of the Blessed Virgin Mary, Mother of God

ISBN/EAN: 9783742862495

Manufactured in Europe, USA, Canada, Australia, Japa

Cover: Foto ©Lupo / pixelio.de

Manufactured and distributed by brebook publishing software (www.brebook.com)

abbe

(Mathieu) Orsini, Patrick Power

Life of the Blessed Virgin Mary, Mother of God

THE PRESENTATION IN THE TEMPLE.

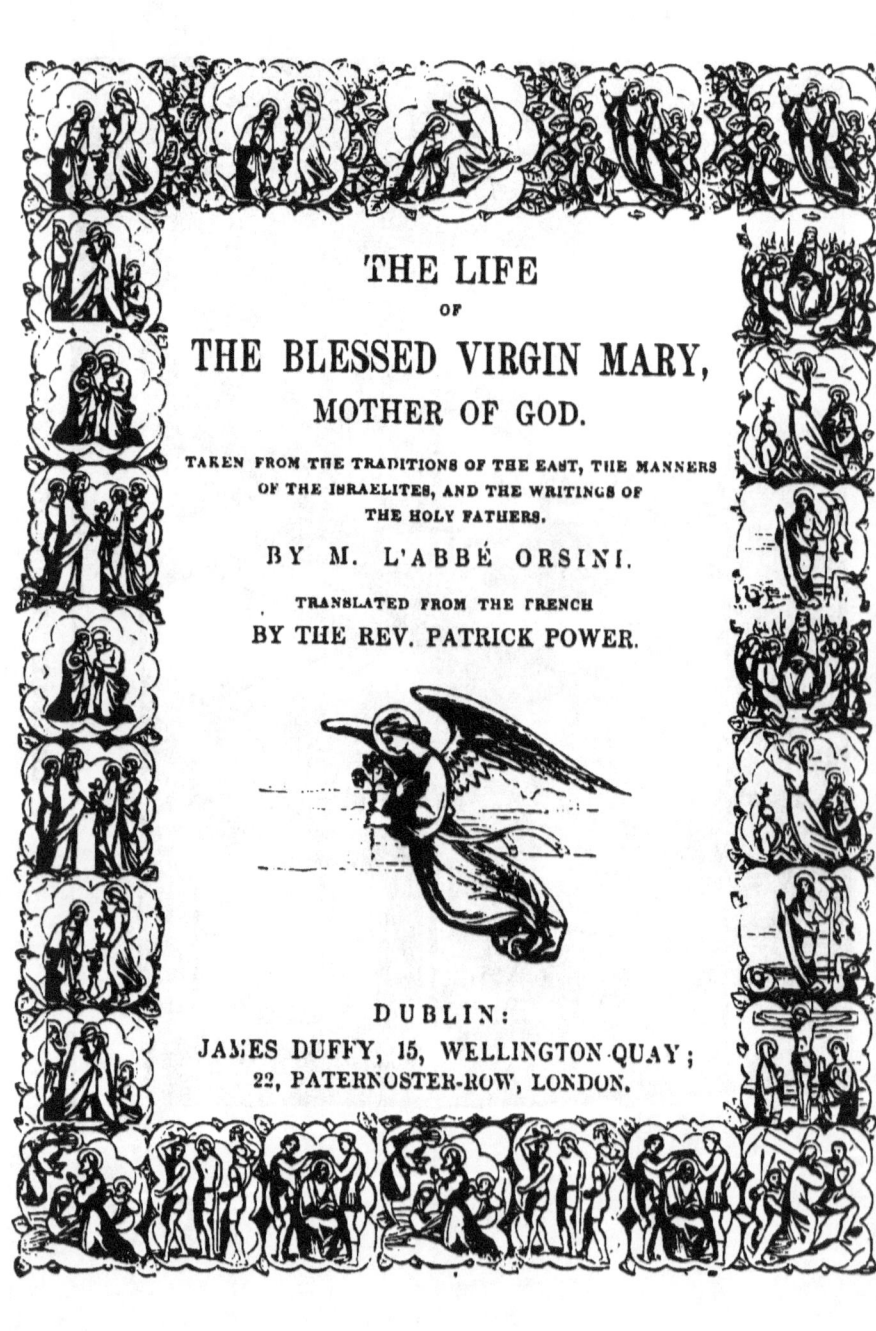

THE LIFE
OF
THE BLESSED VIRGIN MARY,
MOTHER OF GOD.

TAKEN FROM THE TRADITIONS OF THE EAST, THE MANNERS
OF THE ISRAELITES, AND THE WRITINGS OF
THE HOLY FATHERS.

BY M. L'ABBÉ ORSINI.

TRANSLATED FROM THE FRENCH
BY THE REV. PATRICK POWER.

DUBLIN:
JAMES DUFFY, 15, WELLINGTON QUAY;
22, PATERNOSTER-ROW, LONDON.

THE AUTHOR'S PREFACE.

This book, received with such favour and indulgence by the public, is not written through any vain desire of obtaining celebrity; it is a work of patience and of faith, a flower placed on the altar of Mary, with the simple heart of a pilgrim of the good old times. A better historian the Virgin undoubtedly deserved; but one more sincerely desirous to see her name glorified and her devotion extended she could not find.

The history of the Queen of Angels, the mystical rose of the New Law, is a theme so poetical in itself, that it naturally calls forth the most beautiful and refined ideas, as well as the most dignified expressions of language. It is an Oriental recital, reflecting the manners, the glories, and the sites of Asia; and so can it appear strange that the style should be impressed with an Eastern tint?

We have studied the Fathers sufficiently well, to know that they have not undervalued the graces of diction; and that a beautiful style in writing and speaking placed them on equal terms with the pagans, when entering the lists with them. This is what the great St. Jerome calls, in his figurative style, *to cut off the head of Goliah with his own sword*. What can be more sublime and more poetical than certain descriptions of St. John Chrysostom? That sacred orator often held converse with the Oriental poets; and in one of his homilies it is, that we meet with the simile of *the earth embalmed with the perfume of roses*, a simile made use of in later times by Saadi, in his Gulistan. In order to convert the people, we must, above all things, endeavour to gain their attention; to confirm in Catholic belief the masses long agitated by the successive throes of revolutions, tossed about by the whirlwinds of systems, rendered indifferent through lassitude, and open to the virulent attacks of an emboldened sect, which now raises its head higher than ever, for—

Deja de sa faveur on adore le bruit,

we must begin by giving them a taste for reading. The preacher who strips the word of God of all the chaste ornaments of true eloquence, will soon render our churches unfrequented, and will have reason to say, like a certain Greek musician, while standing alone in a public place, "ye temples, listen to my strains!" The writer on religious subjects, who, in a country priding itself on its literary taste and information, makes use of a heavy and prosy style of diction, will fare no better; he himself will sink into utter oblivion, and his book, though it were as intrinsically valuable as gold and precious gems, will become the most useless thing in the world, for no person will open it. St. Basil had been so impressed with this truth, that he strongly inculcated on the minds of the young orators of his day the necessity of close application to the study of polite literature, that they might be able to transcribe its beauties into Catholic works. "Polite literature," says the illustrious doctor, "serves as foliage to cover and ornament the words of wisdom and truth. Moses and Daniel were the two most brilliant stars of the synagogue, for they were well versed in all the arts and sciences of the Egyptians." St. Jerome, rebutting the ante-literary attacks of Rufinus, who accused him of *mingling the ordure of paganism with the word of God*, cooly answered, *that being blind as a mole he*

PREFACE.

ought not ridicule those who had the eyes of a goat. And how comes it, that when the most sumptuous decoration of altars and tabernacles has been always considered, and that even in the best disciplined ages of the church, a good and laudable practice, a practice highly calculated to elevate the majesty of Christian worship, religious literature should be converted into a dreary and dismal waste, on which no one would dare enter, lest he should perish with *ennui* on the way? Is it in this style that the Holy Scriptures, which St. John Chrysostom declared to be full of *pearls and diamonds*, have been written? Is it not every style of composition, from the pastoral to the epic, found in the Bible? The saints of ages long past, ages which we are pleased to call *dark*, had no idea of stripping their religious works of all their literary value. "Why is it," says an illustrious writer of the ninth century, "that we treasure up the relics of the saints, in gold and jewels, and allow their glorious deeds to be clothed only in rude and barbarous forms of expression? Impure tales must be narrated with all the graces of diction, and immortal actions must, indeed, be told in a flat, insipid style! Is beauty of language, and is grace of diction to subserve no other purpose than that of setting off the turpitude of crime and folly? "It would be well," said a pious and learned writer, when dedicating, in the year 1722, the life of a certain holy man to the Bishop of Blois, "could Catholics take such pains in ornamenting the immortal actions of the saints, as sinners do in ornamenting their guilty passions; and could they make it appear that they can ornament virtue better than those profane writers can adorn vice."

Writing for persons engaged in worldly business, as well as for persons devoted to the practices of piety, we have endeavoured to reduce to practice the advice and counsel of those writers whom we considered the most judicious.

Happy, indeed, is the author who falls into the hands of men capable of appreciating a book, and of reviewing it free from all undue influence, and in that spirit of justice which accords well with the mastery of mind, for criticism is a sort of profession in which many engage, but with which few are acquainted; to form a just critic, one must possess a good store of information, have a well regulated taste, and above all, must be characterized for a judicious and just mind; and these are qualities which every one cannot boast of. To M de Chantal, who seizes at once on the whole scope of the author's mind, and in developing it, adorns it; to M. Douhaire, whose high character for just criticism has been appreciated in France, in Italy, and elsewhere; to M. Poujoulat, of European reputation; to M. Bonnetti, whose *Annals* are, perhaps, the best collection we have of Catholic philosophy; to M. Amédée de Quesnel, whose graceful pen cheers on every one who aims at refining and sanctifying manners; in a word, to all the literary men of Paris, of the provinces, and of foreign countries, to whom we cannot individually return thanks, we here sincerely offer them expressions of our sincere gratitude. Their very flattering expressions in our favour have not, however, been unmixed with censure; but thanks to them for both one and the other. To pass censure on a work, in order that its real faults should be corrected, and not for the purpose of satisfying private spleen, is often productive of good and always entitled to respect.

An editor with whom we have the pleasure of being acquainted, has spoken of us in these terms:—" M. l'Abbe Orsini is one of those writers of our time, who best knows its wants, and who has best learned its language; he speaks like a true disciple of M. de Chateaubriand." To compare us with so great a man is, indeed, no slight honour; but God forbid that we should have the presumption of deeming ourselves worthy of it! and if, perchance, our style bears any similiarity, however

PREFACE. vii

slight, to that of the illustrious viscount, we have only to say, as an humble poet of Kurdistan said, under similar circumstances:

"I have sprung, as well as Antar, the celebrated poet, from the garden of Nischabur; but Antar was a flower of that garden, and I am only a bramble of it."

One remark in particular has been made respecting this work, and we think it only right to say a few words in answer to it. The use which we have made of the manners of the Hebrews in throwing light on the life of the Blessed Virgin has not been fully approved of.

There is no one who has visited the East, or who has been conversant with the history and manners of Asia, but will at once see that our labour is based on long and careful research, and that the *imagination is not entirely groundless;* we have not, of ourselves, even invented the customary forms of *adieu,* and the *wishes of a safe journey;* everything has been taken from trustworthy sources, which we have minutely examined, whenever the matter was worth the labour. Our work, moreover, has been read by learned Orientalists, and they have pronounced it *faithfully erudite.* In these times, the historian, as well as the painter, must closely apply himself to the study of local colouring. Once an artist attempts to introduce our Western costumes, and our Northern sites, into a subject taken from the records of ancient Asia, he must be prepared to meet, at the hands of competent judges, ridicule and censure; a literary writer cannot expect to be treated differently; for a work on literature, like a painting, should assume the tint of the sky, the configuration of the sun, the costumes of the country, the customs and manners of the characters, which are described in its pages. In tracing the history of the daughter of the kings of Juda, we have yielded to the exigencies of our theme, and thought it well to avoid confounding the manners of the East with the manners prevailing among us; we have described them, such as they were at the time in which Mary lived. And no other resource was left us to adhere to truth, and to fill up the many gaps of a history, which, in many respects, must resemble the private life of the Israelites at the time of Herod. On reading over the Gospel attentively, we find, almost in every page, allusion made to the national manners and customs—customs and manners to which Christ himself deigned to conform. That the Virgin faithfully followed the example of her Divine Son no one can question. The manners of the Israelites were founded on Scripture and tradition, and this it was that endowed them with a sacred character in the eyes of the entire nation; to depart from long received and established usages, would have been considered no slight transgression. Even the dress worn by the young brides on the occasion of their marriage might be traced to some biblical fact, and to some old tradition of the synagogue.

Besides the flattering testimony of the Press, we have received private letters of approval and sympathy, which, like the gifts of Providence, have descended on us from on high. Prince Orsini, who has been pleased to accept of the Dedication of our work, true Roman prince and patron of literature as he is, has honoured us with a letter of approval, after having read the history of the Blessed Virgin. Here is an extract from it:

"A work so remarkable and so sacred as yours is, indeed, worthy of a more distinguished patron than I can be; I feel sincerely grateful to you, and any words of mine cannot adequately express how deeply I feel the compliment which your goodness and kindness have induced you to pay me. Rome applauds your work, and the glory which you have endeavoured to procure for the Mother of God is already reflected back on yourself." * * *

PREFACE.

"Your work has tended, and will undoubtedly tend yet, to spread through France the affecting devotion of Mary, which St. Bernard formerly propagated with such renown. I feel convinced, that wherever the Church counts her children, 'The Life of the Mother of God' will produce the same good effects; let my name be taken as a guarantee."

That is a guarantee, the value of which we cannot fully appreciate. What better guarantee of success could we indeed have, than that offered us by a man so illustrious and distinguished—a man, whom all the academies of the Italian peninsula are anxious to receive within their walls; whose great merits the Court of Rome renognises and appreciates; whom Brazil implicitly entrusts with her dearest interests; and who fears not, in this age of unbelief, to assume that religious and chivalrous motto: SPES IN DEO! Honour to the land represented by men of such magnanimity of soul and firmness of faith! Honour to diplomatists, who make their country respected, by giving an example of every public and private virtue!

Our Life of the Blessed Virgin has found favour not only in the eyes of the great personages of the land, but also in the eyes of the bishops of the Church. Many instances of honourable approval we could cite, but we shall confine ourselves to that of one more nearly connected than others with us—that of our own bishop, one of the most zealous and illustrious bishops of France. Like the good religious of the olden times, who enchased pearls in the ivory clasps of their missals, we shall take the liberty of inserting, in our humble pages, an extract from the beautiful letter of Monseigneur Casanelli d'Istria. If this book be destined to maintain its position for any time, literary men of future times will be able to learn from these different extracts, that at a time when religious literature received no support in France, there had been Roman princes, ambassadors of foreign countries, and illustrious bishops, who afforded it protection. The following is the extract from the letter of the Bishop of Ajaccio, an extract a hundred times more valuable than the poor work which it ornaments:—

"I should have thanked you before now, for the nice present of your estimable work so kindly forwarded me, and for the pleasure afforded me, by the perusal of a life, to me doubly interesting, both from the nature of the subject, and from the beautiful diction in which you have clothed it. I appreciate this present the more, as it has been made by the Author, and that Author once my fellow-countryman, and one of my priests. I have not been the only person who has appreciated the merits of your book. The approval of all those to whom I have lent it is in accordance with the well-merited praise bestowed on it by the Parisian Press.

"It has afforded me no little satisfaction to see, that the first fruits of your literary labours have been consecrated to the Queen of Angels. Such a beginning cannot but presage the most glorious success in the career on which you have entered."

This work is again offered to the public, accompanied with a sincere desire that it may be productive of good; defects it may have, but what human work is exempt from them? Perfection is that talismanic mountain, the summit of which it has not been given to mortals to reach, and least of all to ourselves.

ORSINI.

CONTENTS.

CHAPTER I.
The Universal Expectation of the Virgin and the Messiah, - Page 1

CHAPTER II.
The Immaculate Conception, - - - - - - - - 28

CHAPTER III.
The Birth of Mary, - - - - - - - - - 44

CHAPTER IV.
The Presentation, - - - - - - - - - - 50

CHAPTER V.
Mary at the Temple, - - - - - - - - - 59

CHAPTER VI.
Mary an Orphan, - - - - - - - - - - 77

CHAPTER VII.
The Marriage of the Virgin, - - - - - - - - 88

CHAPTER VIII.
The Annunciation, - - - - - - - - - 107

CHAPTER IX.
The Visitation, - - - - - - - - - - 118

CONTENTS.

CHAPTER X.
The Virgin Mother, - - - - - - - - - 130

CHAPTER XI.
Mary at Bethlehem, - - - - - - - - - 139

CHAPTER XII.
The Purification, - - - - - - - - - - 165

CHAPTER XIII.
The Flight into Egypt, - - - - - - - - 172

CHAPTER XIV.
The Return from Egypt, - - - - - - - - 184

CHAPTER XV.
Mary at the Preaching of Jesus, - - - - - - 196

CHAPTER XVI.
Mary on Calvary, - - - - - - - - - 214

CHAPTER XVII.
The Death of Mary, - - - - - - - - 232

THE LIFE
OF
THE BLESSED VIRGIN.

CHAPTER I.

THE UNIVERSAL EXPECTATION OF THE VIRGIN AND THE MESSIAH.

IN those olden times which bordered on the infancy of the world, when our first parents, alarmed and trembling, heard, under the majestic shades of Eden, the thundering voice of Jehovah, condemning them to exile, to labour, to death, in punishment of their folly and disobedience; a mysterious prediction, in which the goodness of the Creator shone out resplendent through the wrath of an offended Deity, raised the dejected spirits of both these frail creatures, who, like Lucifer, had sinned through pride. A daughter of Eve, a woman of *masculine* courage, was to crush, under her feet, the head of the serpent, and to regenerate for ever a guilty race. This woman was Mary.[*]

From that time there existed among the antediluvian races, a tradition that a Virgin, beautiful and spotless as

---

[*] According to the Rabbins, the sun, through horror, hid itself at the moment of Eve's transgression. To commemorate this sinister phenomenon the women were obliged to light the lamps in all the Jewish houses during the night of the Sabbath.—*Boulanger, Antiquites devoilees.*

light, should repair, by her divine parturition, all the evil which the woman had caused.

This consolatory tradition, which raised the hopes of a fallen race, had not been effaced from the memory of man at the time of their dispersion over the plains of Sennaar. This consoling, though distant, hope accompanied them over seas and mountains. In later times, when the primitive religion began to decline, and the primeval traditions became clouded in darkness, the tradition of the Virgin and Messiah resisted the action of time, and raised itself aloft over the ruins of ancient creeds, like the evergreen which grows on the ruins of what was once Babylon the Great.*

If we traverse the various regions of the globe, from north to south, from east to west; if we open the religious annals of those countries extending from the land of the orange tree to the burning mountains of the sun, where grows the heliotrope, we shall find the Virgin Mother at the root of almost all their theogonies. At Thibet, in Japan, and in a part of the eastern peninsula of India, the god Fo, whom they honour, in order to save man, became incarnate in the womb of the nymph Lhamoghiurprul, the youthful spouse of a king, and equally remarkable for beauty of person and sanctity of life. In China, Sching-Mou, the most popular of their goddesses, conceived by the mere touch of a water-flower. Her son, brought up under the poor roof of a fisherman, becomes an illustrious personage, and works miracles. The Lamas say that Buddha was born of the Virgin-Maha-Mahai. Sommonokhodom, the prince,

---

* There is found one tree only amidst the ruins of Babylon. The Persians give it the name of Athèle. According to them this tree grew in the ancient city, and was miraculously preserved in order that their prophet Ali, the son-in-law of Mahomet, should be able to tie his horse to it after the battle of Hilla. It is an evergreen, and so rare is it in those countries, that there is only one other of the same species at Bassora.—*Rich's Memoirs.*

the legislator, and the god of Siam, in like manner, derives his birth from a virgin rendered pregnant by the rays of the sun. Lao-Tseu becomes incarnate in the womb of a maiden Negress, *marvellous and beautiful as a jasper*. The Zodiacal Isis of the Egyptians is likewise a virgin mother. The goddess of the Druids was to bring forth a future redeemer.* The Brahmins teach that when a God becomes incarnate, he is conceived by divine operation in the womb of a virgin. Thus, Jagarnat, the mutilated saviour of the world;† Chrichna, born in a grotto, where the angels and shepherds come to adore him in his cradle, have respectively a virgin as mother.

The Babylonian Dogdo sees in a dream a messenger from Oromazes, resplendent with light, laying at her feet superb garments; a celestial ray falls on the countenance of the sleeper, and she becomes as beautiful as the *day-star*. Zerdascht Zoroaster, or rather Ebrahim-zer-Ateucht,‡ the celebrated prophet of the *Magi*, is the fruit of this nocturnal vision. The tyrant Nemrod, informed by his astrologers that a child about being born threatened destruction to his gods and his throne, put to the sword every woman in his dominions who was thought pregnant. Zerdascht is saved from the general massacre by the address and prudence of his mother.§

* Hinc Druidæ Statuam in intimie penetralibus erexerunt, Isidi seu Virgini hanc dedicantes, ex qua filitis ille proditurus erat (nempe generis humani redemptor).—*Elias Schedius de diis Germanis, Cap.* 13.

† Jagarnat, the seventh incarnation of Brahma, is re-produced in the form of a pyramid, without either feet or hands. He lost them, say the Brahmins, in his endeavour to bear the world in order to save it.—*See Kircher*.

‡ Zer-Ateucht signifies *washed with silver*. This surname was given to Zoroaster, because, say the Ghebers, he proved his mission to a Sabean Prince by whom he was persecuted, by plunging into a bath of molten silver.—*Tavernier, t.* 2, *p.* 92.

§ See Tavernier in the passage just quoted.

4   THE UNIVERSAL EXPECTATION OF

The Macenians, who dwell in Paraguay, along the borders of Lake Zarayas, tell that, at a very remote period, a woman of surpassing loveliness became a mother, and yet remained a virgin; that her son, after working many illustrious miracles, raised himself aloft in air, in the presence of his disciples, and then became transformed into a sun.*

The scattered fragments of these various creeds, if united together, will almost furnish us with a history of the Virgin and of Christ, in all its details. Despite her royal origin, Mary is of humble station: so is the mother of Zoroaster. Like her, too, Mary receives a visit from an angel charged with a heavenly message. The tyrant Nemrod, may be taken as the type of Herod. He thirsts for the blood of the young *magi* as rabidly as the sanguinary spouse of Mariamne thirsts for the blood of the infant Jesus. The one, equally as the other, permits his prey to escape. Born of a virgin, as Buddha, our Divine Saviour lives among persons of humble rank. So lived, too, the son of the Chinese goddess. Like unto Chrichna, the angels and shepherds come to pay him homage and adoration, even on the night of his birth; then, after having calmed the tempests, walked on the waters, expelled the demons, raised the dead, he makes his triumphant ascension in presence of five hundred disciples, whose dazzled eyes lose sight of him in a cloud. This is precisely the account which the savage hordes of Paraguay give us.

It is assuredly very strange that these extraordinary legends, when united together, should form the life of the Son of God. That they have been copied from the facts related in the Gospels is impossible, for there is no question that they are of older date. Can truth, then, originate

† See Muratori.

from error? What opinion are we to form of such fantastical likenesses? Shall we say with the later Pagan sophists, and the self-styled thinkers of our own age, equally incredulous as the first, and well worthy of fraternizing on the benches of the school of materialism, that the apostles borrowed these fables from the various forms of belief in Asia? But what grounds of probability are there that men, sprung from the people—men, whose knowledge was confined to the guidance of a bark over the waters of Lake Tiberias, and whose nets were yet dripping at the time of their call to the apostleship—that laborious artisans, compelled, even during their preaching, to toil for their daily bread, could have purloined, and made themselves masters of the sacred books of the Indians, the Chinese, and the Persians? What reason is there to suppose, that Simon Peter, the son of Zebedee, or the learned but austere disciple of Gamaliel, who boldly said to Corinth, that rich and proud city of Greece: "*For me, I know nothing but Jesus, and Jesus crucified,*" should have torn from the form of idolatry—the destruction of which was their peculiar mission—any of her old shreds, to patch them fraudulently on a life so simple and illustrious as was that of Christ? Moreover, it is not merly of Asia that there is question. Not to speak of both the Indies, so imperfectly known under the reign of Tiberius—of China, with its towers of porcelain, whose remote provinces had not tempted even the greedy Romans,[*] how could the apostles communicate with distant America, separated from the old continent by a green cincture of waves, and lost as a pearl in the midst of waters?

---

[*] It was under the reign of Augustus that the Romans received the first ambassadors from the Seres, now called the Chinese. The ambassadors pretended that they spent three years in performing the journey.

But, allowing for a moment that the apostles might —it matters little through what means—have had intelligence of these dark traditions; I will even go further: admitting that, notwithstanding their native simplicity, profound sanctity, their testimony, sealed with their blood, they might have conceived the extraordinary idea of embroidering some fabulous circumstances on the evangelical tissue; the thing would be altogether beyond their power. With what front, for example, could they have attributed to Herod, who was known to the whole city of Jerusalem, and with whose glorious and tragical reign every person was thoroughly conversant, an atrocious and improbable fact revived of some one or other king of Persia, of whom history has preserved but some vague reminiscences immersed in a sea of fables, and who, perhaps, had no existence, except in the reveries of the Ghebers? Can it be supposed that these subtle Pharisees, who had so insidiously contrived to surprise Jesus in his words, were persons to be imposed on by an old Persian story, or that the Herodians would have patiently endured that a prince deified by them, and who had lavished on them every honour and every benefit, should be calumniated under the very portals of his palace? And the voice of this sect of courtiers would not alone be raised in favour of the Idumean. A man of strong passions and violent propensities, but yet susceptible of reciprocating true affection and love; a sanguinary but able politician, a valiant chief, a liberal prince, and an enlightened protector of the arts, Herod, notwithstanding his beastly appetites and his foreign extraction, had left after him friends but too ready to avenge his memory, in case it had been branded by any calumnious imputation.* But the

---

* The parasites of Herod the First, dazzled with the grandeur and magni-

massacre of the innocents is not one of these ordinary and vulgar acts which are lost sight of in the midst of numerous political crimes; there had been madness as well as barbarity in that abominable measure. A man of blood, reputed the friend of Anthony and Augustus—but folly! * *

If the Herodians are silent, it is because the matter is too clear, too public—entirely too recent, to allow of any contradiction; because the place where lived the mothers of the martyrs who, for the honour of being born with Christ, paid the forfeit of their young lives, is only two hours' journey from Jerusalem; the reason is, that entire villages had seen the poignards glisten, and heard the cries of death—the reason is, because at the first contradiction given to the Christians, every person would have stood up saying: *But we were there!* The same line of argument holds equally good in reference to the virginity of Mary, her divine parturition, the visit of the shepherds, directed by the angels, the glorious resurrection, and, in a word— all the prodigies which signalized the coming of Christ. The Apostles wrote during the life even of those who had figured in the scenes of which they make mention; and the life of OUR LORD had been of a term so short, that the shepherds of Bethlehem, who came to adore him in his manger, could converse with the disciples who were witnesses of his ascension. St. Peter and St. John, these apostles so easily intimidated at the time of Jesus, declared in a cool, resolute manner to the scribes and high priests, that they considered them as Deicides, and proved by the miracles of his birth,

---

ficence of this prince, maintained that he was the *Messiah*. Hence arose that sect of the Herodians of whom there is mention made in the Gospel, and whom the pagans had known, for Perseus and his scholiast teach us that even at the time of Nero, the birth of King Herod was celebrated by his followers with the same solemnity as the Sabbath.

life, and death, that Christ whom they crucified—was God. Did the Jews, galled and irritated by this accusation, brand these marvellous facts with imposture? By no means, *they have never denied them;* but to palliate the strange hardness of their hearts, they attributed them to magic learned among the Egyptians. It follows, then, that some reason must exist for the conformity which is noticed among the evangelical facts, and the traditions, more or less intermingled with fable, of these primeval people. But how, then, explain these analogies? Is it a sport of chance or some fortuitous accident? Not by chance does it happen that the mystery of the incarnation of a God in the chaste womb of a virgin is one of the fundamental articles of belief in Asia ; it is not perchance that the privileged women who bear in their wombs this emanation of the divinity are always pure, lovely, holy, and so resembling each other, that they are said to be moulded in a type of a date so remote as to be concealed from us by the night of time ; it is not fortuitously that the divine nature is united to the human nature by a luminous ray. These ideas, which carry with them the impress of primitive epochs, evidently go so far back as the creation of the world. The patriarchs before the Flood—that connected chain of old men who lived to the age of cedars—wishing to form to themselves an idea of a woman, blessed among all other women, whose miraculous parturition was to save the human race, painted her in the colours of Eve before her fall. They invested her with that beauty of majesty and holiness which could originate in the minds of the children of men no other sentiment save that of religious veneration. They compared her to a beautiful star of a delicious, mysterious, chaste, and veiled light, whose rise was to herald that of the Sun of Justice. The means to which God had recourse to render fruitful this virginal womb, strikingly accord with the maternal ideas which govern the theogonies of the various people of the globe. Let us cast a glance for a moment on all the antiquated forms of belief, and we will find that fire is invariably mixed up with them: but fire, according to the Magi, was the earthly emblem of the sun, and the sun itself was but the dwelling of the MOST HIGH, the tent of Adonai-Jehovah, say the Hebrews, who had preserved this primitive idea,* with the deposit of the faith of Abel.

The Scripture tells us, that in the first ages of the world, Jehovah conversed familiarly with the patriarchs. How could he make his appearance to them, since *no man can see God and live?* Moses, who conversed with him face to face, and spoke to him *as to a friend*, saw only the *Schekina*, that is the divine presence, in form of a cloud, at the door of the tabernacle of the covenant. Apparently, it was thus that the Lord manifested himself to the race of Seth, before their ways became corrupted. Deprived of this glorious privilege, which seemed the latest reflection of the brilliant perogatives of Eden, the people descended from Noe sought out, in the works of creation, something pure and refulgent which might have some analogy with the presence of the OMNIPOTENT. The sun, that giant star which forces man to look downwards, appeared to them the most eligible terrestrial *Schekina*, and God seemed to confirm them in this idea by appearing under the form of flame in the bush of Horeb, and on the summit of Mount Sinai. They, therefore, considered the sun as the shadow of uncreated light, and hence originated, without

---

* See the Psalm xxviii. 5. The Persians had the same idea. They suppose that the throne of God is in the sun, (says Hanway,) and hence their veneration for this luminary.

doubt, this belief of the people of Asia—that by a luminous ray the expected Saviour was to become incarnate in the womb of a virgin. Worship, that feeling of love and gratitude, outwardly manifested by acts of religion, is as old as the world, and altars are as old as worship.* The offerings of Adam and Eve, in their state of innocence, were undoubtedly fruits and flowers;† but when sin introduced death into the ways of men—when the head of the human family forfeited, with the sacred shade of the tree of life, his talisman of immortality,‡ in addition to the wild fruits and flowers which the land of exile produced,

---

* It is very probable that the sacrifices of Abel and Cain were offered on some elevated rock or mound, and hence comes the name of altar. The Latin word *altare* appears to be derived from the Celtic *allt*, high, and *ar*, stone.—*Introduc. à l'Histoire Eccl. de Bret.* t. 1, *l.* 5, *p.* 375.

† According to a Pagan tradition, mentioned by Porphyry, (*Traité de l'Abst., liv.* 2,) the primitive men offered on the altars of the gods only flowers, fruit, and tufts of grass.

‡ Man had never been immortal in this world in the same sense as pure spirits, for a body formed of dust should naturally return into dust. Immortality here below man could never lay claim to, by right of birth. Every terrestrial body must perish by the dissolution of its parts, at least when a particular will of the Creator is not opposed to it. This Divine will was manifested in favour of our first parents. God planted in that delightful garden where he had placed mortal man, the tree of life—a plant of Heavenly origin, which was endowed with the peculiar property of repelling death, like the laurel which, as the ancients say, repelled lightning. To this mysterious tree was attached the immortality of the human species. At a distance from this protecting shelter, death seized his prey, and man fell from the highest heaven into his miserable earthly covering. (*Aug. Quæst. Vet. et Nov. Test., q.* 19, *p.* 430). It cannot be called into question, I think, that God could, consistently with justice, expel Adam from paradise after his disobedience, but exile imports sentence of death against man and his posterity. Without the tree of life he was nothing more than a frail, perishable creature, subject to the laws which rule created bodies. Adam becoming mortal brought forth children mortal like himself—the children must follow the condition of the father. In all this God inflicted no wrong on the human race; we are of our nature mortal—he has left us such as we were. To withdraw a gratuitous favour, when the object of that favour destroys the very act which confers it on him, is not cruelty, it is justice.

he offered the firstlings of his flock. This merits a little reflection. Adam who, to the most perfect form of body, united a soul high and intelligent, in which the Lord had implanted the germ of every virtue and every knowledge, could not be divested of the feelings of humanity. His fatal compliance towards Eve points him out to us as loving even to weakness, and therefore susceptible, in the highest degree, of fine and generous feelings. How came it, then, that he should think that the Creator could take complacency in the murder of his creature, and that an act of destruction would be an act of piety? The immolation of animals, which does not in the least accord with the intellectual wishes of a man, and as the people of the primitive ages lived solely on vegetable diet, could be viewed in no other light than that of murder, and so ought excite in the mind of the father of the human race a thousand natural repugnances. For a long time these poor creatures, deprived of reason, but capable of attachment, had formed in Eden the court of this solitary king.* He with them

* We cannot exactly compute the time that Adam and Eve remained in the terrestrial paradise. This stay must, however, be of some duration, and so Milton has supposed, whom we here quote, not as a poet, but as a profound orientalist. If we bear in mind that it was in Eden that Adam learned to classify and to call by name all the birds of the air, all the beasts of the field, and all the fishes of the sea; that he was instructed in all the properties of the different plants, can we conclude otherwise than that all this was not the work of a day? The Persians and Chinese think many ages passed on during the stay of the first man in Paradise. According to the opinion of the Arabians and Rabbins, he continued there only a half day, but this half day of theirs is equivalent to five hundred years; for a day of paradise corresponds with a thousand years. This space of time we think too long. It is commonly believed that Cain the parracide, whose birth is closely linked, in Genesis, with the expulsion of his parents, was born in the 13th year of the world, and from that it will follow that our first parents' stay in paradise was a little more than twelve years. This term, though rather short, would, however, be sufficient for the first man to establish firmly his authority over the animals subject to his dominion, and to become attached to his humble subjects by the ties of habit.

sat down at the same table, drank from the same source, slept on the moss of the same hillock, and his prayer ascended at even to the Master of nature, in union with the weak cry of insects concealed under the herbage, the distant bellowing of the lords of the forest, and the warbling of birds. Involved with man in his misfortune, and its consequent penalty, the innocent companions of his past happy life now shared his exile. Some following their instincts of ferocity, which formed no part of their nature in Paradise, fled into the interior of the deserts, and the secret caves of the mountains, from which they waged a fatal war against man. Others—creatures inoffensive and docile, united themselves to the sad fortune of their master, established themselves about his grotto, and kindly tendered him their milk, their labour, their concerts, their downy fleece. And was it, indeed, among these affectionate slaves, so humbly ranged under his authority, that he should select and mark out his victims? Was he to plunge the knife into the throat of the timid lamb which so gently licked his hand? Ah, once man struck down at his feet a defenceless creature, and witnessed his pangs of agony, that very moment he should become as wan and pallid as an assassin! This idea of immolation was not man's; it was not an act of choice, but of hard submission; it was the imperfect expiation of a fault which willed blood. Who imposed it? He alone who is the sovereign disposer of life and death—God. From the moment that the first man violated the divine precept, God could, consistently with his justice, crush him like an earthen vessel, and destroy, in his person, the whole human race, cursed and corrupted in their source. That he did not wish: his entrails yearned towards this poor rebellious creature, whose life was depending on his mercy, and commuting into exile the sentence of death, merited by the revolt of our first parents, from that time he opened before them, by the pure effect of his mercy, a new and glorious perspective of immortality. According to St. Bernard, this illustrious favour, which Christ was to seal on the cross, was granted in favour of Mary; and to save from annihilation this holy Virgin, involved in the future fate of her race, was the reason why the Most High spared Eve and all her posterity. If we are reluctant in subscribing to this pious, but rather too exclusive opinion, at least let us not scout the thought that, when the Eternal weighed the destinies of man against the blood of his Son, the merits and the virtues of her who was one day to be the Queen of angels, and the consolatrix of the afflicted, made him incline the scale on the side of mercy. Be that as it may, there had been at that time a mysterious revelation in reference to a prophet, born of a prophet, who, by dying on a cross, was to ransom the sins of the world; a revelation, according to the tradition of the Hebrews, renewed at a latter time by an angel of the Lord to the mother of Abel and Seth.

A prophecy, foretelling man's redemption, should, one ought to suppose, be engraven in indellible characters on their memory. But the Creator, knowing the volatile mind of man—knowing that passions, these jarring winds of the soul, would efface from his heart the divine threats and promises, with the same facility as the billows of the surging sea blot out every track that could afford guidance to the pilot—for this it was, that he was willing that the grand promise of the Messiah should not stand alone, but form a part of a scene of terror which might make a strong and lively impression on his forgetful and fickle nature. He instituted sacrifices, and these religious ceremonies were at the same time commemorative, expiatory, and typical.

At the period of the division of the land, and the dispersion of that great patriarchal family which the Lord had preserved to re-people the world, each colony carried with them into these virgin lands, where they repaired to erect their tents, the wreck of the sciences and arts saved from the Deluge,* and that form of worship of which Enoch and the patriarchs had laid the foundation. To these Noe, that fervent servant of God, added the historical and religious traditions, which a long term of life previous to the Flood had enabled him to collect. He spoke of man formed from the slime of the earth, his rebellion, his punishment, his future redemption, for which the world should be indebted to the marvellous parturition of a new Eve. At the view of the bloody sacrifices offered up for the unexpiated guilt of their first parents he taught his descendants to raise their eyes to a more august victim, sitting on the right hand of Jehovah, in the starry recess of heaven, a victim of which the oblation of heifers and lambs was but a figure, and which alone could absorb death and conquer hell. The people at first faithfully retained these primitive notions, which were the foundation of all their various forms of belief.† Altars

---

* It is certain that the primitive race of man, which was rural, but not savage, were acquainted with those arts which ministered to their necessities and pleasures. Scarcely had the children of Adam formed themselves into small communities, when public worship was established among them; when they began to fabricate tents, build towns, forge iron, melt brass, invent musical instruments, and trace the course of the stars. The history of astronomy, according to Bailly, must be traced as far back as the antediluvian age. Lalande attributes to the Egyptians the origin of this science. But the Hebrews, who are in a position to decide this difference, agree with Bailly against his adversary, and inform us that the Egyptians were indebted for the rudiments of astronomy to the traditions rescued from the Deluge.—*See Josephus.*

† The Indians, the Chinese, the Peruvians, and even the Hurons, believe that the first man was formed of the slime of the earth. The Brahmins, who give us such glowing pictures of their *chorcam*, or paradise, place in it a tree, whose fruits had the property of conferring immortality, if permission were

were raised at the confluence of rivers, under the shade of the forests, on the tops of mountains, along the seashore, and on the sandy down where the wormwood paraded its leaves to the desert wind. From the very beginning the silvery light of the moon shone down on these rural temples bounded only by the horizon, and without any other roof than that of the heavens with their glittering stars. At that remote epoch, God met with adoration worthy of him; and so clear, so sublime, so uniform, and so simple, were the ideas formed of true worship, that to himself alone we must trace them back. Yet, an element of immense reach, an element of superstitious alarm, founded on the fearful and recent remembrance of the destruction of the world by water, had glided into the form of worship practised by those who lived after the Flood. In exploring the silent ruins of those high towers,* which could not save from a watery grave the giants of an extinct race; on discovering on the steepest point of the mountains, in the very region of the clouds, the cast off properties of the ocean, man felt himself under the powerful and avenging hand of an angry God, and this thought damped his courage. Looking back on

granted to eat of them. The Persians hand down that the evil spirit Ahriman seduced our first parents under the form of a snake. The history of the woman seduced at the foot of a tree, the consequent wrath of God, and the first fratricide, were traditions among the Iroquois. The Tartars attribute our forfeiture to a delicious and delightful plant. The inhabitants of Thibet assign our misery and fall to the eating of the dangerous plant of *schimæ*, sweet as sugar, and that the knowledge of our state of nakedness was revealed by this fruit. The tradition of the woman and the serpent was in like manner known by the Mexicans, &c.—See *M. Rosselly de Lorques, Christ devant le Siècle*, chap. 9.

* The tower of Babel furnishes us with some idea of the antediluvian architecture. In it we find brick and bitumen used. If, as everything induces to think so, this huge tower resembled the ancient and famous tower of Bel, at Babylon, it was surrounded exteriorly by a spiral staircase, which ascended to the platform, and gave the edifice the appearance of seven towers superimposed.

himself with dejection and anguish, and seeing himself as he really was—an atom before the Eternal—he fearfully demands if the prayers and wishes of him, a poor worm lost in the crowd of numerous other beings, could by any means reach the throne of the Ancient of days. He so despicable, and God so grand! Not daring to pronounce in the affirmative, he believes it a duty incumbent on him to secure some powerful mediator, through whose intercession he might make known his wants and offer his acts of thanksgiving. That mediator he selects among the stars which were the delight of his solitary watchings, and which, as he supposed, were governed by celestial intelligences. Hence the origin of Sabeism, the immediate source of idolatry. In process of time the darkness became thicker, religions were overloaded with rites, the worship of the true God became gradually mingled with that of the stars and the elements. The discovery of the hieroglyphics completed the confusion, and the few truths which were rescued from the total ruin of the ancient forms of belief, were mysteriously concealed in the under parts of the idolatrous sanctuaries, like sepulchral lamps burning only for the dead. They were carefully concealed from the people* who lavishly paid unmeaning acts of adoration to tigers, lions, crocodiles, and even to vegetable substances, and deified their passions and vices. It was then that impostors, trafficking on human credulity, ravelled or designedly broke the already slender thread of

---

* Plato, in speaking of the God who had created the universe, says that he is not allowed to make him known to the people. The books of Numa, written on the bark of the birch tree, and found in his tomb many ages after his death, were secretly burned, as they were thought subversive of the doctrine of polytheism. The Brahmins, who, if we are to believe some travellers, entertain very sublime ideas of the divinity, yet place before the Indians the most hideous idols for their adoration. True religion alone has treated man in the light of immortal and reasonable creatures.

THE VIRGIN AND THE MESSIAH.   17

the patriarchal traditions. Audaciously substituting remembrance for hope, they collected around the cloudy cradle of their false prophets or fabulous divinities, the wonders of the Incarnate Word, and the primitive reminiscences of his high and tragical destiny.

Thus we explain these analogies which seem at first sight incomprehensible. However, all the nations of polytheism received not the mystery of the Messiah as an accomplished fact. A short time previous to the Christian Era, the Druids were still raising in the dark forests of Gaul an altar to the Virgin *who was to bring forth.* The Chinese, instructed by Confucius, who himself had found this oracle in the old traditions, were in expectation of the HOLY, who was to arise in the western regions of Asia, and nearly half a century after the death of the MAN GOD, sent a solemn ambassador in search of him. The Magi, on the faith of Zerdascht, were studying the constellations to find out the star of Jacob, which was to be their guide to the cradle of Christ.* The Brahmins were longing for the glorious *avatar*† of him who was to *cleanse the world from sin,* and demanded him of Wichnow, when laying on his altar, resplendent with jewels, the odoriferous branches of basilisk, a plant endeared to the Indian god. The fiery children of Romulus, conspicuous for their idolatry, and who had formed entire legions of gods, were reading in the books so jealously and artfully watched by the sybil of Cumæ, *the Virgin, the Divine Infant, the adoration of the shepherds, the serpent crushed, and the age of gold restored to the world.*

* Alburfarage (Historia Dynastiarum) says, that Zerdascht predicted to the *Magi* the birth of the Messiah, born of a Virgin; he adds, that at the time of his birth there appeared a strange star which conducted them to the place of his birth, and ordained them to bear him presents. Sharistani, a Mussulman writer, relates, in like manner, a prediction of Zerdascht relative to a prophet who was to reform the world with respect both to religion and justice, and to whom the princes and kings of the world would render subjection.

† *Avatar*, the fabulous incarnation of an Indian divinity.

C

In fine, about the time of the Messiah, all the countries of the East were in expectation of a future Redeemer; and Boulanger, though receiving a truer inspiration on his death-bed, after pointing out how generally that expectation prevailed, illogically designates it a universal chimera.* But if God willed that infidel nations, in the midst of their wanderings, should preserve this belief, the only thread remaining to extricate them from the labyrinth of error; if he compelled even the father of lies to give glory to Christ and to his Mother, and to trace the name of Mary on a leaf of the sybil's book;† if it was his will that the incarnation of the WORD should be the object of the expectation of all, what was this pale and weak glimmer enveloped in profound darkness, in comparison to the magnificent glow which enlightened the children of Abraham?

We are struck with surprise at the view of this prophetical chain, the first link of which commences at the infancy of the world, and the last is forged on at the tomb of Christ.‡ The threat of Jehovah to the infernal serpent includes, as we have already said, the first oracle regarding the Messiah, and that oracle is remarkable on this account, for in revealing the power of God, the honour of Mary is not overlooked: *he who will spring from the woman shall crush thy head*, says the Eternal. These mysterious words, more clearly explained in the sequel to the exiles of Eden,§

---

* Unanimous testimony is of the greatest weight, says Bernandin St. Piere, for a universal error there cannot be.—*Studies of Nature*, Study 8, p. 398.

† Il divoto di Maria del Paolo Segneri, parte prima.

‡ There is a tradition taught in the Synagogue, and recognised as true in the Church, that all the prophets, without exception, have had in view the Messiah as the term of their prophecies.—See *St. Cyprian on the Worship of Idols.*

§ According to a Hebraical tradition, God seeing Adam in despair at the frightful consequences of his transgression, told him by an angel to assuage his grief, for from his posterity would arise a Redeemer, who was to destroy origi-

were handed down by Noe to Sem, who was appointed by
God to be the inheritor of the faith; and Sem, whose term
of life nearly equalled that of his ancestors, could repeat
them to the father of believers. It was then that a benediction, replete with mystery, in which the promise of the
Messiah was included, pointed out that the blessed seed promised to Eve should be the seed and shoot of Abraham. To
the olden traditions immediately succeeded the grand prediction of Jacob. The expiring patriarch, who had seen in
spirit the condition of the twelve tribes when they were
to be in possession of Palestine, announced to his children
collected about his dying bed that Judah had been selected
from among all his brethren, as the stock from which the
kings of Israel were to descend, and as the father of the
Schilo so often promised, who was to be the King of
kings, and the Lord of lords. The coming of Christ is
marked in a particular manner: he will rise up from the
amidst of the ruins of his country, when the *schebet* (the
sceptre, the legislative authority) will be in the hands of
a stranger.* The prophet saved from the waters of the

nal sin, and was to be the salvation of all those who hoped in him.—*Baxn. tom.*
4, *l.* 7, *c.* 25.

* The Christians make application of this revelation to the Messiah, and
by it prove to the incredulous Jews, that he must have appeared long before
now, since, after eighteen centuries, their tribes are mingled, their sacrifices
abolished, their laws extinct; that they have no longer territory or rulers,
and that in every place where they are found they are paying obedience to
foreign laws, and are subject to foreign dominion. To elude the force of this
argument, the Jews pretend, that the word *schebet*, which we translate into
sceptre, equally means the rod which chastises the slave, and hence they endeavour to maintain that though this oracle should regard the Messiah, all that
we can conclude from it is, that their chastisement would continue to his
coming, who would then deliver them—they deny that the word *schil* can be
translated into Messiah. But their ancient books refute their argument.
This prophecy is understood as regarding the Messiah in the *Talmud*, and let
us see how the paraphrase of Onkelos explains this passage: "Juda will not
be without some one clothed with the supreme authority, nor without scribes

Nile, who was called by God to collect and transmit to writing an account of the early ages and the olden traditions of the human race, traditions yet fresh in the memory of the people, willingly lends the support of his striking testimony to the prophecy of Jacob. " Adonai Jehovah," he says, in speaking to the people of God, " will raise up to you, from the midst of thy nation, and from among the number of thy brethren a prophet like unto me ; hear you him. He will bring you the orders of heaven, and the Lord will take vengeance on any who shall refuse to hear him."* And it is of the Messiah that the synagogue always understood this clear text. St. Philip understood it in that sense when, without making exactly the application to our Divine Redeemer, he said to Nathaniel : " We have found him whom the prophets foretold, of whom Moses spoke in the law, Jesus of Nazareth. Towards the end of the mission of Moses, and whilst Israel lay still encamped in the desert, Balaam, whose maledictions in the vale of Sallows a Moabite prince had depreciated,† came to corroborate the expected arrival of the Messiah, and to mark out in a manner precise and clear, the grand epoch of his coming. On the highest peak of Phagor, in sight

among the sons of her children until the Messiah comes." Jonathan, to whom the Jews assigned the first place among the disciples of Hillel, and whom they held almost in equal veneration to Moses, translates in like manner the word *schebet* into principality, and *Schilo* into Messiah. The paraphrase of Jerusalem sides with this opinion Thus, their oldest, most authentic, and respectable commentaries, furnish us with arms to overthrow all their arguments.

* Hence arises that hope of a new law which the Jews were expecting to accompany the Messiah, a law which they placed far above that of Moses. *The law which man studies in this world is but vanity, say their doctors, in comparison to that of the Messiah.*—Medrash Rabba, on Ecclesiastes, 11, 8.

† The plain of Babylon, intersected with rivers and canals, and consequently very marshy, abounds in willows. And hence arises its Scriptural name of the *Valley of Willows*.

THE VIRGIN AND THE MESSIAH. 21

of the cursed lake and the barren mountains of Arabia, the soothsayer, from the banks of the Euphrates, agitated by the Spirit of God, beholds, as with the eye of a seer,* a wonderful vision. His words, interrupted now and then by long and solemn pauses, are thrown out, without either order or method, to the mountain gales, like the shreds of some mysterious discourse linked below with the infernal powers: *I will see him.........but not now. I will behold him,.....but not near at hand. A star will arise from Jacob,.......a shoot will branch off from Israel. He will rule over many people.* To these incoherent expressions succeeded a magnificent picture, but gloomy in colouring, of the conquests of God's chosen people. It is not without design, that the vision of the prophet points out Rome at the apogee of its colossal power. Then it was that Christ was to come on earth to immolate himself for us, on the tree of infamy. The prophet paints in glowing colours this bloody epoch. It is said that cities and empires yet to arise presented themselves before his eyes in the mirage of the desert. He sees the fleet of the Cæsars leaving the ports of Italy and directing their victory-loving prows towards the flat coasts of Syria. He sees the ruin of that Judea, which was not to be in existence for a long time after, and where the chosen people of God could not at that time lay claim to any other possessions, except the possession of some few monuments. Then, seven centuries be-

---

* Though we were in profound ignorance of the great antiquity of the prophecy of Balaam, the manner in which it is expressed sufficiently indicates it so. Balaam, a Chaldean astrologer, does not prophesy as the *seers* of Juda. A vast horizon presents itself before him, and along it he discovers at the same time heaven, earth, and sea; he expresses himself, like one who enter into a detail of everything which he beholds at the moment he is speaking, and which makes the strongest impression on him. This manner of prophesying resembles somewhat that which the highlanders of *Scotland* call *second sight*.

fore the birth of the son of Ilium, and whilst the wild goats of Latium were still quietly browsing on the shrubby declivities of the seven hills, he follows with his prophetic glance the fall of the Roman eagle. Ages glide over, and again, ages, without other promises from Jehovah; but the oracles regarding the Messiah are entrusted to tradition which carefully preserves them, or are consigned in the holy law. Israel sustains an obscure, but incessant and obstinate wrestling against the idolatrous people who surround and press her tribes on all sides. Sometimes she yields to the strange propensity which drags her down to idolatry, and then the fatal sword of the Amorrhites and Moabites is, unknowingly, drawn in the battle of the Lord, and avenges, unwillingly, the injuries of the God of Jacob. But during these varying fortunes, the people forgot not the coming of Christ; they live in the faith of a Messiah. In want of any new revelations, their life even becomes prophetical. Political and religious institutions, local customs and private manners, all tend to the same end, all flow from the same source: everything is bound up with the expected coming of a Redeemer, to be born of a virgin of Juda. With the expectation of a Messiah, is connected that law of Deuteronomy, which requires that a brother should raise up an heir to his brother dying without children, that his name may be perpetual in Israel. It is this last hope of belonging one day, sooner or later, to the celestial envoy, which caused the young and submissive virgin of Galaad to weep on the mountains of Judea; and her only regret in descending into that bloody tomb, to which a father's vow condemned her, was the extinction of her hope of being related to the Messiah. It is to this belief, so general among the Hebrews, that the Thecuite makes allusion, when denouncing to King David the secret plots which were being contrived against her only surviving son; she poetically describes the fear of a mother and Jewish matron, by this touching expression: *Lord, they wish to extinguish my last spark!* How widely does the present incredulity of the Jews contrast with the faith of their forefathers. The great concern of these men of primeval times was the coming of the Messiah; those who died at a time long before the epoch when were to be fulfilled the promises of heaven, died under the firm conviction that these promises would one day be accomplished. On the very brink of eternity, they saluted that distant hope, as Moses, the great prophet, with a deep sigh, saluted that *land of milk and honey*, which the Lord prevented his ever entering. At the time of David and that of his royal children, the thread of the prophecy is again united; and the mystery of the Virgin and Messiah is made known by prophecies yet grander, and as patent as the sun. The holy king, whom the God of Israel preferred to the race of Saul, sees the virginity of Mary and the supernatural birth of the Son of God. *Your birth*, he says, not sullied as that of the children of men, *will be as pure as the morning dew.* Then raising his eyes aloft, he beholds Him whom God hath given him as a son according to the flesh, sitting on the right of Jehovah, on a throne more lasting than the heaven and the stars. From the time of the great prophecy in Eden, to the perfect establishment of the Hebrews in Palestine, the Virgin had been understood rather than revealed in the predictions of the patriarchs and prophets. But from the time of David, the radiant figure of Mary no longer presents any vague outlines, and she who was to infuse the blood of Abraham, of Jacob, and of Jesse-the-Just, into the veins of the MAN GOD, becomes more clearly delineated. David had spoken of her virginal parturition;

Solomon took complacency in tracing her image with such beautiful streaks of his pencil, as to leave far behind in the shade the glowing descriptions given of those peris of the east, those smiling and vaporous divinities which flit across the dreams of the Arabian pastor. He sees her arise from the midst of the daughters of Judea, *as a lily among the thorns;* her eyes are beautiful and mild *as those of the dove;* her lips like *scarlet lace,* a dropping honeycomb; her coming forth aerial *as the odour of perfumes;* and her beauty vies in lustre with *the rising moon.* Her tastes are simple and poetical; she loves to stray in the shady vales, *when the vines are in flower,* and the *fig-tree had put forth her green figs;* her cheeks are as the *bark of the pomegranate,* the tree of Paradise,* and she takes pleasure in listening to the plaintive song of the turtle-dove. Silent and retiring, she veils herself from every eye, and remains concealed within her dwelling, as *the dove which builds its nest in the crevices of the rocks.* She is elected for a mystical marriage in preference to the virgins and queens of every other nation; a crown is promised her by him *who loveth her soul,* and the happy bond by which she is united to her royal spouse *is stronger than death.*† Elias, praying on Mount Carmel for the cessation of that long drought, which after three years split the earth, and dried up the sources, sees the promised virgin under the form of a transparent cloud, which rises from the bosom of the waters, announcing the return of rain. The blessings of the people salute this propitious omen,‡ and the prophet, pene-

---

* The Orientals call the *pomegranate* the *fruit of Paradise.*
† The Holy Fathers remark that the *Canticle of Canticles* is a continual allegory of the Mother of God.
‡ When rain falls in Palestine, there is universal joy among the people; they assemble in the streets, they sing—they become agitated, they cry out at the highest pitch, " Oh! God! be thou blessed."—*Volney's Travels in Syria.*

trating the things of heaven, builds an oratory to the future queen of heaven.* Isaias declared to the house of David, the head of which, Achab, was trembling under the menaces of the stranger, *like a forest shaken by the tempest*, that God would give him an encouraging sign regarding the futurity of Judea, still a long and glorious future. " A virgin shall conceive,† and bring forth a son, and he shall be called *Emmanuel*, that is, God with us..... And there shall come forth a shoot out of the trunk of Jesse, and a flower shall spring up from his root.‡ His name shall be called Won-

* The oratory which Elias built on Mount Carmel was dedicated by him to the Virgin who was to bring forth, *Virgini parituræ*. This Chapel was called *Semnæum*, that is, a place consecrated to an impériére (Empress) which can be no other than Mary, Impériére of Heaven and Earth.—*History of Mount Carmel, Succession of the Holy Prophet*, chap. 31.

† This grand prophecy has been the subject of a long and stormy debate among the Jews and Christians. The Rabbins who have, from the time of Jesus Christ, commented on this text, desirous of destroying the evidence of their own condemnation, and rendering obscure the words of the prophecy, say that the word *halma*, which is found in the Hebrew text, means simply a young woman, although the Septuagint have translated it by *Virgin*. The Fathers have altogether destroyed this objection. "The Seventy Interpreters," says St. John Chrysostom, " are particularly entitled to our belief. They wrote their version more than a century before Jesus Christ—there were many assembled together—their number and their unanimity rendered them more deserving of belief than the Jews of our days, who have maliciously corrupted many parts of the Sacred Scriptures."—*Sermon* 4, chap. 1. St. Jerome, the most profound Hebrew scholar of all the interpreters and commentators of Scripture, pronounces without fear, he says, of contradiction from the Jews, that *halma* in every part of the Scripture in which the word occurs, means solely a Virgin unsullied, and nowhere does it mean a married woman.— *Commentary on Isaias*, Book 3. Luther, who so frightfully abuses true and real knowledge, cries out with that impetuosity and vehemence so peculiar to him : " If at any time a Jew or Hebraist can point out to me that *halma* means *any sort of woman*, and not a Virgin, I will, please God, give him a hundred florins wherever I can procure them."— *The Works of Luther, vol.* 8, *p.* 129. Mahomet himself has borne testimony to the Virginity of the Mother of God. "And Mary, daughter of Imram, who has preserved her virginity and believed the word of her Lord and his scriptures."—*Koran, Surate* 66.

‡ Jesse, called also Isaias, was the son of Obed and father of David. His memory is held in the highest veneration among the Hebrews.

D

derful, Counsellor, God the Mighty, the Father of the World to come, the Prince of peace. He shall be set up as a standard before the people, the Gentiles shall come to beseech him, and his sepulchre shall be glorious." The mystery of the Messiah is wholly unveiled to the eyes of the prophets. Some see Bethlehem rendered illustrious by his birth; others predict his triumphant entry into Jerusulam, and even particularize his gentle and slow mule. They behold him— the Pontiff according to the order of Melchisedech —entering the temple; they know the number of pieces of silver dropped by the executioners of the Synagogue into the hand of the base coward who betrayed his master; they behold the cross, that instrument for the punishment of slaves—the drink of gall insolently presented to an agonized God, and the garment, worked by a mother's hands, for which the rude soldiers cast lots; they hear the nails hacking the bleeding flesh, and sinking with a hoarse sound into the cursed wood. Then the scene changes, like Raphael's pictures, in which the subject, commenced on earth, is finished beyond the clouds. The man of sorrows, the humble Messiah, scorned by his friends, and rejected by his people, looks down triumphantly from the highest heavens on his earthly enemies; all the nations of the earth retain the remembrance of their God, forgotten after so many centuries! The people rally around the standard of the Cross, and the kingdom of Christ will have no other limits than those of the world. All the prophecies are fulfilled to the letter. Jacob foretold that the coming of *Schilo* would be at hand at the very moment when the Jews would cease to be governed by their own laws, importing the fall of their power. Balaam adds that the subversion of the kingdom of Judea would be the work of a people arrived from Italy; and the governor Daniel gives an exact account of the number of weeks which were to flow on up to that time. " Everything which is to happen in the world casts its shadow before," said an illustrious and gifted writer, though now living lonely and retired; " when the sun is about to rise, the horizon is chequered with a thousand varied clouds, and the east seems to be one golden bed of flame. When the tempest is at hand, a deafening roar is heard on the shore, and the billows are agitated as if by a power innate in themselves."

The figures of the Old Testament, according to the holy fathers of the church, are the signs which announce the rising of the *Sun of Justice* and the *Star of the Sea*. To Christ, the Son of God, belongs strength ; to Mary, grace and merciful goodness. She is the tree of life replanted by the hand of God himself in the dwellings of man, and the guarantee of happiness, preferable to that enjoyed by our first parents in the garden of Eden; she is the dove of the ark which carried the olive branch from the dry land ; the sealed fountain, whose waters nothing unclean has troubled ; the holy mountain, from which, without human touch, rolled the stone that shattered the idols, &c. Like that glowing and ravishing countenance, which, by borrowing a thousand scattered beauties from the most lovely women of Greece, a painter of antiquity had formed ; the chaste spouse of the Holy Ghost reflected in her person all those varied and engaging qualities, which the most celebrated women of the old law presented to the admiration of their contemporaries.

With the loveliness of Rachel and Sara, she unites in her person the prudence of Abigail, and the strong resolute bearing of Esther. Susanna, chaste as the flower, whose name she bears ;* Judith, whose lily crown was stained by the blood of Holofernes ;† Axa, whose hand was purchased by

---

* The name Susanna means lily.—*Favyn*, book 2.
† The ancients attributed to the lily the efficacy of neutralizing enchant-

a conquered city; and that glorious but unfortunate mother, who beheld all her sons sacrificed before her eyes, for their adherence to the law, were but faint pictures of her who was to unite in her person all the perfections of woman and angel. After four thousand years, the time marked out by the prophets at length arrives; the shadows of the old law disappear, and Mary arises above the horizon of Judea, like the star which ushers in the day.

CHAPTER II.

THE IMMACULATE CONCEPTION.

A WOMAN destined from all eternity to save the world by co-operating in the union of the divine and human nature, and enclosing in her chaste womb Him, whom neither the heavens nor the earth, nor the vast extent of the sea, could contain; a woman anxiously expected since the formation of the globe, and the avowed end of all those holy generations, which succeeded each other since the days of the patriarchs, must be other than a woman of ordinary stamp, and ought to be endowed with privileges above those of humanity. The pious belief in the Immaculate Conception of Mary flows from this consideration of respect. Heirs of an inauspicious head, degraded in the person of a rebellious father, and branded by the sentence which condemned him, in place of receiving from him the life of grace, we have received the death of sin, and by an alarming destiny, we are condemned to hell even before

---

ments and of removing danger. Judith bound her forehead with a lily crown, that she may courageously enter the tent of Holofernes.—*Comment of the Rabbins on the Book of Judith.*

our birth. This unhappy fate inherent in the human race, cursed as one man in its origin, is common to all, and the Scripture makes no exception in favour of any child of Adam. But the piety of the faithful could not support the thought that the Mother of God should be made subject to the disgraceful sentence, which brands us with the seal of hell, even in our mother's womb. They thought the Sovereign Judge should suspend the general effect of his rigorous law in favour of her who came into the world to co-operate in the incarnation of the Messiah, the most secret and incomprehensible of all the divine counsels. Notwithstanding the silence of the Gospel, there was an opinion, pretty general, that the virgin, in view of her miraculous maternity, had been held, if I may use the expression, suspended on the brink of the abyss, opened under our feet by the disobedience of our first parents, and that her conception had been as immaculate as her life.* Yet, this opinion, redounding to the honour of the Virgin mother, has met with opponents, and powerful opponents, for St. Anselm, St. Bernard, St. Bonaventure, St. Thomas of Aquin, Albert the Great, and many other enlightened and learned persons, all great theologians, and even strongly devoted to Mary, maintain that she had been conceived in sin, and had been subject to the general law, though immediately after, she had been cleansed from it by a special and extraordinary favour.†

* This belief, adopted among the Greeks, was then consecrated by a festival celebrated from the seventh century.

† According to St. 'Augustin, the lineage to which all the patriarchs aspired was Jesus Christ, and Jesus Christ in Mary. And, in truth, says a learned theologian, if nature, in all its efforts, tends to Jesus Christ, who is the Lord of ages, it is not that it contemplates mounting up by its innate virtue to the Son of God—the extent of her power stops with the humble Mary, who was to bring forth the blessed seed, not by virtue of her progenitors, but by the power of the Most High.

But devotion to the Virgin—a devotion of which the Greeks had taken the initiative—prevailed over the opinion of the great doctors of the middle ages. That which had escaped the eagle eyes of the *school*, was made known to the simple and unsophisticated. The writings of the apostles and doctors were opened anew; a close search was made into all these matters regarding the greatness of Mary, which had been handed down to us from age to age, and this rigorous inquiry threw new light on the obscure portion of the history of the Mother of God. If we go back to the times of the apostles, we shall find, even then, the title of most holy and *immaculate* applied to Mary.* The apostle St. Andrew, quoted by the Babylonian Abdias, thus speaks: " As the first Adam had been made of the earth before it was cursed, so the second Adam has been formed from a virgin earth, which was never cursed." The saints and martyrs who lived in the third century, St. Hippolytus, St. Gregory, Bishop of Neocæsarea, Origen, St. Dionysius of Alexandria, style the holy Virgin pure and *immaculate*. St. Cyprian, speaking more clearly and precisely, says, " That there is a very wide difference between other mortals and the Virgin, and that there exists nothing in common between them but nature, without its penalty." In the fourth century, St. Basil and St. Epiphanius pay similar homage to Mary; St. Ambrose compares her to " a straight and glittering stem, which has neither the knot of original sin, nor the bark of actual sin." *Virgo in qua nec nodus originalis, nec cortex actualis culpæ, fuit,*" and St. Jerome compares her to " that cloud of light which has never known darkness."† A priest of Jerusalem, Chrysippus, a very ancient

---

* St. James the Great, and St. Mark, in their liturgy.
† Commentary of St. Jerome on the 77th Psalm.—" Deduxit eos in nube

author, after investing Mary with the title of *immaculate*, adds that " she has nothing in common with her perverse people, she who, from her nature, without sin or stain, resembles the rose planted on a soil set thick with thorns."

St. John Chrysostom calls the Virgin "most holy, *immaculate*, blessed above all creatures, glorious Mother of God." In the fifth century, St. Augustin could not endure even the mention of Mary's name when there is question of sin,* and St. John Chrysologus affirms that everything has been saved in the Virgin: *Merito ergo Virgini salva sunt omnia.* St. Fulgentius, who flourished at the commencement of the sixth century, says that "the holy Virgin was altogether excluded from the original decree." It is wrong, says St. Ildefonsus, Archbishop of Toledo, who flourished about the middle of the seventh century, " to wish to render Mary, the Mother of God, subject to the laws of nature; it is certain that she has been free and exempt from the stain of original sin, and that she has removed the malediction of Eve. This holy bishop did not rest content with the expression of his sentiments in relation to the immaculate conception of the Blessed Virgin; in his life written by the Benedictines, it is mentioned, that he gave orders that a solemn feast should be observed through all Spain, in honour of the conception of the Mother of God. We also find in the laws of the Visigoths, that the king Ervige passed a law, compelling the Jews to refrain from servile works on the Christian festivals, and among these festivals, occurs the feast of the Conception of the Virgin. St. John Damascene, who died about the year 780, in treating of the

diei; nubes est beata Virgo, quæ pulchre dicitur nubes, diei, quia non fuit in tenebris, sed semper in luce."

* It is necessary to remark that St. Augustin then defended the doctrine of original sin against the Pelagians.

conception of Mary, says, that she was pure and *immaculate.*
"You are all beautiful, O Mary!" says the humble and learned
Abbot of Celles, " you are all beautiful in your conception,
being created to become the temple of God. The stain of
sin, whether mortal, venial, or *original,* has never infected
your soul." Mahomedanism itself pronounces in favour of
the immaculate conception, and the Arabian commentators of
the Koran have adopted, after their own fashion, the opinion
of the Catholic theologians supporting this doctrine. "Every
one of Adam's race," says Cottada, " from the very moment
of his coming into the world, is marked on the side by
Satan; we must, however, except Jesus and his Mother,
for a veil was interposed by God between them and Satan,
which preserved them from his fatal mark." This chain of
witnesses favouring the immaculate conception of Mary,
breaks off rather suddenly in the ninth and continues so
during the tenth, eleventh, and twelfth centuries. Very
few authors of distinction wrote, during that space, in
favour of that opinion, but many eminent for their learning
and holiness wrote in support of the contrary. By way of
atonement, the feast of the Conception of the Virgin was
established in various kingdoms. From the time of the
first Henry, King of England, and Duke of Normandy, this
feast was celebrated at Rouen, with extraordinary solemnity.
"It was instituted," says the old chroniclers, " on account
of the blessed apparition presented to an abbe, in whom implicit reliance can be placed, who, during a violent storm,
had encountered the perils of a shipwreck." An old copy
of the history of the antiquities of Rouen adds, that "from
the very time of the institution of that festival, an association was founded of the most illustrious persons of that city,
who, even yet, on every year, select from among themselves
the head of the confraternity, which holding out a *puy* or

platform to all orators, in every tongue, offers a valuable
premium to those who, in the most ornate, appropriate, and
perfect style, should celebrate the praise of the Virgin Mary,
on the subject of the holy conception, by hymns, odes, son-
nets, ballads, royal chants," etc.* Thus the Virgin, full of
grace, presided at the revival of poetry, and her immaculate
conception furnished with pious themes the land of minstrels.
From Normandy the feast of the conception passed over the
sea, and was established in that extensive kingdom, then
Catholic, but afterwards......! but then her kings and
haughty barons had a deep reverence for OUR LADY. At
the same period this feast was also established in Lyons,
notwithstanding the remonstrances of St. Bernard, who reproached the canons of Lyons with the celebration of the
immaculate conception, without previously consulting the
Apostolic See.† Renold of Hombieres, Bishop of Paris,
dying in 1288, bequeathed a considerable sum to establish
the office of the Immaculate Conception of the Virgin. In
1394, Don Juan the First, King of Arragon, instituted, by
royal patent, the Feast of the Immaculate Conception in all
the provinces of Spain which had not succumbed to the
yoke of Mahomedanism; and his ordinance conveyed that
the kings, his predecessors, the objects of Mary's protection
and favour, had previously solemnized that feast in a
manner worthy of her. This ordinance, as a gem in Mary's
crown, is too intimately connected with the nature of this
work to allow us to omit its insertion here:‡—

* Antiquities of the City of Rouen, by N. Taillipied, Doctor of Theology.
† "*Nam, si sic videbitur,*" he says, " *consulenda erat prius Apostolicæ Sedis
auctoritas et non ita præcipitanter atque inconsulté paucorum sequenda simpli-
citas imperitorum.*" St. Thomas, in his " Summa of Theology," says also
that this feast has been tolerated, though not approved of by the Church.
‡ See the Book of the Privileges of the Kingdom of Valentia, for the year
1394.

"We, Don Juan, by the grace of God, King of Arrogon and of Valentia, etc.

"Why is it that some persons feel astonished that the Blessed Mary, Mother of God, should have been conceived without original sin, whilst they entertain not the slightest doubt that St. John the Baptist had been sanctified in his mother's womb by that same God, who, descending from the highest heavens, and from the throne of the most Holy Trinity, was made flesh in the blessed womb of a virgin? What favours, think we, could the Lord have refused to a woman who brought him forth by means of the astounding miracle of her fruitful virginity? Loving his Mother equally as himself, he must have encompassed her conception, her nativity, and the other phases of her holy life, with illustrious prerogatives.

"Why call in question the glorious conception of a Virgin, whose extraordinary privileges and favours, which cannot command sufficient admiration, Catholic belief forces us to acknowledge? Is it not the greatest subject of wonder to all Christians, that a creature should have given birth to her Creator, and that she should have become mother without the loss of her virginity? How can the human mind adequately sound the praises of this glorious Virgin, whose prerogatives of divine maternity, combined with the lustre of stainless virginity, and her elevation above the prophets, and all the saints, and all the choirs of angels, the Omnipotent destined her the possession of, without the slightest corruption. To cast on her the imputation of original sin, on her, to whom the angel, commissioned by heaven, addresses these words:—'*Hail, Mary, full of grace: the Lord is with thee; blessed art thou amongst women;*' it must follow, that at the first instant of her conception she stood in need of come special grace and favour. Let those who speak so improperly, then, be silent; let those who have only vain and frivolous objections to propose against the immaculate conception, so privileged and pure, of the Blessed Virgin, feel a blush of shame at giving them publicity, because it was only meet that she should be endowed with purity so spotless, as to be inferior only to the purity of God himself. It is only meet that she who had brought forth a Son, the Creator, and Father of all things, should have been ever, and should be now, most pure, most lovely, most perfect, having by a divine decree, been chosen before all ages, to bear in her womb Him, whom the whole world and the highest heavens cannot contain.

"But we, who among all Catholic kings, without any merit on our parts, have received so many graces and favours from this Mother of mercies, we firmly believe that the conception of this Blessed Virgin, in whose womb the Son of God deigned to become man, has been entirely holy and spotless.

"Thus, with a pure heart we will honour the mystery of the immaculate and glorious conception of the most holy Virgin, Mother of God, and we, and all those of our royal household, shall every year celebrate its festival with solemnity, in the same manner that our illustrious predecessors, of glorious memory, have celebrated it, having established, in honour of it, a perpetual association. It is for this purpose we ordain that this festival of the Immaculate Conception shall be celebrated with all possible solemnity and respect every year in perpetuity, in all kingdoms subject to our obedience, by all the faithful, whether religious or secular, by all priest and all other persons, whatever may be their condition and state; and that from henceforward we strictly prohibit all preachers, and all those who deliver public lectures on the Gospel, from saying, publishing, and advancing anything which in any manner may act prejudicially to, or derogate from, the purity and sanctity of this glorious conception; but, on the contrary, we ordain that preachers and all others who might have formed opposite opinions should maintain strict silence, as the Catholic faith requires not that the contrary opinion should be either supported or professed, and that such as hold in their hearts our pious and salutary opinion should, by discourse, make it known, and earnestly show forth their devotion, in celebrating by the praises of the Most High, the glory and honour of the blessed Mother, who is the queen of heaven, the gate of paradise, the help of Christians, the assured port of salvation, and the anchor of the hope of sinners who place their trust in her. By the tenor of these presents we expressly ordain in perpetuity, that henceforward, any preacher, or any other person among our subjects, of whatever rank or condition he may be, who should not faithfully observe this general ordinance, shall be expelled from their convents and houses; and that so long as they maintain this adverse opinion, they shall as our enemies, remain without the bounds of our kingdoms. So willing and ordaining, with full knowledge and mature deliberation, under pain of incurring our displeasure and anger, all and every one of our servants who are or who will be on this or the other side of the sea, to observe and cause to be observed with the greatest diligence and respect our present edict, as soon as it shall be made known to them, and that each in his district, shall, in the usual places, publish it solemnly and with sound of trumpet, so that no person can show cause of ignorance, and that the devotion of the Immaculate Conception of the Most Blessed Virgin, which the faithful have long preserved in their hearts, may be increased more and more, and that we may no longer hear certain persons of the opposite opinion giving expression to their sentiments. In faith whereof we ordain that these presents be despatched, authorized by our seal attached.

"Given at Valentia, on the second of February, the day on which is celebrated the Festival of the Purification of the Most Blessed Virgin, the year of our Lord, 1384, and the eighth of our reign."

The doctrine of the Immaculate Conception had been banished from the chairs and schools for a very long space of time, when many religious* orders, but particularly the order of St. Francis, who devoted itself, body and soul, to that doctrine, undertook its revival. The Franciscans, who first publicly professed it, both by word and writing, maintained it by arguments so strong and convincing, that not only the great mass of the faithful, but the most learned bodies in Europe, enthusiastically adhered to it. The doctors of the Sorbonne, in their assembly in the month of February, 1576, declared that they considered the question of the immaculate conception of the Virgin as a point of faith (*de fide*). In another decree these same doctors, following, they said, in the footsteps of their ancestors (*majorum nostrorum vestigia sequentes*), bound themselves by oath to maintain that opinion. The law with regard to this is precise: "We resolve and declare that no person shall be

---

* Montfaucon, who travelled through Italy about the year 1698, having visited, at Pavia, the library of Beleridus, so renowned for his piety, was greatly surprised at observing that the immense collection of books solely consisted of treatises written by the Franciscans, in defence of the immaculate conception. An engraving placed in the front of one of these books, which was written by *Fra* Alva, represented the holy Virgin seated on the clouds; over her was a circle, flanked with towers, and in every tower a Franciscan who combated against the impugners of the immaculate conception.

admitted for the future into our Faculty unless he binds himself by oath, as we have done, to support, during his life, the doctrine of the immaculate conception." "*Statuentes ut nemo deinceps huic nostro collegio adscribatur, nisi se hujus doctrinæ assertorem semper pro viribus futuram simili juramento profiteatur.*" So acted in like manner the Universities of Mayence, Cologne, Valentia, Alcala, Coimbra, Salamanca, and Naples. The Franciscans, on their parts, commenced to celebrate this feast under the name of *the pure and immaculate conception,* and to commemorate, in the office of the day, the special grace which preserved Mary from the stain of original sin. And the Holy See not only tolerated this festival, but favoured it in an illustrious manner by granting to it the same privileges and indulgences which had been granted to the feast of the Holy Sacrament. In 1618 the viceroy of Naples, together with his court and army, registered a vow in the church of Notre Dame la Grande, to believe and defend the immaculate conception. In 1624, the order of the knights of the Duke of Nivers was confirmed at Rome under the title of the knights of the immaculate conception of the glorious Virgin, *immaculatæ conceptionis gloriosæ Virginis.* The councils have favoured this opinion. The Council of Basle, in the session of the 21st of September, 1429, thus speaks: "There has been raised in this holy council a difficult question on the conception of the glorious Virgin Mary, Mother of God, and on the beginning of justification. Some say that her soul, during some time, or at least during some moments, had been subject indeed to original sin; others support, on the contrary, that God's love for her extended even to the first instant of her creation; that the Most High, who had formed her himself, and that the Son, who had chosen her for his Mother on earth, endowed her with singular and extraordinary graces; that Jesus Christ had redeemed her in a supereminent and particular manner, by preserving her from the stain of original sin, and sanctifying her from the first instant of her conception.

" Having then carefully examined the arguments and authorities, which for many years have been advanced on both sides, in the public acts of this council; having besides paid due attention to many other things on the same subject; everything maturely weighed and considered, we decide and declare that the doctrine which teaches that the glorious Virgin Mary, Mother of God, by a peculiar privilege and a preventing and operating grace, had never been contaminated by the stain of original sin, but that she had always been holy, immaculate, and exempt from both original and actual sin; we declare that the doctrine which teaches all this is a pious doctrine, conformable to ecclesiastical worship, to Catholic faith, to right reason, and to Holy Scripture, and that as such it ought to be so approved, maintained, and followed by all Catholics, as that no person for the future should be allowed to preach or teach the contrary. Reviving, besides, the institution of the festival of the blessed conception, which, by an old and laudable custom, was celebrated on the eight day of December, both at Rome as well as in other churches ; it is our will and command that this feast be celebrated on the same day, under the name of the Conception of the Virgin, in all the churches, monasteries, and communities of the Catholic religion, and that canticles of joy and thanksgiving be sung in honour of it."

The council grants even indulgences to this solemnity. The Fathers of the Council of Trent have formally declared, that when framing their decree on original sin, they had no intention of including the immaculate and blessed Mother of God.* Two parties sprung up in the Church on this nice and critical question. Both sides could boast of, among their ranks, celebrated doctors, and learned theologians. Some thought to support the purity of the doctrine of the Church, to the prejudice of which it is easy to fall into indiscretion, *et sapere plus quam oportet* ; others wished to defend, at all hazards, the glorious perogatives of the Mother of God. The Court of Rome allowed, at first, a free arena to these theological disputations ; in her sovereign and reflecting wisdom, she maturely weighed the arguments advanced on both sides. In carefully examining the opinions of the fathers and ancient doctors, she found a great number of probabilities in favour of the so much disputed perogative of the Blessed Virgin brilliantly reflected from apostolical tradition. From that time her sympathy was accorded to the defenders of the immaculate conception. Pope Sixtus IV. confirmed this festival, and Pope Paul V., and Gregory XV., prohibited not only public *theses*, but private discourses and secret conversations against the mystery of the spotless conception. But Rome, with that prudence by which all her acts are characterized, felt unwilling to stigmatize the contrary opinion, through respect for the holy and illustrious names which supported it. She has never allowed that such an opinion should be censured as heretical, rash, scandalous, or even erroneous. She could prescribe as an article of faith, the belief in the immaculate conception of the Virgin ; but she rests satisfied with insinuating it, fully aware that the piety of the faithful required not a formal decision to render to the mother of mercies, to the consolatrix of sinners, to her whom the Church styles our

---

* " Declarat hæc sancta synodus non esse intentionis suæ comprehendere in hoc decreto ubi de peccato originali agitur, beatam et IMMACULATAM Dei genitricem."

mediatrix with Jesus Christ, every honour which comports with her dignity. A voice to whose weight too much importance cannot be attached, the great voice of Bossuet, is raised in this question; the *buckler of religion* is gloriously placed in front of the Blessed Virgin. " There is in the opinion of the immaculate conception a certain innate force, which brings conviction to devout souls. . After articles of faith, I see nothing more certain. It is for this reason, that I feel no surprise that the school of the Parisian theologians obliges all her children to defend this doctrine. As for me, I feel joy and satisfaction in following, at this time, her intentions. After having been nourished with her milk, I willingly submit myself to her ordinances, and particularly so, as such ordinances seem to me to be in accordance with the wishes of the Church. The sentiments of the Church redound to the honour of the conception of Mary. She does not oblige us to believe her *immaculate ;* but she gives us to understand, that this belief is pleasing to her. There are things which she commands, wherein we make known our obedience; there are other things which she only insinuates, wherein we can show our affection. Our piety requires, if we be true children of the Church, not only to obey the commands but even to bend to the slightest indications of the will of a mother so beneficent and holy."* Since the eagle of Meaux gave expression to these fine sentiments, this devotion has daily gained ground. In Spain, where an association of the immaculate conception was established in 1506, by Cardinal Ximenes, the festival perpetuating the memory of this glorious prerogative of Mary is celebrated with the greatest solemnity. There is scarcely a sermon preached there,

* Sermon on the Conception.

which does not commence in these words : "*Sea alabado el sanctissimo sacramen'o de el altar y la immaculada concepcion de la Virgen Maria, Neustra Senora, concebida sin pe peccado original en el primero in stante physico y real de su animacion.—Amen !*" " Praise be to the Most Holy Sacrament of the altar and to the immaculate conception of the Virgin Mary, our Lady, conceived without original sin at the first physical and real instant of her life.—Amen !" And this doctrine has not only been received for many centuries by the Spanish Church, but the country of Ferdinand and Isabella has so adopted it, that the profession of faith in the immaculate conception is the ordinary way in which the people greet each other.* This doctrine is held in the highest esteem through all Italy, and France as highly respects it. " It is a fact of which we are desirous to give undeniable proofs," says the Archbishop of Paris, " and we sincerely wish that it should be made known even in the most remote parts of the Catholic world. In our diocese this devotion has gradually cast its roots deeper and deeper, and disasters and calamities, so far from weakening it, have only strengthened, increased, and extended it with wonderful progress." The devotion of the immaculate conception is now, after the many violent storms with which it had to contend, indigenous to the soil of France. Assuredly, we cannot for a moment doubt that HE who saved the angels of heaven from the fall of their rebellious fellow-spirits, had preserved the queen of angels from the common fall of man, and that God said to Mary, as Assuerus said to Esther:

---

* Entering a house in Spain, the first words which visitors pronounce, before wishing good day, are these, " Ave purissima ;" the owners of the house immediately answer, " Sin peccado concebida sanctissima."

THE IMMACULATE CONCEPTION. 43

"This law regarding the whole world was not intended for you."

[The foregoing chapter was written by the author, before the ever memorable 8th December, 1854, when it was solemnly defined by the infallible authority of the Catholic Church, that "IT IS A DOGMA OF FAITH, that the Most Blessed Virgin Mary, in the first instant of her conception, by a singular privilege and grace of God, in virtue of the Merits of Jesus Christ, the Saviour of the human race, was preserved exempt from all stain of Original Sin." "It is good for us to be here, under the Glorious Pontificate, which marks an epoch in the centuries of the Church. The name of Pius was crowned with martyrdom in the first who bore it; and twice in this half-century those who bore it have been confessors, and exiles. It is not, therefore, from the exile of the reigning Pontiff that this century will take its character and its greatness. But the age will be marked in the history of the Church by a dignity more divine. As the fourth century was glorious by the definition of the Godhead of the Consubstantial Son, and the fifth by that of His two perfect natures, and the thirteenth by that of the Procession of the Holy Ghost, so the nineteenth will be glorious by the definition of the Immaculate Conception."—*Dr. Manning.*]

CHAPTER III.

THE BIRTH OF MARY.

TOWARDS the decline of the religion and temporal concerns of the Hebrews, at the time marked out by the prophets, when the royal sceptre was wielded by the hands of a foreigner, as the prophet Jacob had long since foretold, there lived in Nazareth, a town of Lower Galilee, and not far distant from Mount Carmel, a just man, named Joachim,[*] of the tribe of Juda, and of the race of David, by Nathan. His wife, who, according to St. Augustin, was descended from the tribe of Levi[†] was called Anna, a name in Hebrew signifying *gracious*.[‡] They were both just before Jehovah, and walked with an upright heart the way of his commandments;[§] but the Lord seemed to have averted from them the light of his countenance, for one great blessing was

---

[*] A writer of the life of Mary (Christopher of Castro, Jesuit of Scagna), with the Rabbins, St. Hilary and other holy fathers, on inquiry discovered that the father of Mary had the two names, Heli and Joachim. The Arabians and the Mussulmen recognised him under the name of Amram, son of Mathan, and drew a distinction between him and another Amram, father of Mary, the sister of Moses.—*D'Herbelot, Bibliothéque Orientale*, tome 2.

[†] St. Augustin *on the Unanimity of the Evangelists.*

[‡] The Mahomedans, inheritors of the Arabic traditions, recognised the blessed mother of the holy Virgin under her own name, Hannah. According to them she was daughter of Nakor, and wife of Amram.—*D'Herbelot, Bibliothéque Orientale, tome* 2.

[§] St. Anne and St. Joachim were publicly honoured by the Church from the earliest ages. St. John Damascene passes a grand eulogium on their virtue. The Emperor Justinian I., about the year 550, erected a church at Constantinople, under the invocation of St. Anne. The body of the Saint was brought, it is said, from Palestine to Constantinople, in the year 710. (See Godescard, t. v. p. 319.) Luther previous to his fall, had a great devotion towards St. Anne. To this saint it was that he vowed to embrace the monastic state, after seeing one of his companions fall before his eyes struck by lightning.

THE BIRTH OF MARY.

wanting to render their lives happy—they were without children—to them a saddening and dejecting thought, as in Israel sterility was the brand of shame. Joachim, who entertained a strong affection for his wife, as well for her sweetness of disposition as for her other eminent virtues, was unwilling to add to her unhappiness, by giving her letters of divorce, which then the law freely granted.* He closely guards her; and these holy spouses, with humble resignation to the decrees of heaven, passed their days in labour, prayer, and acts of charity. Such eminent virtue must, assuredly, meet with its recompense. After twenty years of sterility, Anne miraculously conceived and brought forth that blessed creature, who, of all the elect, was the most perfect, holy, and pleasing in the eyes of the Lord. In the beginning of the month Tisri,† the first of the Jewish civil year, and whilst the incense of holocausts was rising to heaven for the expiation of the sins of the people, that predestined Virgin was born, who was to wash out the primal transgression in the blood of Christ.‡ Her birth, like that of her Divine Son, was unattended by any outward show. Her parents, though descended from a long line of

---

* The Pharisees introduced this abuse of the law of divorce, so much stigmatized by our Lord. Their doctrine was, that a wife could be divorced for the most trivial cause—as for example for having overdone the meat of her *landlord*, or simply for not being pretty enough. This was the sentiment of the celebrated Doctor Hillil.

† The eighth of September. Baronius is of opinion that Mary was born in the year of Rome 733—twenty-one years before the vulgar era, on the 8th of September, at day-break, on Saturday. The *Nain* of Tillemont tells us that the Virgin was born in the year 734. This opinion is generally followed.

‡ Let us see what the Turks teach, in reference to the birth of the Blessed Virgin. The spouse of Amram (Joachim) said to God, when she had given the light to her daughter: " My Lord, I have brought forth a daughter, but no man will be comparable to her. I have given her the name of *Miriam* (Mary). I recommend her and her future race to you, to oppose Satan, who has been stoned."—*Surate*, iii. b. 36.

kings, were of the people, and apparently led a retired and obscure life. This mysterious rose, which in latter times St. John beheld clothed with the sun, as with radiant drapery, was to blow on a poor and naked stalk before the parching blast of adversity.* The cradle, unlike that of the Hebrew princes, had no gilded trappings to enhance it; it was redolent neither of the perfume of spikenards, nor that of myrrh, or aloes: of flexible saplings it was woven, and the little arms, that were at a future day to lull to sleep the Saviour of the world, were now compressed by coarse linen bandages. The infants of royalty, whilst yet enveloped in their purple swaddling clothes, see homage paid them by persons of the greatest rank and distinction in the state, who even then call them, " Your Highness!" the child who was to become the Spouse and Mother of God, familiarized her first smile with poor unknown women of obscure descent, who, reflecting, perhaps, on the lot of the lowly born, and the disregard and contempt in which they were generally held, were saying in tones of sadness, *one slave more!* But the holy mother of the Virgin, appreciating the value of the rich gift bestowed on her by heaven, revealed to her, it is thought, by an angel, profoundly gave thanks to the Lord, and breaks forth into a canticle of thanksgiving and praise—still preserved by tradition—which portrays the excessive maternal joy of her heart: *Cantabo laudem Domino meo, quia visitavit me et abstulit a me opprobrium inimicorum meorum. Et dedit mihi, fructum justitiæ multiplicem in conspec u tuo. Quis annuntiabit Filis Ruben*

---

* Isaias had foretold him in these words—"*A branch will shoot up from the stock of Jesse.*" But the word trunk or stock in Hebrew means, as St. Jerome remarks (Isaias, chap. ii.), a trunk without branches or leaves—denoting, as the holy doctor further remarks, that the august Mary was to be born of the race of David, when that family would have lost all its former splendour, and would be nigh extinct.

quod Anna lacet! Audite, audite, duodecim tribus Israel, quia Anna lactat!......

"Oh! excellent gift," cries out St. John Damascene, overflowing with those sentiments of love and gratitude with which every rational creature should be animated at the thought of the birth of Mary. "Oh! inexpressible gift! Oh! the incomparable munificence of our God! All nature cries out in transports of joy at the birth of Mary. Oh! how all men should rejoice in the hope of being delivered from corruption, and glory in that happy epoch, when she who had been born without corruption or stain, was to bring forth the Creator of the world." The Church regarding the nativity of Mary as an event which, in grandeur and importance, yields only to that of the birth of Jesus Christ, sounds forth in every Christian temple her solemn accents of profound joy, on the day commemorative of that event. On the eighth of September, the day set apart to commemorate that happy event, she cries out with transport, "Your nativity, O Virgin Mother of God, has filled the whole world with joy, for of you was born the Son of Justice, Jesus Christ, our God, who, freeing the whole human race from the curse under which they groaned, has loaded them with benefits; and overcoming death, has bestowed on us eternal life." It was customary in Israel, that the child, on the ninth day after birth, should, in a family meeting, receive that name by which it was afterwards to be known. The daughter of Joachim received from her father the name of *Miriam* (Mary), which in the Syriac tongue means *lady, mistress, sovereign,* and which in Hebrew has the signification of *star of the sea.* "And, surely," says St. Bernard, "the Mother of God could not receive a more appropriate name, or one which could better express her high dignity. Mary is, indeed, that lovely and brilliant star which shines down on the expansive and stormy sea of this world. Such, potent efficacy and such marvellous beauty does this divine name possess, that the bare mention of it melts the heart, and the mere insertion of it brightens the page." "The name of Mary," says St. Anthony of Padua, "is sweeter than a honeycomb to the lips, more flattering than enchanting music to the ear, and more delicious than the purest joy to the heart." "*Nomen virginis Mariæ, mel in ore, melos in aure, jubilium in corde.*" Twenty-four days after the birth of a daughter, the Jewish mother with her first-born repaired to the temple, and was there solemnly purified. In conformity with the law of Moses, she then offered to the Lord a lamb or a pair of turtle doves. The pair of turtle doves was the offering of the poor; it was, too, the offering of the spouse of Joachim. But the gratitude of the pious mother was not limited to the customary sacrifice. A worthy imitator of Anna, the wife of Elcana, she offered to the Lord a more unspotted victim—a more innocent dove than those which had fallen palpitating and bleeding under the priest's knife. To suspend from the walls of the temple a votive crown of the purest gold was beyond her power, but the crown of her old age—the blessing of her life—she laid down at the feet of the Most High, and entered into an engagement, that as soon as her daughter arrived at the years of discretion, and could distinguish good from evil, she would lead her again to the temple,* and there consecrate her to the service of the holy place. The father of Mary ratified the vow, which then became obligatory.† The ceremony over, Joachim and Anne re-enter the

* See Mach. Book IV.
† There were among the Jews two sorts of vows. The first, *neder*, was a simple vow, which could be redeemed; and such was the vow of Anne, mother of Mary. The second, *cherem*, was strictly obligatory, binding under all cir-

THE BIRTH OF MARY. 49

road of their native province—a province in no way remarkable for giving birth to illustrious men, and the last place out of which Israel expected a prophet to arise*—and regained their humble dwelling, always open to the needy and the stranger. It was here that the child of benediction, the child of grace and favour spent her early years—those years which were so delightful to her parents, and grew up like one of those lilies, of which Jesus Christ has spoken, and which possess, according to the poetical expression of St. Bernard, the odour of hope: *habens odorem spei.* As was customary with the women of her country, Anne herself nursed her daughter.†

The understanding of Mary, like the day in these delightful regions of the sun, had scarcely an aurora, but shone out full from the most tender age. Her precocious fervour, the wisdom with which her discourses were seasoned, and that at a period of life when other children enjoy a purely physical existence, afforded sufficient grounds to her parents to judge that the hour of separation had come; and when Joachim had offered, for the third time, to the Lord the firstlings of his small tenement, and the fruits of the little heritage of his fathers, both parents, grateful and resigned, set out for Jerusalem, to lay down in the sacred precincts of the temple the treasure which the HOLY ONE of Israel had given them.

cumstances; and everything promised by such a vow could not be recalled. Every Israelite could alienate by this sort of vow everything belonging to him—houses, lands, beasts, children, slaves, &c., and things thus vowed could never at any price be purchased or redeemed.

* Can anything good come from Nazareth? asked Nathaniel of those who spoke to him about Christ. Nazareth was a small and contemptible place, says St. John Chrysostom, and not only Nazareth, but all Galilee.—*Sermon* ix.

† In Judea, women did not consider themselves dispensed from nursing their own children. In the Scriptures we find mention made of only three nurses—those of Rebecca, Miphiboseth, and Joas; we must observe, moreover, that Rachel was not a native, and that the others were princesses.

CHAPTER IV.

THE PRESENTATION.

THE waves of Cison* were rolling on in all their pride, but red and angry from the violence of the equinoctial gales—the green mountains of Galilee were surcharged with snow, when the parents of Mary undertook their journey to Jerusalem. The reasons which induced them to quit their native province during the rainy season we know not. It may be, that they were desirous of assisting at the grand solemnities of the feast of the dedication; it may that they wished to square the time of their setting out with the period of the service of Zachary, the high priest, who dwelt in Hebron or Ain, and who was called to perform his sacerdotal functions in the temple only at regular stated intervals.† Compelled in a most inclement season, with a young and tender child, to undertake a journey of many days, these pious and prudent wayfarers, in setting out for the holy city, selected not the wild and cavernous route which winds through the arid plains, the foaming torrents, and the deep ravines of the mountains of Judea and Samaria. There winter reigned in all

---

* The Cison is a small river flowing between Nazareth and Mount Carmel, insignificant and scanty, like the other rivers in Palestine, in the summer; it becomes very considerable during the rainy seasons. The army of Sisara, general of the forces of Jabin, were drowned in this river, in their endeavours to force a passage through it.

† " According to the regulation of David, the Jewish priests were divided into twenty-four classes or courses, each of which, in turn, served during a week in the temple of Jerusalem. Each course was subdivided into seven parts, each of which served in turn during that work, and each part of that subdivision had that portion of the service assigned him which fell to him by lot. Zachary was of the course or service of Abia."—*Prid. Hist. of the Jews.*

its severity. They descended by the embalmed declivities of Carmel into the fertile and sandy plains of Saron, where the temperature is so mild, that the orange trees, bananahs, and date trees were then in full bloom.* On arriving at that side of the city, they enter Jerusalem through the gate of Ephraim, and after passing on through some winding and dreary streets, lined on both sides with large, heavy, square-built houses, without windows, and whose terraced roofs were but a poor imitation of citadels, they stopped in the oriental part of the city, before a house of unpretending appearance, which tradition assigns as the dwelling of St. Anne.† When Mary was recovered from the fatigues of her journey, Joachim paid a visit to his relatives in Jerusalem, and providing himself with a spotless lamb, together with a measure of wheaten flour, as an offering to the Lord,‡ he ascended to the temple, in company with his numerous friends dressed out in their holiday garb. In passing through the outer court where the stranger must arrest his steps under pain of death, the *cortege* grows larger by the addition of a great number of officers belonging to the royal household, of Pharisees, Scribes, and illustrious bodies, assembled together through some secret disposition of Provi-

---

* Volney beheld, along the coasts of Syria, orange trees laden with fruits and flowers in the month of January. "With us," he says, "each month has a different season ; there, almost every hour has a different season." At Tripoli he was oppressed by the July heats, and in six hours afterwards he felt the cold temperature of March, on the neighbouring mountains. Again, he experienced the severe cold of a December day among the mountains, and a short journey brought him to the plain where the flowers were in full bloom.

† A monastery has been erected over this house of St. Anne. The monastery is now converted into a mosque Under the Christian kings, a religious order dwelt in it.—*Intr. de Paris à Jerusalem*, t. ii., p. 211.

‡ The solemn presentations were accompanied by a sacrifice. Anna, mother of Samuel, offered sacrifice when leading her son to Silo. Father Croiset thinks one had been in like manner offered at the time of the consecration of the Blessed Virgin. It was almost impossible that it could be otherwise.

dence, under the porch of Solomon.* Undoubtedly, God willed that the happy Virgin, chosen by him from all eternity to be the Mother of Christ, should appear in the house of prayer in apparel suited to her high destiny. Pious authors,† associating the world of spirits with this earthly festival, have even insinuated, that the invisible guardians of the temple, surrounding Mary on all sides, overshadowed her with their white wings, cast under her feet the odoriferous flowers of paradise, and celebrated her coming with melodious canticles of praise. They stopped a moment on the marble steps of the *Chel;*‡ there the Pharisees paraded their *tephilim* § and threw back over their haughty brows a skirt of their *talid*, composed of white and fine wool,|| and ornamented with purple granados and violet *cordons;* the daring captains of Herod were enveloped in their rich cloaks negligently tied by golden clasps, and the daughters of Sion wrapped themselves more closely in the folds of their veils, *through respect for the angels of the sanctuary.*¶ The divine child and her gorgeous retinue then passed through the gate of bronze, which closed the sacred precincts against the profane. In the frozen regions of the North, large basilicas are required as a shelter from the injurious effects of the cli-

---

* *Primarius quoque hierosolymitas viros et mulieres interfuisse huic deductioni, succinentibus universis angelis.*"—(*Isid. of Thess.*)

† St. Andrew of Crete, Georges of Nicomedia.

‡ The *Chel* was a space of ten cubits between the court of the Gentiles and the court of women.

§ "The *tephilim* were small bits of parchment on which four sentences of Scripture were written with a peculiar sort of ink. These *typhilim*, or *phylacteries*, were much used at the time of Jesus Christ, consituting badges of distinction, which drew forth from him reproaches."—*Basnage t.* 5, *liv.* 7.

|| "A sort of cloak worn by the Jews at the temple during prayer. Some folded it about the neck, others covered the head with it; and this latter custom was the one more generally observed."—*Basnage, t.* 5, *liv.* 7.

¶ " Ideo dubet mulier potestatem habere supra caput propter angelos.— *Ep. St. Paul to the Corinth.*, *chap.* 11, *v.* 10.

THE PRESENTATION. 53

mate; and so we have vast cathedrals which are capable of containing many thousands. But in ancient Asia, the temples were exclusively devoted to the functions of the priests: the people prayed without. In Israel, the *the holy assembly* was usually held in the court of women. The second court was so designated, because the Jewish women, assimilated by the old law to slaves, could advance no farther. Separated from their sons and husbands, who remained in the area of the porch, or under the arcades of the perystile, during the ceremonies of the Hebraical worship, they prayed apart in the upper galleries, with their heads lowly inclined towards the house of Jehovah, whose gorgeous roof of cedar, with its tapering gilded spires, they perceived at some distance. The ceremony of the presentation had certainly been performed in the court of women, and not in the interior of the sanctuary, as some authorities have supposed. It opened by a sacrifice. The gate of Nicanor, turning noiselessly on its brazen hinges, to allow the victim to pass on, opened in perspective a view of the temple of Zorobabel, with its votive crowns, its golden plated doors, and its walls of huge and polished stones, on which the hand of time had traced that tinged filemot which characterizes the ancient buildings of the Levant. Grandeur and magnificence distinctively marked every part of the house of Jehovah; and yet it had fallen off much in splendour and holiness! There was something indescribably wanting and incomplete in its imposing ceremonies; its priests were not the anointed of the Lord; the vessels of the temple were unconsecrated, the ark had disappeared, and with it the *Schekina ;* the stones of the *rational*, that brilliant and latest oracle in which God made known his will to the Aaronides, had lost their prophetic lustre, and no longer predicted either defeat or victory.* But a day that was to shed lustre on the holy house seemed about to arise, and already the East was giving indications of the light. The priests and the Levites, assembled in the outer court, received from the hands of Joachim the victim of *prosperity*.† These ministers of the living God had not their brows bound with laurel or green smallage, like the priests of idols. A sort of mitre, with a coarse linen band, a tunic of linen, long, white, and without folds, tied round by a long embroidered cincture of golden and purple dye, composed the sacerdotal costume, and which was worn only in the temple. After having thrown over his left shoulder the flowing ends of his cincture, one of the *Chananeans*‡ took the lamb, and turning its head towards the north, struck the sacred knife into its throat, pronouncing at the same time a short invocation to the God of Jacob. The blood, which flowed into a brazen vessel, was deposited in a reservoir, for the purpose of sprinkling the corners of the altar.§ That over, the priest spread out on a large golden plate the bowels, kidneys, liver, and fat of the victim, which the different Levites presented in

---

* " God made use of the precious stones which the high priest carried on the *rational*, for the purpose of presaging victory ; for before encamping, a flash of light issued from it, by which the people were given to understand that the Sovereign Majesty was present, and prepared to aid them. But since I have commenced writing two centuries have elapsed, and during that space of time the the *rational* never emitted that light."—*Josephus' Ant. of the Jews*, b. 3, c. 8.

† Whenever a favour was demanded of God, or thanksgiving returned for one, that was called a sacrifice of prosperity.

‡ " The ordinary sacrificing priest."—*Josephus*.

§ " At the four corners of the altar of holocausts, where the priests remained when they were offering sacrifice, there were four small pillars, a cubit each in height. These pillars were hollow, and received a portion of the blood of the victims. These were the corners of the altar, of which mention is made so frequently in Scripture."—*Prideaux Hist. of the Jews*.

THE PRESENTATION.   55

turn, after having carefully washed them in the fountain
square. On the oblation he placed incense and salt; then
ascending with naked feet the gently inclined steps which
led to the table of the altar of holocausts, he poured out
libations of wine and blood,* cast into the glowing flame,
fanned into life by no human breath,† a little wheaten
flour, diluted in a golden cup with oil of the purest olives,
and then laid the peace offering on the glowing piles
furnished by the extensive woods of Sichem,‡ which the inferior officers of the temple and carefully sought out and
stripped of their bark.§ The remaining portion of the
sacrifice, with the exception of the breast and right shoulder,
which belonged to the priests, was returned to the husband
of St. Anne, who, conformably to the custom of his country,
divided it in small portions among his near relatives. The
last sound of the sacerdotal trumpets was dying away along
the porticos, the sacrifice was still burning on the brazen
altar, when a priest descended into the court of women, to
terminate the ceremony. Anne, followed by Joachim, and
bearing Mary in her arms, advanced, her head covered, towards the minister of the MOST HIGH, and if we are to believe an Arabic tradition, inserted by Mahomet himself in
the Koran, she presented him the youthful servant of the
Lord, pronouncing at the same time, in subdued, moving
accents, these touching words: "I am come to offer you

---

* Each sacrifice required the employment of a great number of priests and Levites. Basnage assures us that the mere sacrifice of a lamb required the presence of eighteen priests.

† "The Jews neither used the mouth, or bellows of any description, to light the fire of the altar. They excited the flame by pouring oil on glowing coals." —*Prideaux*.

‡ "Wood was carried from the territory of Napoli, for the sacrifice of the temple. The country of Sichem is to this day a woody country."—*Corresp. of the East*, t, 4, p. 166.

§ Prideaux's History of the Jews.

THE PRESENTATION.

the present which God has given me."* The priest, in the name of HIM who renders fruitful the womb of mothers, received the precious deposit, which gratitude confided to him, and gave his benediction to Anne and Joachim, as Heli the high-priest had done before, under similar circumstances, to Elcana and his happy wife. Then extending his hands over those assembled, who bent down to receive the pontifical benediction:† "O Israel," he says, "That the Eternal may direct his light towards you; that he may grant you prosperity and peace in all things!" A canticle of joy and thanksgiving, with a melodious accompaniment of the sacerdotal harps, ended the presentation of the Blessed Virgin. Such was the ceremony which had taken place, in the latter days of November, in the holy temple of Sion. Those who looked no farther than to outward appearances, beheld only a youthful child incomparably beautiful and remarkably fervent, consecrated by her mother to God, who had bestowed her in recompense of that mother's fastings and tears; but the angels of heaven, who were hovering over the sanctuary, recognised in this delicate and amiable creature, the Virgin of Isaias—the spouse whose mystical hymn Solomon had chanted—the heavenly Eve, who came to blot out the transgressions which the sinner Eve could not wash out with her

---

* "According to a Mahomedan tradition, when St. Anne had brought into the world the Blessed Virgin, she presented her to the priests, saying at the same time, as is seen in the Koran, *dhouncon hadih alnedhirat*; that is, here is the offering which I present you with. Hossain Vaez makes an addition to these words in his Persian paraphrase, *kihez an khodai*, meaning, for it is a gift which God has bestowed on me, or rather more literally, for it is from this gift that God is to come."—*D'Herbelot, Bibliothéque Orientale, t. 2, p.* 620.

† " Whilst the pontiff was giving his benediction, the people were obliged to place their hands on their eyes and to conceal their faces, for they were prohibited from looking at the hands of the priest. The Jews imagined that God was behind the high priest, and looked through him with extended hands; they durst not raise their eyes towards him, *for no person can see God and live.*"—*Busnage, liv.* 7, *ch.* 15.

THE PRESENTATION. 57

tears*—the adopted and cherished daughter of God the Almighty—she whom Adam had formerly contemplated from the sublime heights of paradise, as the only plank of salvation which remained to rescue him from shipwreck.

Filled with joy at seeing the aurora of the world's redemption glittering at last, the angelical choirs respectfully hailed this young plant, sprung from the root of Jesse, which was to grow at the foot of the altar of the MOST HIGH, as the olive tree of peace and of the renewed alliance. What was then passing in the soul of Mary, in that soul lovingly blowing under the breathing of the Holy Ghost, where unalterable peace reigned, and pure love and light dwelt? By what holy bonds was she united to HIM by whom she was preferred to the virgins and queens of so many nations? That is a secret between herself and God; but there is every reason to suppose that never was there an offering so favourably received; and St. Evodius of Antioch, St. Epiphanius of Salamis, St. Andrew of Crete, and numerous other Latin Fathers, are unanimous in their belief that the consecration of the Virgin was the most pleasing act of religion that man had until then paid to God. We know not the priest by whom the Holy Virgin was received among the daughters of the Lord. St. Germanus, Patriarch of Constantinople, and Georges of Nicomedia, think that he was the father of St. John the Baptist. The ties of kindred by which Zachary was united to the family of Joachim, the high rank which he then held in the priesthood,* and the tender affection entertained by Mary for him and St. Elizabeth, stamp this opinion with a very high degree of probability. Be this as it

---

* To furnish us with some idea of the repentance of Eve after her transgression, the Rabbins say, that the lake Tiberiades was supplied by her tears.

† "The Jews believed that St. John the Baptist was greater than Jesus Christ, as he was the son of a *high priest*."—*St. John Chrysostom, Sermon* 12.

F

may, the blessed daughter of Joachim was solemnly admitted among the *almas*, or young virgins, who were brought up, remote from every eye, under the sacred shadow of the altar. That Mary had spent the earlier and most delightful years of her life in the temple is proved by apostolical tradition, the writings of the Fathers, and the opinion of the Church, which ordinarily gives not its sanction to doubtful facts.* Nevertheless, some heretics have treated this circumstance as altogether fabulous, and even Catholic writers themselves have considered this passage in her life as obscure and concealed under the veil of time long past, on which it is very difficult to throw light. The denial of heretics can be easily accounted for, but the extreme prudence of Catholic writers appears rather strange, for if ever Christian tradition had the impress of authenticity, it is this assuredly. St. Evodius, who first made mention, in an epistle entitled *Lumen*, which Nicephorus has handed down to us, of this particular and glorious passage in the infancy of the Blessed Virgin, flourished at the time of the apostles and the Mother of God. He was bishop of Antioch, a city of Syria, into which flowed both Jews and Christians; and the temple, in which the new converts followed, with deep reverence, the traces of the Son of God and his divine Mother, was yet standing in all its glory. This tradition, which flowed from the Church of Jerusalem, a church which was composed, without taking into account the disciples of Jesus Christ, of a great number of the relatives of the Virgin and St. Joseph, was consecrated at a very opportune time by a religious monument, proving the fact to demonstration in the eyes even of Protestants themselves.† The greater number of the Fathers, and in

---

* The Church has instituted in honour of the presentation of the Blessed Virgin, a festival, which is celebrated on the 21st of November.
† Gibbon himself was forced to acknowledge the authenticity of religious

particular St. Jerome,* who livedon the very site of man's redemption, and at a time when the traditions were of recent date, have related the fact and adhered to it as true. This traditionary belief we can then rank among the best ascertained historical facts.

CHAPTER V

MARY AT THE TEMPLE.

IN the fortified enclosure of the temple, on the site where the Christians of Jerusalem erected an oratory, which was afterwards enlarged by the companions in arms of Godefroy, so as to form, under the invocation of the Blessed Virgin, a beautiful church with a gilded† cupola, which the knights

---

traditions in Palestine. "The Christians fixed," he says, "by an *undoubted* tradition, the scene of each memorable event"—Vol. 4, p. 101. An avowal, indeed, of great weight, coming, as it does, from a writer so learned as the English historian, and from one so hostile to religion. Chateaubriand says, "If anything in this world can be proved to demonstration, the Christian traditions at Jerusalem admit of no doubt as to their veracity."

* St. Epiphanius, St. Gregory of Nyssa, St. Gregory of Nazianzen, St. Germanus, Patriarch of Constantinople, Georges of Nicomedia, St. John Damascene, &c.

† The mosque of Omar (el Aksa) brings to the minds of Christians the ancient Temple of Solomon : *el-sakhra* is built on the site where Mary lived from the age of three years to the time of her espousals with Joseph. This spot was at that time, connected with the temple of Solomon, as, at this day, *el sakhra* is an appendage of the mosque of Omar. Before the Crusades, *el sakhra* was' only a chapel—the Franks enlarged it so as to form a spacious church surmounted by a gilded cupola. When the victorious Mahometans hurled down the great cross which glittered on the cupola of the *sakhra*, the exulting tones of the Mussulmen and the piteous cries of the Christians were so vehement and loud, that, as an Arabian author observes, it appeared as if the world was about to be dissolved.—*Corr. d'Orient.*, t. 5. According to Ben Schonah, the tumult excited in the city was so great, that, to appease it, the interference of Saladin himself was required.

templar, with feelings of joy and delight, so frequently ornamented with the spoils of the Saracens, in that enclosure was raised that part of the religious edifice which was consecrated the virgins devoted to the Lord. Here it was that Zachary conducted his youthful relative.[*] Although, in Israel, virginity was considered a virtue only for a certain limited time, and which should soon give place to conjugal virtue, it was not, however, without its peculiar prerogatives and honours. Jehovah loved the prayer of chaste children and unspotted virgins, and when he was about to redeem the human race, a virgin, and not a queen, did he select to co-operate in the great work. Thus, when the *seers* of Judea unfolded to the chosen, but often chastised people, the prophetic picture of their defeats or victories, they always attached to it a smiling or weeping virgin who might personify the provinces and cities. In the exterminating wars in which the broad sword of the Hebrews had cut down the women, children, and the old men of Moab, the virgins were spared; and the high priest, who was prohibited by a severe law from rendering the funeral services to the friend, *the beloved of his soul,* and even to the prince of his people, could, without the slightest censure, assist at the funeral

---

[*] St. Germanus affirms that it was St. Zachary who undertook to place the Virgin in the temple. The Arabic traditions also mention that God charged Zachary with the protection of the Virgin, *Ouacafalha Zacharia.* The Koran, in the *surate,* which treats of the family of Amram, in addition to this circumstance, makes mention of an extraordinary legend current among the Christian tribes of the desert. The legend goes, that Zachary, who went from time to time to visit his young protegée, invariably found with her a profusion of the most delicious fruits of the Holy Land, and that at a time when their season was long past. This extraordinary circumstance at length compelled him to ask, by what means she procured these delicious fruits. Mary made answer, "*Hou men and Allah iarzæ man tascha begair hissa.*" "Everything which you see comes from God, who provides for those he pleases, without account or number."—*D'Herbelot, Bibliothéque Orient.,* t. 2, Art. *Miriam.*

of his virgin sister. The virgins or *almas* figured in the ceremonies of the Hebraical worship, before that worship possessed a temple. Under the guidance of Mary, sister of Moses, we see them celebrating, by dances and canticles of triumph, the passage of the Red Sea.* These dancing bands of young girls, transplanted from Egypt to the desert, survived a long time among the Hebrews. The virgins of Silo, who seemed, from the time of the Judges, to have been more particularly consecrated to the service of Adonai than the other daughters of Israel, danced to the music of canticles and to the sound of harps, a short distance from the holy place during a feast of the Lord, when they were carried off by the Benjamites. This serious event was no check to that custom, which ceased not until that disastrous epoch when the ark was taken away, and the first temple was destroyed. It is probable that all the *almas* had the privilege of being numbered among these sacred choirs, provided their reputation had not in any way been tarnished. But among them a select number was distinguished from the others, who surrounded the altar with more fervour and perseverance. Whilst the ark of the Lord was still encamped under tents, *the women who watched and prayed at the door of the tabernacle* offered to God the bronze mirrors which they had brought with them from Egypt. These were assuredly pious widows who had declined entering into any new engagements in order that they should be unceasingly employed about the things of heaven, and also *almas*, devoted by their parents to the the service of the sanctuary, and placed under the protection of these holy women. In this light St. Jerome explains that passage of

---

* "Mary and her *youthful companions* (the almas), at the passage of the Red Sea, sung canticles of thanksgiving with an accompaniment on the timbrel."—*R. Sal. Yarhhi.*

Exodus. As the vow of parents was ordinarily redeemable, and as the redemption, fixed at a moderate sum* was always paid at the end of a few years,† these temporary vows were called *a lending to the Lord.*‡ I have lended to the Lord, said Anna, when conducting little Samuel to Silo ; *Idcirco et ego commodavi eum Domino.* After the return from captivity, the influence of the Persians, by whom the women were expelled from these religious solemnities,§ seriously affected the institution of the *almas.* They no longer formed a distinct body in the state, nor a conspicuous figure in the ceremonies of worship. Under the pontiff kings they lived shut up, and their days flowed on in such close retreat, that when they ran in confusion and disorder about the high priest, Onias, at the moment when all Jerusalem stood confounded at the attempted sacrilege of Heliodorus, the Jewish historians considered the fact so strange and marvellous, that they inserted it in their annals. Let what may be said, there had been at the time of the presentation of Mary, virgins attached to the service of the second temple. The institutions of the early Christians are a convincing proof of it, and St. Ambrose, as well as

* Moses, by an express law, had fixed on a sum of *fifty sicles* at most.
† " Children under this sort of bondage forfeited not their rights to their paternal inheritance, and could purchase their freedom if their parents neglected doing so."—*L'Abbé Guénée.* Josephus (*Ant.* book 4,) remarks that men and women, who, after having voluntarily consecrated themselves to the ministry, were desirous of relaxing their vows, paid a certain sum to the sacrificing priests, and that those who were insolvent were left to the *discretion of the* priest.
‡ See Father Croiset.
§ " In Bombay, the descendants of the Persians have a temple consecrated to fire worship. They assemble together in great numbers on the exterior of the temple, clothed in glittering costume and covered with party-coloured turbans, and salute the rising sun, or offer their acts of adoration to his departing rays, by prostrating themselves before him. Their wives are not then seen, that being the particular time for going to fetch water from the wells."— Buckingham.

St. Jerome, have affirmed it.* But how did Mary pass her time during her stay in the temple? What were, during this interesting epoch of her life, her employments, her tastes, her habits, her devotional practices? With regard to this point we possess very few authentic documents. A traditionary life of the Mother of God, considered by St. Epiphanius, who lived in 390, as then of a very old date, enters, no doubt, into details of that nature, but nowhere is it now to be found. The gospel of the birth of the Virgin has been rejected by the Church, and St. Jerome, who has mentioned the reception of Mary among the daughters of the Lord, gives no further particulars. To fill up this gap in a history which it would appear God was pleased to envelope in darkness, we possess but a few broken links, some few unconnected passages of the Fathers, from which it is difficult, however carefully arranged they may be, to form a satisfactory sketch. But it matters little. Like the Indian workman who ties up the broken web, thread by thread, and patiently endeavours to unite its ends by unravelling and knitting the threadbare and worn woof, let us proceed energetically to the work, and collect the scattered shreds of the precious tissue of the Virgin's life, to tie up the woof again if we can. With the enduring patience of Banian, we shall endeavour to avoid all matters of conjecture—respect for the subject matter will prevent such a course—but shall strive, with the aid of the best authorities, and a long course of study on the manners of the Hebrews, to give, as precise as we can, and as nearly approximating

---

* "It is known that the early Christians, and particularly those of Jerusalem, who were of Jewish extraction, preserved some of the institutions of the old law; among these we may rank those of virgins and widows, whom we find attached to the primitive churches, exercising the different good works appropriate to their sex."—*Fleury's Manners of the Isr. and Christians*, p. 115.

MARY AT THE TEMPLE.

the truth as possible, some idea of the almost cloistered life spent by Mary in the temple. Old legendary writers have thought well to throw around the early childhood of Mary prodigies and marvels almost without number. We shall pass over in silence such miraculous occurrences, as having no proof to support them; but there is one thing on which we shall for a short time dwell, and that is, an inaccurate, or rather an inadmissible assertion, which has been taken on trust, and without mature examination, by holy personages and religious writers.* Because the Virgin had been always holiness itself—a thing which no one questions—a conclusion is then drawn that she ought to have been placed in the most sanctified part of the temple—that is, in the holy of holies, an inference materially false. The holy of holies— the impenetrable sanctuary of the God of armies—was closed against the whole tribe of the Hebrew priesthood, with the sole exception of the high priest, and even he entered there but once a year—not, however, without many fasts, washings, and ablutions. He entered it environed with a dense cloud of perfumes, which was interposed between him and the divinity, *whom no man could behold and live*, says the Scripture. Again, he remained there but a few moments, during which the people, prostrated on the ground, broke forth into groans and sighs, lest they should die. Then a grand entertainment was given to his friends, that they may rejoice with him at escaping such imminent peril.† From this let us judge if it were possible that Mary could be brought up in the holy of holies. The local traditions of Jerusalem, equally as common sense, protest strongly against this bold opinion. The *Sakhra*,

---

* St. Andrew of Crete, Georges of Nicomedia, Gibieuf, &c.
† Prideaux, Basnage, *Hist. des Juifs, liv.* 5, *chap.* 15.

originally a Christian church, built on the very site of the
apartments of the Virgin, is a dependency quite distinct
from, and by no means enclosed in, the mosque of Omar.
Yet the mosque of Omar is built on the very site of the
temple. Father Croiset, in his "*Exercises of Devotion*,"
has not adopted this tradition, but unwilling to reject it altogether, he steers a middle course. According to him the
mother of God was not brought up in the holy of holies;
but the priests revering her admirable virtues, gave her permission to go and pray there from time to time. The learned
Jesuit, in adopting this *mezzo termine*, has overlooked many
things. The first: that woman, among the Hebrews, was
considered an impure being, assimilated to a slave, and on
whom prayer was scarcely obligatory;* that she was confined
in a court out of which there was for her no egress, and
that the interior of the temple was a place prohibited her,
even though she were a prophetess or a daughter of royalty.
The second: that the priests could not grant Mary a privilege of which they themselves were deprived; and could they
even grant it, availing herself of it would, according to
the formal text of the law, expose her to certain death.
Again, leaving out of question the influence of these religious fears among the priests of Jehovah, they would in no
way have permitted entrance into the holy of holies, because it was a matter of vital importance to keep concealed

---

* "The uncleanliness of woman, according to the Rabbins, dates from the seduction of Eve by the serpent, and cannot be removed until the coming of the Messiah. Her prayer is not so obligatory as the prayer of man. She is not even bound by the greater part of the affirmative *commandments*. The Jews, even to this day, offer their morning prayer thus: '*Blessed be thou, O Lord, King of the universe, for not having created me a woman.*' The humble woman, on her part, says, in a spirit of resignation: '*Blessed be thou, Lord, for having created me according to your will.*' "—*Basnage's Hist. of the Jews*, t. 5, p. 169.

from the people the knowledge of the disappearance of the ark—a disappearance which would have thrown them into a deep and fatal despondency.

The second version is equally as inadmissible as the first.

The education which Mary received in the temple was as well attended to as the sciences of that time and the manners of the Hebrews would admit of. It regarded principally domestic duties, from which the wife and daughter of Cæsar Augustus, even under the imperial roof, and in the midst of the delights of Rome, did not deem themselves dispensed.* Brought up in the strict observance of the law of Moses, and conforming herself to the habits of her people, Mary arose at the first song of the birds, at the hour *at which the bad angels are silent, and at which prayers are more favourably heard.*† She dressed with the greatest modesty, through respect for the glory of God, whose eye penetrates everywhere, and who beholds, even in the darkest night, every act which man performs. While dressing she returned thanks to God for another additional day, and for having preserved her during her sleep from the snares of the evil spirit.‡ Her toilet was of short duration, for there was nothing *recherche* about it. She wore neither bracelets nor pearls, nor gold chains *inlaid with silver*, nor purple tunics, like the daughters of the princes of her nation. A purple-coloured dress, as beautifully shaded as the flower of the field; a white tunic, drawn close by a cincture, with both ends flowing down gracefully; a long veil, the folds of which, artlessly but gracefully arranged, hung down so as to cover at once and entirely the whole countenance, and

---

* Augustus never wore any other clothes than those woven by his wife or daughter.
† Basnage, t. 4, p. 306.
‡ Basnage.

a *chaussure* suited to the dress, formed the eastern costume of Mary.* After the customary ablutions, the Virgin, her companions, and the pious matrons, who were responsible to the priests and to God for this sacred deposit, proceeded towards the tribune, where the *almas* took their seats in the place most distinguished.† The rising sun was now gilding with its golden rays the distant mountains of Arabia—the eagle was whirling in the clouds—the sacrifice was burning on the altar—the sacerdotal trumpets were sounding, and Mary, her head bent under her veil, was repeating with fervour the eighteen prayers of Esdras,‡ and demanding of God, with all Israel, the Christ so long promised to the world, and still so long withheld. " O God ! glorified and hallowed be your name in this world, which you have

---

* The Annunciads of Genoa wore, in the 16th century, the habit of the Blessed Virgin ; that is, *the lower part white, and the upper azure colour, in order that the memory of her should be always present to their minds. The slippers of the Choir Nuns were also made of azure-coloured leather.* (*Rule of the Annunciads of Genoa*, chap. ii.) Lamartine, in his Travels in the East, has remarked the costume of Mary, as that worn by the women of Nazareth. " They wear," says the poetic traveller, " a long, azure-coloured tunic, tied close by a white cincture, its end trailing on the ground—the projecting folds of the white portion of the dress fall gracefully over the blue." Lamartine traces this costume so far back as the time of Abraham and Isaac—a supposition by no means improbable. We see that only a slight difference exists between the costume adopted in the 16th century, and that observed by the French traveller.

† Origen, St. Basil, St. Gregory of Nyssa, and St. Cyril, have handed down to us a tradition, which assigns to virgins a place of honour set apart in the peristyle appropriated to women.

‡ " The most solemn part of the Jewish prayers is that which is called *Shemon eh-Eshre*, or the eighteen prayers. It is said they were composed and instituted by Esdras for the great synagogue. Rabbi Gamaliel added to them a nineteenth against the Christians, a little before the destruction of Jerusalem. The eighteen prayers are of great antiquity, and it cannot be questioned, that they were recited at the time of our Lord, and that he offered them to God, conjointly with the assembly, whenever he was present in the synagogue. Every person, arrived at the years of discretion, was obliged to offer up to God, thrice a day—morning, noon, and night—these nineteen prayers."— *Prideaux's History of the Jews.*

created according to your own good pleasure, *thy kingdom come,* let redemption flourish, and let the Messiah come speedily."* And the people responded in chorus, "Amen! Amen!" Then were chanted forth the concluding verses of that beautiful Psalm, attributed to the prophets Aggeas and Zachary: "The Lord loosens those who are in chains; the Lord enlightens the blind; the Lord raises up the fallen; the Lord loves the just.

"The Lord takes care of the stranger; he will take under his protection the orphan and the widow, and he will destroy the ways of sinners.

"The Lord shall reign for ever. Your God, O Sion! shall reign through all generations."†

The reading of the *schema,*‡ and the benediction of the priest, who presided at the public prayer, terminated the ceremony, which was renewed every day, morning and evening.§ After the fulfilment of this primary duty, Mary and her youthful companions returned to their customary occupations. Some plied with their agile fingers the cedar distaff, others shaded the veils of the temple with purple, violet, and blue, and worked on them *bouquets* of flowers, whilst

---

* This prayer, which is called *kaddisch,* is the oldest of all those which the Jews have preserved, and as it is read in the Chaldean tongue, it is thought to be one of the prayers composed at the return from Babylon. (Baan. t. 5, p. 314.) Prideaux affirms that it was in use a long time before the coming of our Lord, and that the Apostles, together with the people, had frequently offered it up in the synagogues. It was recited during the service, and the assembly were obliged to respond many times, *amen.*

† Leon de Monide.—*Maimonede.*

‡ Leon de Modena, cap. 11, p. 29. By the *Schema* is meant three different sections of Deuteronomy and Numbers. It is a sort of profession of faith, which is recited evening and morning, by which a belief is professed in one only God, who has taken his people out of *Egypt.*

§ It is certain that the Blessed Virgin assisted very often at the public morning and evening prayers. These prayers were more efficacious than any others; and Hebrew doctors assert, that no other prayers were *heard by God,* except *these.*

MARY AT THE TEMPLE.   69

groups inclining forward over the Sidonian loom, applied themselves to the execution of the various designs of these magnificent carpets, which elicited the eulogiums of all Israel *on the valiant woman*, and which Homer himself has extolled.* The Virgin surpassed all the daughters of Israel in those beautiful pieces of work, so well appreciated by the ancients. St. Epiphanius tells us, that she excelled in the art of embroidery, carving, and gilding;† her incomparable skill in the spinning of the thread of Pelusium‡ is still traditionary in the east, and the western Christians, in order to perpetuate the remembrance of it, have given the title of the *thread of the Virgin* to those pieces of net-work, equally remarkable for their glittering whiteness and almost aerial texture, which are seen fluttering over the hollows of the valleys during the early hours of an autumnal day. The same motive it was that induced the grave and pure spouses of the primitive Christians, when about to enter into the ties of wedlock, to undertake a long journey, for the purpose of laying on the altar of the queen of angels, a distaff surrounded with fillets of purple and loaded with spotless wool.§ The Church of Jerusalem had consecrated, betimes, this *souvenir* by placing among its treasures the distaffs of Mary.‖

* See the Iliad, book 6.
† " In the middle ages, in remembrance of the pieces worked in linen by the Virgin, the weavers were ranged under the banner of the Annunciation; the artists of gilded brocade and silken stuffs placed themselves under the protection of *Our Lady the Rich*, and had her image fixed on their banner, loaded with the most magnificent description of embroidery."—*Alex. Monteil vie des Français des divers etats.*
‡ " The clothes in which the principal priests dressed in the morning were composed, says Misnah, of the fine linen of Pelusium, a city of Egypt, celebrated for its linen." *Et Pelusiaco filum componere lino.*
§ This custom exists still in some villages of the north and west of France.
‖ These distaffs were sent in the *suite* of the Empress Pulcheria, who deposited them in the church of the Guides, at Constantinople.

Whilst engaged in these practices of religion and piety, the Virgin found some leisure moments to devote to the culture of the sciences, and her brilliant and well poised genius was visibly developing itself, like a beautiful palm whose roots are watered by the running stream. St. Ambrose tells us that she perfectly understood the sacred books, and St. Anselm thinks that she was an adept in the language of Moses—the old Hebrew, which Josue made use of when he arrested the course of the sun and moon in the valley of Aialon, and in which God traced with his omnipotent finger, on the *precious and very dense stones*,* the ten precepts of the Decalogue. It is not a great stretch of the imagination to suppose that Mary, in studying the idiom of Anne and Debora, became initiated, during her solitary watches, in the lofty and mysterious conceptions of the *seers* of Israel, or that she had received from the sanctifying spirit, by whom she was so richly endowed, a breath of poetical inspiration resembling the harmonious breeze which passed over the Eolian harp of David.† It cannot be said, that she, the youthful prophetess who endowed the new law with a canticle so beautiful, could be a stranger to the noblest and most delightful inspirations of genius. Apart from the sacred character, which recommends it to us Christians, the *Magnificat*, in the opinion of all nations, holds a conspicuous place among the poetical composi-

---

* A Hebrew tradition. *See Basnage.* " According to some oriental writers, the tables of the law were of ruby or carbuncle; but the most common opinion among the Arabians and Mussulmen is, that they were emeralds, on which the characters were so traced, that they could be read on every side."—*D'Herbelot, Biblio. Orientale.*

† According to an old Jewish tradition, David had a harp which sounded during the night when a *peculiar wind* was blowing. Basnage has ridiculed the idea of such sounds awakened by the breath of night, and treated this assertion as folly. The invention of the Eolian harps, whose magic sounds delight the English parks, supplied the Rabbins with this idea.

tions of the highest order. Mary united in her person unparalleled sanctity, and talents of first-rate order. The living ark, who who was to contain the Saviour of the world, could not be possessed of too many accomplishments. When light wishes to be condensed, say the orientals, it selects the carbuncle as a tabernacle! A poet, slavishly fawning on Augustus Cæsar, once said to him, that it required many ages to produce a work like him, and that, since the days of the creation, all nature's efforts were directed towards his formation. Such expressions, applied to the sanguinary nephew of Cæsar, are extravagant to absurdity; but if applied to the Virgin, are true to the letter. In truth, Mary is nature's *chef-d'œuvre*, the flower of primitive generations and the marvel of centuries. The world has never seen, nor ever will see, so many perfections united in a mere daughter of man. This illustrious and blessed creature possessed, in the highest degree, grace, holiness, and grandeur. Conceived in friendship with God, sanctified before her birth, she was a perfect stranger to those passions which raise up whirlwinds in the soul, and to those grovelling propensities which spring up like reptiles in the midst of the mire of the heart. Since the grievous transgression of Eden, *man is inclined to evil from his youth;* the greatest saints had been sinners before they entered on the ways of sanctity, and the gold of their virtues had not been always without alloy. But the Virgin was never a slave of hell; she was brought forth, like the pomegranate, with a royal diadem on her head, and her soul, irresistibly impelled towards virtue, swam in a pure and transparent atmosphere, where sin could find no access. The remembrance of her many virtues is still cherished among infidel nations. The Persians give her the title of the holy and glorious Mary.[*] The Turks give her the addi-

[*] D'Herbelot, Bibliothèque Orientale.

tional title of *Seddika*, which means just,[*] and the Christians assert that she alone possessed more merit in the sight of God, than all the angels together.

In truth, the saintly acts and virtues of Mary resembled those flakes of snow which fall in silence on the inaccessible summit of lofty mountains; the declining eve yields not in lustre to that of the next day—purity is added to purity, and whiteness to whiteness until there is formed one shining cone, on which the light plays, and which, like the sun, forces man to lower his eye. To no other creature has it been granted to present before the Sovereign Judge a similar life. Jesus Christ alone has surpassed her, but Jesus Christ was the son of God.

Mary entered the temple of Jerusalem like one of those spotless victims which the Spirit of the Lord presented before the vision of Malachy. Beautiful, youthful, nobly descended, and with just pretensions to any match, however high, among a people who often placed beauty on the throne.[†] She bound herself to the corners of the altar by a vow of virginity, lisped forth by her infantine lips, but which at a later time her heart ratified by a perfect renunciation of the pomps and vanities of the world.

Of such a vow, unheard of until then in the annals of the world, Mary *leaped over the hedge* which separated the old from the new law, and so plunged by anticipation *into the sea of evangelical virtues*,[‡] as to afford us grounds for

---

[*] D'Herbelot, Bibliothéque Orientale.

[†] It is well known that David, Solomon, and other kings of Juda, often placed in their royal couches or regal beds women of mean origin. The celebrated Sulamite of Solomon was, it is said, a young girl from the country near the small village of Sulam, situated a short distance from Jerusalem. At the time of Mary, Herod the Great had married Mariamne, the daughter of a simple priest, on account of her beauty.

[‡] St. John Chrysostom.

saying that she had already sounded its depths, when her Son came to reveal it to the children of men. God does not suddenly alter his ways; he announces, he prepares a long time beforehand, the astounding events which are to change the face of the world. The Messiah needed a precursor, and he was found in the person of St. John the Baptist. The new law required some preliminary, and the virtues of Mary preceded the Gospel, as a cool delightful morn precedes the glorious day. St. Epiphanius, quoted by Nicephorus, has handed down to us a glowing picture of the Virgin. This portrait, drawn in the fourth century, from traditions now destroyed, and from manuscripts no longer in existence, is the only one which we possess. The Virgin, according to this bishop, was not tall in stature, though above the middle size; her countenance, slightly bronzed, like the countenance of the Sulamite, by the climate of her country, had that rich glow so peculiar to ripe corn; her hair flaxen, her eyes sparkling, with a black mellow pupil, her eyebrows black and arched, her nose aquiline, her lips ruby, the cast of her countenance oval, and her hands and fingers long and slender.

All the fathers vie with each other in their description of the beauty of the Virgin. St. Dionysius, the Areopagite, whose testimony is of the greatest weight, as he had seen the divine Mary, tells us that *she was so beautiful as to dazzle the sight, and that he would have adored her as a goddess, had he not known that there was only one God.* But it was not to the aggregate of physical perfections that Mary was indebted for her surpassing loveliness; it emanated from a higher source. St. Ambrose thought so, when he said that this engaging exterior was only a transparent veil, which gave a view of all the virtues of her mind, and that her soul, the noblest and purest that ever was created, if we except that of Jesus Christ, shone forth clearly and visibly in her countenance. The physical loveliness of Mary, reflected, but at a distance, the intellectual and imperishable beauties of her mind. She was the most beautiful of women, for she was the most chaste and the holiest of the daughters of Eve.* God has made a palace from the mother-of-pearl of the green sea:† but what is the outward shell without the pearl? The Fathers have not been deceived in what they have handed down to us regarding the person of Mary. A large portion has been devoted to the moral beauties of the mind, which alone will not be the food of worms. We shall endeavour, then, to collect these little precious gems, which are scattered through their writings, and form a mosaic, which may present us with a second portrait of her who, as St. Sophronius says, was *the garden of the delights of the Lord.*

Mary's every action was accompanied by the nicest feeling of modesty: kind she was, affable, compassionate, and the alms of the young child often fell unperceived into the box attached to one of the columns of the temple, into which Jesus, at a later time, saw fall the widow's mite. She spoke but seldom, and always to the purpose; a lie never sullied her lips; her voice was soft and pleasing, and an indescribable unction accompanied her tones, so as to diffuse a holy calm over the mind. She was ever foremost in the performance of laborious duties, most exact in fulfilling the divine law, profoundly humble, and perfect in every virtue. She was never seen out of temper, was never the cause of offence, neither did she sadden or jeer any one. Detesting pride,

---

* " Neither climate, nor food, nor bodily exercise, form human beauty, but that moral sentiment of virtue, which cannot exist without religion. Beauty of countenance is the true index of the soul." *Bernardin St. Pierre's Studies of Nature.*

† *Bahr-al-Akhdar*, a name given to the Persian Gulf.

she was modest and reserved in speaking, and simple and unaffected in manners. Though beautiful, to appear abroad gave her no concern; though young, on dress she bestowed not a thought; though of illustrious birth, a proud and haughty bearing she abhorred; and though poor, riches she despised, and from the eyes of the world carefully concealed the rich treasures of her mind and heart. In her company one experienced additional purity and additional fervour; for her presence, calm and soothing, seemed to sanctify everything around her, and her look detached altogether the mind from the consideration of sublunary affairs. Her politeness consisted not of an empty form of deceptive and unmeaning expressions, it was an expansion of universal kindness gushing from the heart. Her looks already revealed the Mother of Mercy, the virgin, of whom it has been since said, "*She would ask of God pardon for Lucifer, if Lucifer deigned to ask for pardon.*" The fastings of Mary, according to St. Ambrose, were long and rigorous. The fasts of the East, the mention of which fills with so much alarm the frail portion of our northern populations who say that only hale old men should be bound to that law, consisted in a privation of all things, which commenced in the morning and ended at the rising of the stars.* During that time Mary refused whatever could flatter the taste or delight the heart. She undertook the most toilsome duties, and performed those acts of mercy, the most disgusting to natural feelings. She clothed herself in the most wretched garments, slept on the bare ground, and during these days of mortification and tears, which often lasted for entire weeks, she partook only of a slight repast, consisting of bread baked in

---

* The Jews believed that there could be no proper fast, except that on which the sun did not go down.

the ashes, bitter legumes, and a cup of water from the fountain of Siloe.* Her prayers were long and frequent, and whilst so engaged, her mind was so recollected and attentive, that her soul seemed absorbed in adoration before the Eternal. The howling of the tempest, and the clashing noise of thunder, which caused Cæsar to fly for protection into the subterranean vaults of his palace,† passed on unheeded by the young virgin. Completely absorbed in her religious duties, her soul rested at the feet of the great Author of the universe, far beyond the limits of the world, and the region of the winds.

"No person," says St. Ambrose, "was ever so gifted as Mary, with such a high degree of contemplation; her spirit, always in accordance with her heart, never for a moment lost sight of HIM whom she loved more ardently than all the seraphims together; her whole life was one continual practice of the most pure love of her God, and when sleep oppressed her eyelids, her heart was still watching and praying.‡

Such were the virtues, such were the occupations of Mary in the temple. As the diamond glistens among other precious gems, so did she shed a lustre among the companions of her infancy.§ Her candour and modesty were such, as to induce her to plead forgiveness for her high perfections. The old men, who had grown grey in the service of the priesthood, never passed her without bestowing on her their blessings, and they always deemed her the most beautiful ornament of the holy house.

---

* Basnage, b. 7, chap. 18.—Fleury's Manners of the Israelites.

† If we can credit Suetonius, Augustus had almost a childish fear of thunder and lightning. At the least appearance of a storm he hid himself under the vaults of his palace, where the thunder could not be heard, nor the flashes of lightning seen.

‡ St. Ambrose, De Virgi., lib. 2. § Comparison of St. Jerome.

CHAPTER VI.

MARY AN ORPHAN.

WE must allow, however strange it may appear, that the history of the Virgin is barren of facts, and full of gaps. We might compare it to the majestic ruins of one of the ancient cities of the desert. Here we behold gigantic columns, their bases as firm as those of the mountains; there we see porticos which the Arab, a lover of the marvellous, proclaims to be the work of the *genii* ; farther on, temples in ruins, which the imagination can still reconstruct; and then, as far as the eye can reach, one sterile sandy prospect, without even a blade of grass for the camel of the Bedouin. To supply the defects of the Apostles, who had been too much engaged, it would appear, with the grand and conspicuous figure of Christ, to devote any attention to his terrestrial family, the Fathers have led us into the knowledge of the virtues of St. Anne. With them, we have entered under her humble roof, we have been witnesses of her vows, of her fervent prayers, of the joys of her prolonged maternity, of the effusions of her gratitude; but here the thread of tradition becomes so slender, that it suddenly snaps, and the remaining portion of the life of St. Anne is almost mere conjecture. The mother, whose many tears and fasts procured for her the virgin of Isaias, who surrounded that virgin with such excessive love, who carried her in her arms to the Lord,* and with tears deposited her in the sanctuary, appears but for one moment on the scene, and then is heard of no more. It cannot,

---

* The Glories of Mary, by St. Liguori, chap. 3.

however, be supposed, that the spouse of Joachim remained nine years without paying a visit to her daughter. The outward buildings of the temple, where the children consecrated to the God of Israel were brought up, could not be interdicted to the mothers of these children. A mother, too, has rights sacred and religious, all nations have declared such rights imprescriptable ; and moreover, Scripture informs us, that Anna, the wife of Elcana, was not prevented from seeing her son on the solemn festivals; and that on every visit she paid him, she invariably presented the young prophet, whom she had *lent* to the Lord, with a tunic, woven by her own hands. After the birth of Samuel, Anna brought forth many other children, who grew up before her eyes, as young olive trees, and who shared with the servant of the temple her maternal solicitude. St. Anne had only Mary,* the sun of her happiness, the hope of her old days, the source of all her earthly joys. There can, then, be no question of doubt, that, accompanied by her spouse, she paid her a visit on every occasion that her piety attracted her to the temple; and that, moreover, she sat up at night to weave by the glow of the lamp, or the clear, silvery light of the moon,† the virginal robes of her child. It is thought that St. Anne and St. Joachim returned to their home after the presentation of Mary, and that they remained there some years, before finally settling down at Jerusalem. Joachim, who was not an artisan, as Joseph was, in all pro-

---

* St. Anne was supposed to have given birth to another daughter called Mary, born twenty years before the Blessed Virgin. That tradition has not been received by the Church.

† "The Jewish women plied the distaff together, in summer, by the light of the moon; for the Jewish doctors authorized the husband to divorce his wife, when the women who were engaged at the distaff, during the light of the moon, were guilty of detracting him."—*Sotok.*, *cap.* 6, *p.* 250. This custom of spinning by the light of the moon still exists in Corsica, where a great many other oriental customs are practised.

bability was engaged in the cultivation of the little heritage
of his ancestors, and was in the enjoyment of that blessed
mediocrity, which sages, grandees, and poets have so much
ambitioned, in those moments of despondency when they
upbraid fickle fortune.* Churches were erected at Sephoris, at Nazareth, at Jerusalem, on those very places
which formed a part of his patrimony, but the vineyard or
farm of his fathers must be in the environs of Sephoris;
that it was which made him return into Lower Galilee.
Joachim was an Israelite in the strictest sense of the
word, and greatly attached to the law of Moses. Accompanied by his wife and a party of his relatives—such was
the custom of the Hebrews —he repaired to the temple on
all the solemn festivals, and it is supposed that his desire
to see his daughter was a further inducement to him to be
present at the sacred ceremonies. With what joy his vir-
tuous and holy companion put on her travelling veil, to
wend her way to the holy city! How long and tedious
must those paths appear to her, which she beheld at a distance winding in a serpentine form across the mountains
and valleys! She, attracted by her eye, jumped over
twenty miles in imagination, before in reality arriving at
them, the shrubs, the tufts of laurel roses, the huge green
oaks or sycamores, which spread out in the distance on her
way; for each of these points gained, she was the nearer to
her daughter, that daughter who was a gift from the Lord,
a child of miracle, whom an angel proclaimed the glory of
Israel! With what emotion must she have greeted, at the

* According to St. Gregory of Nyssa, the father of the Blessed Virgin was
an *honourable burgess*, remarkable for his piety and fear of God. P. Valverde
tells us that Anne and Joachim had been in easy circumstances, and that they
bestowed their superfluities on the temple and on the poor.—*See also F.
Ribadeneira's Life of the Saint*, p. 45.

bottom of the valley, the pillar of Antony, which towered aloft, on its base of polished marble,* in sublimity and terror, as a protection to the house of prayer; and how affected must be her tender and holy soul at sight of the temple, which contained her child and her God! At the approach of night, and when the sacerdotal trumpets were summoning the people to prayer,† Anne hastened to pay her adoration to God, and cast a look upon her daughter, whom she had not seen for entire months. The porch, with no other vault than that of heaven was lighted up by the dazzling glare of the chandeliers,‡ blended with the faint glimmering of the stars.

The thousand lights seemed multiplied under the porticos ornamented with fresh garlands,§ and the high priests passed on through the congregated people, in their rich and gorgeous dresses, imported from the Indian coasts, by means of the caravans of Palmyra.‖ From time to time the symphony of harps seemed blended with a murmuring sound similar to the roaring dash of billows¶ on the shore, and caused a number of Hebrews, who had arrived from the

---

* The tower of Antony might be considered the citadel of the temple; it had been long before the palace of the Asmonean princes. The rock on which it stood was inaccessible on every side, and was fifty cubits in height. Herod incrusted it with marble from the bottom to the very summit, so as to allow of neither ascent nor descent.

† The religious festivals of the Jews always commenced at night.

‡ These chandeliers were of gold, and were fifty cubits in height; the light which they shed was seen, say the Rabbins, who are not naturally prone to exaggeration, at an almost incredible long distance from Jerusalem; even in the city the houses were so illumined, that the cooks, without the aid of lamps, were able to cull the grain for the pottage.—*Talemund Traite Succa, fol.* 3; *see also the Third Letter of a Jewish Convert, by M. Drach.*

§ "These green garlands were hung up during the feast of Tabernacles."—*Basnage, liv.* 7, *ch.* 16.

‖ "The vestments which the priests wore at night during the solemn festivals, were imported from India at a vast expense."—*Basnage.*

¶ The Jew and Arabs pray in a loud tone.

banks of the Nile, the Euphrates, and the Tiber, to bend the knee in prayer before the only altar of the God of their fathers.* In the midst of this immense throng of native and foreign believers, Anne, who was engaged in fervent prayer, raised her head but for one moment, the moment when Mary and her youthful companions, dressed and veiled in white, passed on, and, like the wise virgins of the Gospel, with lamps in their hands.

The festival over, Anne, having previously blessed and embraced Mary, re-entered, with Joachim, the mountain path on her way home. She set out from Jerusalem at a slow pace, without once looking back, and brought with her that happiness and those dear reminiscences which were to fill up the whole space of time that was to elapse before the next festival.

When old age and toil had exhausted the strength of Joachim, and when he could no longer labour on his paternal farm, he formed the resolution to go and take up his abode near his daughter. Both husband and wife bade a final adieu to Lower Galilee, and came to dwell in Jerusalem, in a quarter of the city contiguous to the temple. Anne's greatest wishes were now crowned. She could now serve the Lord in his own holy house, and an opportunity daily offered of seeing Mary. How often, during the delightful evenings of summer, when plying the distaff on the floor of her dwelling, must she not allow it to slip from her immoveable fingers, whilst her maternal look was pensively fixed on the gilded roof of the temple! "*Where a man's treasure is, there also,*" says the Scripture, "*is his heart.*"

---

* "Whilst the temple was in existence the Jews had a particular devotion to repair to it. More than eleven hundred thousand persons perished during the siege of Jerusalem, as many had then congregated there from all parts, to be present at the feast of the passover."—*Basnage, liv.* 7, *ch.* 11.

St. Anne could abridge the duration of this painful separation, the law of Moses accepting compensations. Such, however, was not her wish; her gratitude towards God spoke higher and louder than her maternal tenderness, and when the voice of religion is attended to, the voice of nature is silenced. The Virgin had spent nearly nine years within the inclosure of the temple,* when now, for the first time, a dark cloud passed over the bright and serene heaven of her young life. Her dearly beloved father Joachim the Just, became seriously ill, and symptoms of approaching dissolution immediately developed themselves. Alarmed at his state, his kindred and friends hastened to him, and gave him a thousand pledges of affection and sympathy. An inseparable and laudable bond of union existed among the different families of Juda. The dying man calmly smiled on his friends and relatives. Like Jacob, he had been a long time a wayfarer on this world, and it mattered little to him that the wind of death was about to lay low his earthly dwelling; for far beyond this corruptible planet, he beheld in spirit the happy regions where he was to repose for ever in the bosom of Abraham. When his strength, nigh exhausted, proved to the old man that his life was fast ebbing, he makes a public confession of all his faults, as was customary with the Hebrews, and offers to the Sovereign Judge his death in expiation of the sins inherent to our nature, and from which the most just man is not exempt.† This duty over, Joachim calls for his daughter to bestow on her his parting blessing. Mary comes;‡ her fervent

* Father Croiset's Eexercises of Piety, b. 18, ch. 39.
† Basnage, b. 7, chap. 24.
‡ It was a custom, which can be traced so far back as the patriarchs, that children should receive the blessing of their dying parents. Mary should conform to this custom; her retirement in the temple was not of the nature of a monastic enclosure, and St. Joachim was then living in Jerusalem.

prayers for the recovery of the author of her days had not been heard. A *jealous God* wished to estrange, by degrees, from all earthly attachments his chosen spouse, that she may learn to lean on him as her only protector.

Pious authors have thought that at the moment Joachim extended his hands to give his farewell benediction to his daughter the glories for which heaven destined his child were suddenly revealed to him from on high; then the joy of the elect was diffused over his venerable countenance; he let fall his hands, inclined his head, and died.

The chamber of death then resounded with loud lamentations and shrill piercing cries; the women beat their breasts and tore their hair;* the men strewed their heads with ashes and rent their garments; all the windows of the house† were thrown open, and then was lighted up, alongside the remains, the bronze lamp with its numerous sockets—that lamp of death, which shed its mournful tints on the pallid but serene countenance of the just man. This done, the body was given up to the care of those who were charged with the washing and interment of it.‡

On the following day a large *cortège*, among which could be noticed the mourners and musicians,§ drew up before

* St. Jerome remarks that, in his time, there was some among the Jews, who even then slashed their flesh, and made themselves bald by plucking out their hair, which they sacrificed to death.

† "Among the Jews, those who touched the dead bodies were considered defiled and unclean. When the doors are closed, they consider the house of death a sepulchre, and consequently defiled; on the contrary, when the doors are open, uncleanliness is supposed to have departed."—*Maimonide.*

‡ Basnage, b. 7, chap. 24.

§ Jesus Christ met these musicians, the tones of whose instruments were loud and noisy, at the door of the centurion, whose daughter he raised from the dead. Maimonide says, that the poorest Jew was obliged to hire two musicians and a mourner at the interment of his wife, and that the rich, in proportion to their possessions, should have a greater number. See also Fleury's Manners of the Israelites, p. 106.

the house of mourning. The nearest relatives entered the upper room where Joachim had been laid out in the customary way, and placed his remains on their shoulders.

They passed on through the streets of Jerusalem, chanting forth the canticles of death, which sounded high above the soft and plaintive strains of the flutes, and the loud lamentations of the women who bewailed the dead. Anne and Mary were present at the funeral, and walked along, their heads bowed down, with the matrons of their family, from whose eyes tears were flowing in torrents.[*]

The *cortège* passed through the sheep-gate, which since then is called by Christians the Virgin's gate. On arriving at the place of burial, the sound of the flutes and the lamentations of the mourners ceased for a short time, and the chief mourner thus addressed the mortal remains: "God be blessed, who had created and cherished you, who had sustained and then taken away your life. O dead! he knows in what number you are placed, and he will one day raise you up. Blessed may he be who gives and takes away life."[†]

A little clay was then placed on the head of the deceased; the coffin was nailed down, and a gloomy grot was opened, called the *house of the living*,[‡] where the patriarch was to take his last sleep, waiting for the other members of his family. Heartrending cries were then heard on all sides. Anne flung herself on the coffin, to take one last farewell of her husband, and immediately was borne off in a swoon.

---

[*] Wives and children assist at the funerals of their husbands and fathers. The widow of Naim walked in the funeral procession of her son. Joseph was the chief mourner of his father. This custom is still observed in Judea.

[†] Leon de Modena, Customs of the Jews.—*Buxtorf, Syn. Heb.*, p. 502.

[‡] "The sepulchre ought to be called the *house of the dead*, yet the name of the *house of the living* was given to it as a mark that a soul, after being separated from the body, still survives. The Pharisees are supposed to originate that name."—*Basnage, b.* 7, *c.* 24.

When the holy remains of the just man were committed to the earth, a large stone was placed at the mouth of the sepulchral grotto, and to remove it thence was prohibited *under sentence of excommunication*. Cries and wailings then commenced anew, and the spectators plucking, three different times, a tuft of grass, and casting it each time behind them, pronounced in wailing tones: "*they shall flourish like the grass of the fields*." These rites terminated the obsequies of the descendant of the kings of Juda, the father of Mary, and the grandfather of Jesus Christ according to the flesh.[*]

This, her first affliction, and only the prelude of many others, rent the heart of the Holy Virgin. Now commenced her apprenticeship with affliction and sorrow. On the very threshold of childhood the hand of misfortune clasped her, but the illustrious child recoiled not in her path. She mourned, it is true; for her soul, like that of her Divine Son, was neither callous nor insensible, but she emptied to the dregs the bitter chalice in addressing herself thus to God: "O Jehovah, let thy will be done!" The mother and daughter went into mourning after the manner and style of the Hebrews; their weeds consisted of coarse camlet, confined and narrow, called *hair-cloth;* the head and feet naked; the face concealed under the skirts of their dress, observing a rigorous fast, and an inviolable silence, they remained prostrate on the ground during seven days, crying and lamenting with their relatives, and praying for the soul of the deceased.[†]

The seven days past, Anne caused the lamps of the synagogue to be lighted up, and then requested prayers to be offered up for her husband, not forgetting alms proportionate

---

[*] See Fleury's Manners of the Israelites. Leon de Modena, Cont. Relig. des Juifs. Basnage, liv. 7. Correspondence of the East, t. 5.
[†] The 49th Psalm was recited. *See Leon, p.* 18; *Lightfoot on John, p.* 1,072.

to her means. Mary, on her part, fasted every week on that day which saw her for the first time an orphan, and prayed morning and evening for the repose of the soul of her father. These fasts and prayers for the dead continued during the space of eleven months.*

Welcome misfortune, provided you come alone! is a saying of the Greeks. To this first affliction was soon added another of a more poignant nature, and another source of sorrow followed in the wake of the sorrow for Joachim. The lamp of death was scarcely extinguished in the mournful house of St. Anne, when it became necessary to light it anew. The last tears shed by the Virgin for one of the authors of her existence, had scarcely dried up, when the loss of the other† caused them to flow again. One night Mary, accompanied by one of her relatives, went down from the temple into a dark and narrow street, where her mother lived. A single lamp flickered in the upper room. At the entrance she met the weepers, whose faces boded no joyful news. They were sitting in silence; these women were, and remained too, in waiting. St. Anne rallied whatever little strength remained to her, to enable her to bless her child. She recommended her in feeling words to her relatives, but above all to HIM who is the father of the orphan, and then she slept the sleep of the just.‡

Mary, bathed in tears, hung over the icy and clammy countenance of her mother; her flaxen hair became entangled with the grey hairs of her deceased parent. It was said that she endeavoured to revive her by her tears; but it is only the breath of God that can re-animate the dead. After the first burst of natural and legitimate sorrow she

* Basnage, liv. 7, p. 182.
† According to Father Croiset, St. Anne and St. Joachim died within a hort interval of each other.
‡ Religious historians assert, that the Holy Virgin was present at the death of her mother; such is in accordance with the manners of the Hebrews.

closed the eyes of her sainted mother, imprinted on her cheek a sorrowful and impassioned kiss; the last parting adieu of her nation.*

The grief of the youthful Virgin was deep, silent, and patiently endured. Having no longer any other protector in this world but Providence, she fled for refuge to the bosom of God; and thence, as from a still and secure haven, she listened to the distant noise of the warring winds of the world, and learned full well how vain and transitory are the cares and concerns of this life, rank, distinction, grandeur, power, beauty, riches, which glitter and pass on only for a moment like the bubble on the surface of a winter torrent, which bursts almost as soon as it is formed. It was at this time of loneliness and reflection that Mary, as a historian remarks, registered her vow of perpetual virginity.† It is nowhere seen that Anne and Joachim were conscious of such a vow being made, and without their concurrence it was invalid in the eye of the civil, as well as the religious, law. After their death, Mary, though still under tutelage, must consider herself as at full liberty to dispose of her person, and then it was that she selected the Lord for her heritage, and devoted herself by vow, unlimited as to time, to the service of his altar, with the fixed resolution of never leaving the holy place. The Virgin, like her illustrious ancestor, learned by experience, *that one day passed in the tabernacles of the God of Israel was better than a thousand others;* and preferred the last place in the holy house, to the first under the roofs of Cedar.

---

* This custom is of ancient date; for Philo speaking of the lamentations of Jacob at the unexpected death of his son, mentions as one of the sources of his sorrow, his being deprived of the consolation of closing his eyes and giving him the parting kiss. The Hebrew children received the blessing of their dying parents, closed their eyes, and accompanied their last remains to the place of burial."—*History of the Institutions of Moses.*

† Descontures, Vie di la Sainte Vierge, p. 27.

CHAPTER VII.
THE MARRIAGE OF THE VIRGIN.

WHETHER Joachim, on his death-bed, had entrusted the Virgin to the special protection of the priesthood, or whether the magistrates, on whom devolved the duty of providing for orphans, had themselves selected guardians from the illustrious family of Aaron, to whom she was allied on the maternal side, or that the guardianship of children devoted to the service of the temple belonged by right to the Levites, one thing is, however, certain, that after the death of the pious authors of her existence, Mary had guardians from among the sacerdotal race. If we be allowed to hazard an opinion, we should say that it is very probable, that the duties of this guardianship were particularly entrusted to the pious spouse of Elizabeth, as his high reputation for virtue, together with his claim of a near relative, would point him out as peculiarly fitted for that office.* The

---

* The Jews, as well as Celsus, Porphyry, and Faustus, have argued from this relationship, that the Virgin was of the tribe of Levi. Catholic doctors

anxiety and desire which the Blessed Virgin manifested, two or three years later, in travelling all Judea, to present her congratulations to the mother of St. John the Baptist, and her prolonged stay in the highlands of Hebron, would, indeed, point out that closer ties than those of mere relationship existed between them. According to the modes of observance strictly adopted among the Hebrews, the roof under which Mary dwelt during a visit so prolonged, must be as sacred as the paternal roof itself. Whoever the priests were, on whom devolved the guardianship of the blessed daughter of St. Anne, they strictly acquitted themselves of the obligations imposed on them; and when the Virgin had attained her fifteenth year, they thought to unite her in marriage to a spouse worthy of her. This project filled Mary with no little anxiety. Her lofty, pure, and contemplative soul had divined the gospel, and virginity appeared to her to be the most perfect, the most holy, and the most honourable state which a woman could embrace. A very ancient author cited by St. Gregory of Nyssa, relates, that she refused for a long time, but with a great deal of modesty, complying with the intentions of her guardians, and that she supplicated, in humble tones, her family to consent to the life which she was leading in the temple—a life innocent, retired, and exempt from every tie, except the ties of

have combated that opinion : they maintain, that Mary was of the tribe of Juda, and of the family of David. St. Matthew tells us that Jesus Christ was called the son of David, according to the flesh; but he could not be said to be the Son of David, except through Mary, as he had no father among men. When it is urged, how Mary, being of the tribe of Juda, could be a cousin of Elizabeth, who was of the tribe of Levi, St. Augustin answers, that there is no difficulty in the solution; as a man of the tribe of Juda may have taken as wife a woman of the tribe of Levi ; and that the Blessed Virgin, the issue of this marriage, might be the relative of Elizabeth on the maternal side. It is proved, moreover, that the prohibition against a member of one tribe entering into union with a member of another, did not include orphans inheriting paternal property.

H

the Lord. Her request caused no little surprise among those who had the disposal of her person. That which she implored as a favour was nothing less than sterility, that is opprobrium, a state solemnly accursed by the law of Moses;* a state of celibacy she made choice of, that is, a total extinction of the name of her father, a thought little less than impious among the Jews, who considered it a dire calamity, if their name should not be perpetuated in Israel. The vow of virginity, by which she bound herself to God, could not be urged by her as a plea, for such could be annulled by the mere will of her family. Woman, at any epoch of her life, was always considered a minor before the establishment of that immortal code which has enfranchised man, and placed the woman and the slave on terms of equality with him.

The solicitations of the Virgin met with little sympathy among the priests of Jehovah; they had not arrived at such a high pitch of perfection, and to these men of science, and penetration the angelical and holy soul of Mary was a book SEALED WITH SEVEN SEALS OF BRASS. Her ideas, far in advance of her age, and hurtful to the prejudices of her nation, could not be comprehended, and everything she urged as grounds against accepting a state so totally opposed to her most cherished inclinations, availed but little. What reason had she to think, moreover, that God himself was not against her? Her marriage with a just man who could give testimony of the purity of his life, remove her from the importunities of the young Hebrews, who would have sought for her hand even in the temple,† and protect her as well as her Divine Son in the hour of

---

* Origen remarks, that the law affixed a malediction on sterility; for it is written, *cursed be he who has not perpetuated his race in Israel.*

† St. Augustine, *de Sancta Virg.*, cap. 4.

adversity, may have entered into the secret views of Providence. This was the only way that remained of concealing the mystery of the incarnation from the malevolent investigation of a perverse world, who might have made such a miracle the grounds of abominable conjectures, and who might be influenced by misguided zeal, perhaps, to stone the mother of the Messiah, as a creature lost to every sense of honour and feeling of shame;* for the Hebrews never ranked mercy in the number of their favourite virtues, and God himself reproached them by the mouth of his prophet, *with having hearts as hard as stone.*

To these reasons, strong and convincing, yet hidden, in the impenetrable night of God's counsels, was added another, drawn from the source of the antediluvian traditions and from national pride, which alone would have left very slight chance of success to the mild and humble opposition of the Virgin. Perpetual chastity, considered by Christians the queen of virtues, was reputed unmeaning by the disciples of Moses, who for many centuries lived in the anxious expectation of the King Messiah. A young flower of the root of Jesse, a daughter of David, was not at liberty to withdraw herself from the yoke of Hymen. She owed a son to the ambitious piety of her family, who, for all the treasures of the Great King, would not have renounced the hope of counting one day among them the Liberator of Israel. This hope, which had supported the flagging spirit of the Jews at the time that the Assyrian had transplanted them on the banks of the Euphrates, was tempered into a fierce desire of vengeance after the Romans became masters of Asia. The Hebrews expected that the day was not far distant, when the eagles

* See St. John Chrysostom, Sermon 3; and Father Ligny's Life of Christ, vol. i., p. 12.

would be forced to fly before the emerald* standard, and when the device of the Maccabees† would float above that of the Roman senate. Never had the oracles regarding the Messiah appeared so near of accomplishment, and such a time by no means favoured the request which Mary was imploring.

The guardians of the Virgin, unheeding her antipathies and representations, summoned a *reunion* of her nearest relatives, all, as herself,‡ of the race of David and the tribe of Juda, in order to proceed to the selection of a husband. Among those who urged pretensions to her hand, many there were equally remarkable for youth, beauty, and valour; others there were possessors of broad and fertile lands, flocks, vineyards, and olive plantations. The captains of Israel would have added to the dowry of Mary, a part of those spoils and those slaves taken in battle; the Nabals of the tribe would have dressed her in the embroidered stuffs of India, and the double-dyed Tyrian purple; whilst the sons of commerce, who trafficked in the emeralds of Egypt, the gems of Iran, and the pearls of the Persian Gulf, would have laid down at her feet diamond necklaces, costly bracelets, and ear-rings of such value as would suffice for the ransom of a prince. But these illustrious suitors were weighed in the balance and found wanting. Disregarding all the advantages arising from youth, beauty, rank, fortune, and glory, the priests, Mary's guardians, and the elders of her family, fixed their choice

---

* "The Standard of the Jews was green."—*Calmet.*
† "Who among the Gods is like unto you, O Eternal:—*mi camocha baelim Jehovah?*"
‡ Every daughter inheriting a property, was bound to marry with a person of her family and of her tribe, and not with her nearest relative, as Montesquieu has said, in order that inherited possessions should not pass from one tribe to another.

THE MARRIAGE OF THE VIRGIN.

on a poor man, who gained his bread by the sweat of his brow, Joseph, the carpenter of Nazareth.

When we take into account the incomparable loveliness of Mary, the education which she received in the temple, the respectable connexions of her family, her quality as heiress —no slight consideration among the Jews, who were obliged to endow their wives and receive nothing in return,* this decision of her family would appear astounding, had not the fathers made known to us that Joseph was selected by lot, and the clear expression of the divine will.†
An old tradition quoted by St. Jerome, and preserved among the historic records of Mount Carmel, informs us that the suitors, after having prayed to HIM who presided over lots, placed, in the evening, their almond rods in the temple, and that on the following morning the dried and withered branch of Joseph the son of Jacob, the son of Mathan, was discovered fresh and blooming, like that which had of old secured the priesthood to the Aaronites. In the same historical records it is told, that at the sight of this miraculous appearance, which crushed all his hopes, a young man of high lineage, connected with the most distinguished families of Judea, and inheritor of a large property, broke his rod in all the frenzy of despair, flew for refuge into one of the grottoes of Carmel, and became a companion of the disciples of Elias.‡

When the election of the guardians was decided, the announcement was made to Mary, and the incomparable young

---

* "When about being married, the bride received from her parents only the necessary requirements for dress and appearance. The bridegroom furnished the dowry."—*Mosaical Inst.*, v. 2, chap. 1.

† Jerome in Dam., b. 4, chap. 3; Greg. N. Homily on Nat. Niceph., b. 2, chap. 7.

‡ This young person, named Agabus, became celebrated afterwards for his sanctity, and lived and died a Christian.

THE MARRIAGE OF THE VIRGIN.

girl, though accustomed to the most refined and delightful occupations, though brought up in the midst of perfumes, melodious canticles, and the fairy-like splendour of the holy house, yet hesitated not a moment to devote herself to a life of obscurity, to the most common occupations, and to the most painful duties, as the partner of the humble and aged artisan, presented to her by her relatives.* Report goes, that it was made known to her by divine inspiration, that this just man would stand in no closer relationship to her than that of a protector, a father, a guardian of her chastity, and what more could she desire? The Lord had heard her prayer, and in allowing her to remain faithful to her vow, she forfeited not the merit of obedience. The contemplated union between Joseph and Mary ought, one should think, cause no little surprise in Nazareth and Jerusalem, for a great discrepancy with regard to age, fortune, and state existed between the parties. We should, however, greatly deceive ourselves by supposing that this union, apparently so unsuited in every respect, was regarded by the Jewish society, a society of unsophisticated and primitive habits, as an altogether disparaging match. Without holding a very distinguished rank in the state, the profession of an artisan was far from being considered vile or degrading in Israel.† In the genealogy of the tribe of Juda, we find a family who were engaged in the manufacture of fine linen, and another

---

* Desconture's Life of the Blessed Virgin, p. 49; Life of Jesus Christ, by P. Valverde, vol. i., p. 72.

† Artisans still enjoy no little respect in Jerusalem. "In Palestine and in Syria," says Burchardt, "the trades' corporations are almost as equally respected as they had been in France and Germany during the middle ages. A master tradesman holds a rank and position in society, equal to that of a second class merchant; he can marry a person from among the most respectable families of the place, and has ordinarily more influence in this locality, than a merchant whose fortune is thrice greater."—*Travels in Arabia.*

at potter's work, whose memory is held in respect; and the Scripture has handed down to posterity the names of Beleseel and Hiram. We know that St. Paul, though brought up to the profession of the law, and the celebrated and learned Hillel, applied themselves to the mechanical arts, and thought it a matter at which they need not blush. Yet more, every Israelite was an artisan; for every head of a family, no matter what position in life he might hold, was bound to see that his son was acquainted with some profession or trade, unless, says the law, he is desirous *he should grow up a robber.**

The Jews, whose patrimony was in the hands of a foreigner, had no other alternative, whilst awaiting that grand epoch which was to re-establish their fortunes, than exile, or a miserable pittance in the bosom of their native mountains. Those whom love of country induced to abide by the latter alternative, forfeited not their character for independence, and remained ready to embrace any employment that may offer. Israel had no *castes*, as Egypt and India. The religious belief of the people, and their being descended from the patriarchs, were their only sources of pride. " To be descended from Abraham according to the flesh," says the eagle of Meaux, " was a distinctive mark valued above all other things." A person of the very lowest and poorest class among the Hebrews, considered himself a prince in comparison to a foreigner.†

There had been, however, among the Jews as among the Arabs, some tribes and families of greater distinction and lustre than others. The tribe of Juda, who bore the na-

---

* The Turks have adopted this salutary law, the Sultans themselves are obliged to learn some profession or trade.

† In losing their nationality, the Jews have not surrendered this opinion. They still maintain it.

tional standard at the head of the *thousands* of Israel, on the day of battle, and from which the sceptre was not to be taken away until the coming of Christ, always possessed pre-eminence; and the house of David was the one most distinguished and honoured among the families of Juda. Joseph, though poor, was descended from the house of David. The blood of twenty kings flowed through his veins; and Zorobabel, one of his ancestors, it was who led back the chosen people of God from the land of exile. From that time the lustre of his house became gradually dimmed; his family glided down into the ranks of the people, like the family of Moses and Samuel, but its illustrious origin cannot be forgotten. In our own days the last of the Abyssinians, who drag on a miserable existence at the foot of Hedjaz, are yet respected as the descendants of Aaron-al-Raschid, and no family of Arabia would consider their honour stained by forming an alliance with them.

The blessed daughter of Joachim considered it no dishonour, as far as we can see, to wed the *Carpenter*. But if we consider, in a higher point of view, this union, which seems, at first sight, so ill suited, we shall see that it was, in reality a noble alliance. A man whose only merit consisted in lands, vineyards, sicles of gold—things which often change masters, and are both fleeting and perishable—was not the spouse selected by God for the Virgin endeared to heaven. A just man, the most perfect of all his works, he bestows on her. The Lord could not allow himself to be influenced by mere play-things, which are calculated to dazzle common eyes.

He recognises no distinction among the poor frail creatures who for an instant only crawl the earth and then become the prey of worms. *Man judges according to appearances*, says the Scripture, *but Jehovah regards the heart.*

If God makes choice of the humble Joseph as the spouse of the Queen of Angels, as the adopted father of the Messiah, the reason is, that he possessed treasures of grace and holiness enough to excite the envy of the celestial intelligences; the reason is, that his virtues made him the first man of his nation, and that his name had a higher and more conspicuous place than the name of Cæsar, in the book of life, in the heraldic records of eternity. The Virgin was not entrusted to the most powerful, but to the most worthy. The ark, which the princes and warriors of Israel dared not approach lest they should be struck down by the hand of death, drew down the blessings of heaven on the house of a simple Levite, whose poor roof afforded it a shelter.

The espousals of Mary were celebrated with that simplicity so characteristic of the primitive times. Joseph, in presence of her guardians and some witnesses, presented her with a small piece of silver or a gold ring, saying: " If you consent to become my spouse, accept of this pledge." Mary in accepting the ring was solemnly bound, and a sentence of divorce only could, from that day forward, restore her to liberty. The scribes drew up the marriage article; it was concise and altogether free from all technical terms.* The husband promised to honour his wife, to provide for her

---

* Here is the literal copy of the marriage contracts of the Hebrews, which can be traced back to the remotest period, and which Joseph and Mary must necessarily adopt. " In the year......the day......the month of......Benjamin, son of......, has said to Rachel, daughter of......become my spouse according to the law of Moses and of Israel. I promise to honour you, to provide for your support and maintenance, according to the custom of Hebrew husbands, who honour their wives and support them as seems meet. I give, first...... (the sum fixed on by the law), and promise you, together with support, clothes, and all other things necessary, conjugal love, a thing common to people of every nation. Rachel has consented to become the wife of Benjamin, who, in order that the dowry should be proportionate to his means, willingly added to the sum before mentioned, the sum of......"—*Mosaical Inst.*

support, her maintenance, and her wearing apparel, according to customary practice of the Hebrew husbands, and fixed on her a dowry of two hundred *zuses* (50 crowns), a dowry fixed by custom on the daughter of a prince equally as on the daughter of a poor labourer, but which may be increased in proportion to property. A short benediction in thanksgiving to God, the institutor of marriage, concluded the ceremony. The benediction was given by one of the guardians who represented the father of the bride. Marriage, which had not then been raised by our Lord to the dignity of a sacrament, was considered by the Hebrews a ceremony purely civil. As was customary, some months were allowed to flow on between the ceremony of the espousals and the final union. That time was spent by the relatives and friends both of bridegroom and bride in making every arrangement so as to make their appearance with *eclat*. In the East marriages have been always celebrated with extraordinary magnificence; but among the Hebrews, whose feasts are confined exclusively to those of a religious character, and who are unacquainted with either the gladiatorial exhibitions of the circus, the chariot races, the public shows, the representation of naval engagements, or theatrical amusements, the solemnities of marriage afforded a spectacle impatiently looked forward to by the whole city. Thus when the inspired prophets of God depicted the desolation of Juda, and pointed out in the distance the black flag of slavery floating over the highest pinnacle of Sion: "Jerusalem," they cried out, " thy streets shall become as silent as the desert, and as mute as if enslaved; the sounds of harps and timbrels shall no longer be heard in thy devastated inclosure, and the Lord shall put an end to *the joyous canticles of the new bridegroom and bride.*" The gospel often makes allusion to these sort of nuptial feasts, which are in

THE MARRIAGE OF THE VIRGIN. 99

no way reprehended by Jesus Christ, but rather sanctified by his presence. . The nuptials of the Blessed Virgin were celebrated at Jerusalem, and the most distinguished members of her family considered it their duty to appear at them with that splendour so peculiar to the East, a splendour which seems to us as only suited to some imaginary fairy land.

Not to invite all her relatives on an occasion so solemn would have been an unpardonable insult. The plea of extreme poverty would not be received, for they themselves would become responsible for the necessary expenses.

Though the holy union of Joseph and Mary presented nothing which could savour of the vain pleasures of the world, and the enjoyments of the age; though the chaste spouses were perfectly convinced of, and fully knew, the nothingness and vanity of all things here below; still they sacrificed to ancient usages, and, through respect for the time-honoured customs of their ancestors, they submitted to this momentary outward show, which was to pass over their lives, as the flash of lightning shoots across the clouds.

On a mild and beautiful winter's day,* at the very moment when the new moon was slowly rising over the mountains,† there was seen a long procession of women gorgeously attired, wending their way towards the dwelling of Mary. The resinous torches, borne by slaves, lighted up their golden cinctures, their rosaries of pearls, their jewelled crosses worn at the breast, and their Persian tiaras set with

---

* In the middle of the sixteenth century the Church gave permission for the solemnization of this feast. It was celebrated on the 22nd of January, the day on which it is thought that the marriage of Mary and Joseph had taken place. The city of Arras celebrated this feast on the 23rd of January, and some of the churches of Flanders on the 24th of the same month.

† There were particular days for marriages among the Israelites. The time of new moon was generally chosen, and Wednesday was selected in preference to any other day of the week.

diamonds.* These daughters of Sion had preserved the custom of painting their persons, fully practised at the time of Jezebel, their eye-brows and eye-lashes were painted black, and the extremeties of their fingers red as the berries of the eglantine.† Introduced into an inner room, which the young and holy betrothed, together with some pious matronly relatives, occupied, they returned thanks to God who gave her a protector in the person of a husband, and then complimented her on the marriage, the joys of which they had just come to partake of. Mary received their greetings with an humble grace and a native dignity which enchanted the assembly; for "she possessed in a very high degree," says St. Ambrose, "that feeling of propriety and that delicacy of refinement which mark nobility of birth." Her wedding dress, as far as mere conjecture will allow of description, must have been simple and elegant, for in all things she was governed by good taste, and no person knew better what was becoming her sex and position. On this solemn occasion she forgot not that she was the betrothed of Joseph and the daughter of David, and avoided that neglect and carelessness in dress which might be considered by her family as showing a want of proper respect for them. She knew well how to reconcile what she owed to the world with the simplicity which the humble circumstances of her

---

* See Isaias, chap. 3. "We, Europeans," says M. de Geramb, "can form no conception of the extraordinary parade of grandeur attending marriage feasts in the East. The wedding dress of the women is generally purple velvet trimmed with gold, and set off with diamonds and pearls, &c." M. de Lamartine was dazzled by the gorgeous costumes and the great profusion of precious gems paraded by the women of Syria, at the wedding of one of their countrywomen. This magnificence must be even greater at the time of the Blessed Virgin. St. John makes allusion to it in his Apocalypse: "*And I, John, saw the holy city, the new Jerusalem, coming down out of heaven from God, prepared as a bride adorned for her husband.*"—xxi., 2.

† The extremities of the fingers of the Syrian women are usually tinctured with red.

THE MARRIAGE OF THE VIRGIN. 101

husband required. Her dress, similar to that worn by the Jewish virgins on festival days, was probably composed of Tyrian purple. As a memorial of the primitive times and the patriarchal manners of her fathers, she wore, like Rebecca, golden ear-rings and bracelets—an humble but indispensable present which Joseph deemed it his duty to send some days before the ceremony*—and to which were added by those among the Jews who were in easy and comfortable circumstances, pearly necklaces and gorgeous dresses glittering with diamonds. In place of the golden crown† placed on the heads of those brides from among the opulent classes, there was placed on the flaxen and curled hair‡ of the Queen of Virgins a simple garland of myrtle. In spring time an additional one of flowers§ would have been added. A Sidonian veil, ornamented with embroidery in silver or gold, covered her from head to foot, and floated around her like a misty cloud.‖ A canopy covered with rich stuff awaited the bride outside: it was carried by four young Israelites.¶

* "The Christians of Damascus have retained this custom. Some days before the nuptial feast the bridegroom transmitted to the bride a pair of bracelets set in gold or diamonds, according to the circumstances of the future husband, a piece of cloth fringed with gold, and one hundred and sixty piasters to defray the expenses of the wedding."—*Oriental Correspondence, Letter* 147.

† "The crown of the bride was usually golden, and made after the form of a tower, like that of Cybele. These sort of crowns came originally from Persia. They were destroyed during the seige of Jerusalem by Titus, as a sign of mourning. Some scribes still permit crowns of myrtle and roses, worn by the young brides among the lower classes."—*Basnage, b.* 7, *chap.* 21.

‡ "Among the Hebrews everything connected with the attire of the women was regulated according to the old traditional modes of dress. Hairdressers were called in to curl the hair of the young brides, because, as the Rabbins gravely tell us, Jehovah himself arranged in ringlets the hair of Eve, when he united her to Adam in the garden of paradise."—*Basnage, chap.* 21, *p.* 393.

§ Basnage.

‖ These nuptial veils, embroidered in gold or silver, are still used through all Syria.

¶ The order of this nuptial pomp, which can be traced back to the remotest

Mary has on either hand two matrons; the one on the right, representing St. Anne, and the other, perhaps Mary of Cleophas, whose strong and courageous love led her up Calvary's steep, and who is sometimes taken for the sister of Mary, so great was her affection for her.* The nuptial *cortége*, waving, as a token of joy, myrtle and olive branches, marched on to the sound of harps, flutes, and timbrels, which measured the time. The bridegroom, his forehead ornamented with a curious sort of crown, transparent as crystal, and peculiar to his native place,† proceeded onward, surrounded by a number of friends, who manifested their joy, at one time by singing, at another time by dancing, again by shrill, lengthened cries, which a modern traveller, who has discovered these usages in Syria, compares to those loud, noisy shouts given by the haymakers and vintagers on the hills of France during the autumn season. The women of Israel, following the happy pair, cast olive branches under their feet, and from time to time the bride was obliged to arrest her steps, that her clothes might be spinkled with rose water.‡ Mary also should have her day of triumph in Jerusalem. Having arrived at the house in which the cere-

---

times, still exists in Egypt. Niebuhr thus describes an Egyptian marriage: "The bride, veiled from head to foot, walks on under a canopy borne by four men. A great number of slaves march before her. Some play on the tambourin, others sprinkle her with rose water. A great many women and musicians, mounted on asses, follow her. The procession takes place at night, and lighted torches are borne by slaves."—*Niebuhr's Travels in Arabia*, b. 1.

* According to M. Peignot, a faithful historian, and who has been particular in his researches in reference to this subject, this holy woman was the wife of Celophas, brother of St. Joseph, and consequently sister-in-law of the Virgin. See historical inquiries regarding the person of Jesus Christ and Mary, p. 249.

† "This crown," say the Jewish doctors, "which contained a mysterious record, was composed of salt and sulphur. The salt was as transparent as crystal, and divers figures were traced on it by means of the sulphur.—*Mischna, Tit. Sotah*, chap. 9, s. 14.

‡ This custom, as well as many others, was borrowed from the Egyptians.

mony was to be performed, the friends of the bridegroom and the companions of the bride cried out with one voice, *Blessed be he who comes!* Joseph, covered by his *taled*, and Mary by her veil, are seated, one by the side of the other, under the canopy ; the bridegroom then puts a ring on the finger of his companion, saying : *Behold*, you are my wife according to the rite *of Moses and of Israel*. He then removes his *taled*, and places it over his wife, in imitation of what passed at the marriage of Ruth, who said to Booz: *Spread thy coverlet over thy servant.* *

A near relative poured wine into a cup, tasted of it, and then handed it to Joseph and Mary, accompanying the act with a thanksgiving to God for having created man and woman, and for having instituted marriage. Then a handful of wheat was scattered as a symbol of abundance, and a young child dashed the cup to pieces. †

The whole party who surrounded the bridegroom and bride gave thanks to the Lord, and then passed into the banquetting hall. Joseph and Mary arose also, but before following their guests, some secret words were exchanged ‡ between them, in presence of heaven and those stars which announce the glory of the Omnipotent. *You will be as mother to me*, said the patriarch to the Blessed Virgin, *and I will respect you as even the altar of Jehovah*. From that time they were no other in the eye of the religious law than brother and sister in marriage, although their union should be fully maintained. § The rejoicings continued seven days,

---

* Buxtorf.

† Basnage, b. 7, chap. 21. Instit. of Moses, etc., b. 7, chap. 1, p. 336.

‡ St. Thomas is of opinion that St. Joseph and the Blessed Virgin, immediately after their marriage, mutually consented to make a vow of virginity.

§ This vow of chastity in marriage, which has furnished the philosophers of the school of Voltaire with so many impious sarcasms, was not a matter unknown among the Hebrews ; generally it was made at the dictation of passion

as at the time of the patriarchs. The week of the marriage festivities having expired, Joseph and Mary, escorted by a great number of their relatives, forming a brilliant cavalcade, re-entered on the way to Galilee. The little caravan sets off to the sound of cymbals, and continues so until the fountain of Anathot* is gained, and then those living in Jerusalem take leave of Joseph and Mary, with tears in their eyes, blessings on their lips, and their hands placed solemnly on their breasts. The Nazareans pursue their journey. They pass over the mountains of Samaria where the eagle from his ærie on high looks down on them, careless of their presence. Sichem, with its groves of evergreens, its streams of limpid water, and its majestic edifices, then presents itself to their view. They leave behind them Garizim with its red coloured sides, where are pointed out the ruins of a schismatical temple, the disgraceful rival of the house of sanctity, delivered to the flames by John Hircanius. Then the lofty heights of Mount Hebal were left in the distance; and now they passed Sebaste, where are erected new palaces under the protection of Augustus, and which Herod took a servile complacency in ornamenting, as being the only altar on which he could sacrifice to the genius of Rome.

and anger, whilst that of St. Joseph and Mary was dictated by piety. If a husband said to his wife: *You are to me as a mother*, the conjugal rights were no longer allowed him, and a stronger reason for his being deprived of them was, when the altar of Jehovah, the temple or the sacrifice, were interposed in making this vow. The woman sometimes vowed in like manner, and although their vows were not fully approved of, as being in most cases the effects of passion and maledictions, they were not the less, on that account, obliged to fulfil them religiously.—*Basnage, chap.* 19, *p.* 352; *Leon de Modena, chap.* 4.

* The relatives accompanied the wedding party as far as the dwelling of the husband, provided he lived at no great distance from the place where the marriage festivity took place. This custom is still observed by the Arabs. The wedding party separated at Anathot, a town five leagues from Jerusalem as being the first stage.

About mid-day, on the second day's journey, Mount Thabor came in sight, its verdant summit clearly delineated against the pale silvery sky of Galilee; then were seen the lofty ridges of Libanus, its snows and cedars hid in the clouds. From the woody declivities of Hermon, where the goats are seen browsing on the tender branches of the shrubs, they descended into a delightful vale, extending, like a large parterre, between hills overspread by green oaks, myrtles, vines, and olives. Fields of barley, wheat, and trefoil, in full verdure, gently undulated under the cooling breeze of the approaching Spring, a Spring earlier and more temperate than that of our northern climate. A clear and golden light played over this fertile land, where vegetation was already strongly developing itself; and the blue waters, which the summer's heat should in a short time dry up, flowed on in silvery streams into this new Eden. Opulent villages peeped out now and then between the colonnades of palms, and then from time to time was seen, perched on the craggy point of a rock, an isolated fortress guarded by soldiers still national, and charged with a protecting mission, who measured their swords only with nocturnal depredators, or the Arabs of the desert. This delightful and cool vale, confined within a dark shady border of high mountains, was the valley of Esdrelon, at the extremity of which appeared a little town picturesquely situated on a hill's side, and shining like a rare flower in the midst of the surrounding hamlets. This delightful and pleasant town was Nazareth, the native town of the Virgin, the cradle of Christ.*

* The philosophers of the last century, to advance their peculiar opinions, have made every exertion to depreciate Palestine. The impression made by them on the minds of their readers still continues, and the impoverished and depopulated condition of that country, which scarcely yet breathes freely under the sabres of the Mussulmans, is calculated to confirm that impression in the minds of superficial readers. However, there is no doubt that, not

THE MARRIAGE OF THE VIRGIN.

Undoubtedly, Mary could not unmoved look on that town, in which she had for the first time opened her eyes to the light, and the recollection of which, faint, though not effaced, was conjured up in her dreams. She had quitted it when a child, for the splendid walls of the temple; she was now returning to it, beautiful, young, accomplished, a virgin at her return as well as at her departure.

The travellers entered the house of St. Anne, an old and mysterious dwelling, partly sunk into a rock like the pro-

---

taking into account the environs of Jerusalem, the sterility of which has never been denied by any one, we will not recognise in that country, and particularly in that part which formerly belonged to the Canaanites, the promised land of Moses. We shall then give two descriptions of Galilee, one written eighteen centuries ago, as a proof of this assertion. " Galilee," says Flavius Josephus, " is divided into upper and lower, both equally fertile. The soil is both heavy and light, abounding in pasturage, capable of producing every variety of vegetable substance; extensive plantations of vines and olives are there seen. It is watered by torrents which rush down from the mountains, as also by numerous springs and rivulets, which afford a constant supply of water when the torrents are dried up by the summer's heat. The nature of the ground is such, that persons the least inclined to labour, willingly lend themselves to its culture, and so the whole country is in a state of cultivation, and no district is seen lying unproductive. The inhabitants are robust and warlike; the towns and villages are many, and so thickly populated, that the smallest town can count 15,000 souls."—*Josephus.* "If we are to give a description of Galilee," says a modern traveller, " we cannot point out France as a country resembling it, but must look to the Agro Romano. Around Nazareth, as around Rome, the sun presents the same configuration of light. Nature, like the Gospel, is there in all its sublimity. Galilee is a miniature of the Holy Land, and when we beheld it under its varied aspects, we could well understand what it had been at the time of Jesus Christ. To an artist, Galilee is an Eden; in nothing is it wanting; it possesses the fruitful soil of Judea, with the luminous solitudes of Palestine and the verdant fecundity of Samaria. Garizim and the Mount of Olives are not more sublime than Hermon and Thabor, nor are the blue flats of Ascalon more imposing than the perfumed banks of lake Tiberias.

" The soil of Galilee everywhere presents us with historical and miraculous recollections, and on it we find stamped the traces of heroes and the impress of God, and in contemplating the heights of Thabor, we feel convinced that there was the land in which a Man-God dwelt, so blended are religious remembrances and the wonders of heaven and earth."—*See Letters from the East.*

phetical grottos of the olden times,* and which soon was to
become more holy than the temple of Jerusalem, the house
of Jehovah himself. The women of Nazareth greeted with
blessings the arrival of the youthful bride, who like the
Rebecca of Isaac, advanced veiled and bashful. Whilst
those who had known her from childhood were congratulating her, Mary entered this peaceable, paternal dwelling,
which seemed still impregnated with the good odour of the
virtues of Anne and Joachim.

CHAPTER VIII.

THE ANNUNCIATION.

IT is easier to imagine than to describe the peace and happiness enjoyed by Joseph and Mary during the first months
of their chaste union. The peace of God reigned in their
humble dwelling, and their time was divided between prayer
and labour; the one rendered less toilsome when accompanied
by the other. According to an ancient custom, a custom
still observed among the Arabs, and in many other parts
of the East, Joseph plied his trade in a place some distance
removed from that where Mary dwelt.† His workshop,
where Jesus Christ himself laboured, was a low apartment,

---

* Some houses, like that of St. Joseph, are still seen at Nazareth. They
are small, slightly elevated, and communicating with a grotto in the side of a
mountain.

† "This house of St. Joseph is a hundred and thirty, or a hundred and
forty paces distant from that of St. Anne. The place is still called *St. Joseph's
Stall*. This workshop has been converted into a moderately-sized church.
The Turks destroyed a portion of it, but a chapel still remains, where the holy
sacrifice of the Mass is still celebrated."—*Pilgrimage to Jerusalem by Abbé
Geramb*.

ten or twelve feet in length and as many in width. A stone bench presented itself outside to any chance passenger or wayfarer, who, while reposing on it, was shaded from the burning rays of the sun by an awning of matted palm leaves.* It was here that the industrious artisan fashioned ploughs, yokes, and rustic chairs. Sometimes the cottages of the valley were erected under his eye, and at others his arm, still robust, felled the high sycamores and the black firs of Mount Carmel.† The remuneration received by him for so much labour and fatigue was very trifling, and even this small pittance he shared with the poor and needy.

On her own part, his affectionate and blessed companion was far from spending her time in indolence and ease. Endowed with an enlightened, well-balanced, and judicious mind, without looking back on the past with regret, or looking forward to the future with hopes too sanguine, seeing the world as it really is, and viewing her position in its proper light, she conformed to it without difficulty, and was prepared and willing to fulfil, with scrupulous exactitude, its sacred obligations. From the moment of her taking possession of her maternal dwelling, she clothed herself with poverty as with an honourable garment sent her by God, and became, as suited to the humble state in which Providence had placed her, a young and unsophisticated child of the people. All those light and elegant labours belonging to refined life were immediately laid aside, and replaced by the fatiguing duties and monotonous occupations

---

* Workshops similar to this are still seen in the Levant. See Burchardt's Travels in Arabia, b. 1st.

† St. Justin, Martyr, (dialogues with Tryphon,) mentions that Jesus Christ assisted his reputed father in making ploughs and yokes. St. Ambrose tells us, that St. Joseph was employed in hewing wood trees, in building houses, and in other works of that nature.

THE ANNUNCIATION. 109

of economical housekeeping, the mistress of the house having neither slaves nor servants.

The delicate fingers of Mary, hitherto engaged in weaving silken tissues, were now employed in twisting from the foliage of the date tree, or the flowers plucked from the banks of the Jordan, the mat which covered the threshold of her homely dwelling. Her distaff was charged with the coarsest flax ; she was obliged to grind wheat and barley,* and knead the coarse yellow flour into round and slender cakes. Covered with a white veil, an old fashioned vessel on her head,† she went to fetch water from a well a few paces distant,‡ like the wives of the patriarchs of old, or to wash, like the princesses described by Homer, her blue dress in the running stream. Jesus Christ, witness of the toilsome duties of this noble woman, has sometimes made allusion to them in his parables: and these unpretending occupations of Mary are preserved in the evangelical tissue, as the sea-flower is preserved in amber.

We behold this industrious and frugal woman placing the

---

* There are hand-mills in every Jewish and Arabian house ; there is pointed out still at Mecca, in a beautiful house, supposed to belong to Khadidje, a hollow where, it is said, Fatima, named the *Illustrious*, daughter of Mahomet, and wife of Ali, turned her hand-mill, even in the days of her renown.—(*See Burchardt's Travels in Arabia.*) The Arabian women are still engaged in this laborious occupation. Under the reign of the son of Clovis, St. Radigonde, Queen of France, in imitation of the Blessed Virgin, ground all the corn which was consumed during the Lent.—*Private Memoirs of the French.*

† "These pitchers are earthen vessels disproportionate in height. The Nazareans carry them on the head, and it is no little matter of surprise with what agility and lightness they walk, notwithstanding the weight, together with bringing a child in their arms."—*Abbé Geramb.*

‡ "This fountain is called the *Fountain of Mary*. Tradition hands down that the divine mother of Jesus was in the habit of going herself for water ; as a confirmation of this, it may be remarked that water is very scarce at Nazareth. The way leading to this fountain, where the pious mother of Constantine caused to be erected some beautiful reservoirs, is lined with fruit trees."—*Abbé Geramb.*

leaven into three measures of meal, * sweeping the house diligently until she found what was lost,† and economically patching the old garment. ‡ When Jesus sought out for a similitude for the purpose of enforcing purity of heart, he drew it from the remembrance of the neatness of her who carefully cleansed the *interior and exterior of the cup*,§ and in eulogizing the offering of the widow, *who gave it not out of her abundance, but from her indigence*, he cast a thought on Mary. Thus the poet of Chio represents to us justice, under the figure of his mother, a poor and lowly born woman, weighing with exactness the wool which she was about to spin for the support of herself and her son, and maintaining a character for probity and honesty towards the rich, though sunk in the depths of misery and poverty.

At nightfall,‖ when the birds were retiring to sleep in the leafy bower, Mary laid on a clean and polished table, the work of Joseph's hands, small loaves of barley and rye, savoury dates, milk, fruits, and dried pulse, of which consisted the frugal meal of the descendant of the princes of Israel. This sort of diet, simply prepared, was the food of the ancient Hebrews, a sober race, who, when necessity required it, found no inconvenience in living on bread and water.¶ With regard to the Virgin, she lived on such spare diet, that some ancient writers, in love with the marvellous, supposed that she was fed by angels.

When Joseph, relieved from the toilsome duties of the

---

* Luke xiii., 24.
† Luke xv., 8.
‡ Luke v., 36.
§ Luke xi., 39; and Matthew xxii., 25.
‖ "The people usually eat after the day's labour, and at a late hour."— *Manners of the Israelites*. The principal meal of Joseph and Mary was taken at six o'clock.
¶ See Fleury's Manners of the Israelites.

THE ANNUNCIATION. 111

day, entered at sunset his confined, low-roofed chamber, his young companion was there to meet him, who immediately presented him with tepid water to bathe his feet, and cold limpid water from the fountain, contained in a vessel cleansed from every unclean * spot, to wash himself before partaking of his repast.

This grave and simple man, with his fine patriarchal figure, in which every passion was lulled to rest, this angelical young woman, all eagerness to serve him with the solicitude of a dear cherished child, formed a group worthy of the golden age.†

Joseph and Mary were in the enjoyment of this delightful and happy state for the space of two months,‡ when the hour marked by the Ancient of days, in his divine decrees, for the incarnation of his Christ, arrived.

The angel Gabriel was sent by God into Galilee, and appeared to the Blessed Virgin, at the moment when, with head inclined towards that point where stood the temple, she was offering to the God of Jacob her evening prayer.§

The angel, one of the seven who stand on the right hand of God, prostrated himself before the spotless Virgin, and beholding her already on that elevated throne raised above that of the angels and saints;∥

---

* Many precautions were taken by the Jews to preserve the vessels from which they eat and drank from every uncleanness. Not only were they particular that they should not belong to strangers, but they guarded against a thousand other circumstances which might render them unclean.—See Mischna.

† "*Non dedignabor parare et ministrare, quæ erant necessaria Joseph,*" an ancient writer puts into the mouth of the Virgin, and such is only in accordance with usages still in existence.

‡ Father Croiset's Exercises of Piety, b. 18, p. 68.

§ The Orientals, when at prayer, are turned towards a certain point of the heavens, that called the *kebla*. The Jews are faced towards the temple at Jerusalem, the Mahometans towards Mecca, the Sabeans towards the South, and the Magi towards the East.

∥ It is generally supposed that the visit of the angel took place in the evening.

THE ANNUNCIATION.

"Hail Mary, full of grace," he says, reclining his radiant brow, "the Lord is with thee; blessed art thou amongst women."

Mary felt alarmed at the appearance of this shining messenger, who was the bearer of the commands of the Eternal. It may be that, like Moses, she dreaded to see God and die; it may be, as St. Ambrose thinks, that her virginal purity took alarm at the appearance of this son of heaven, who, like a ray of light, entered the solitary cell into which no man could gain admission; or it may be that the submissive attitude and high eulogium of the angel disconcerted her humility. Let the cause be what it may, the gospel mentions that she was troubled, and sought, but in vain, for an explanation of this extraordinary visit, and the hidden meaning of this mysterious salutation.

The angel, perceiving her anxiety, sweetly said to her:

THE ANNUNCIATION.

"Fear not, Mary, for thou hast found grace with God. Thou shalt conceive in thy womb, and shalt bring forth a Son, and thou shalt call his name JESUS. He shall be great, and shall be called the Son of the Most High. The Lord God shall give unto him the throne of David his father, and he shall reign in the house of Jacob for ever, and of his kingdom there shall be no end." Mary, growing more and more surprised, and not being able to reconcile the title of mother with the vow of perpetual virginity made by her in the house of God, said to the angel Gabriel with simplicity: "How can this be done, because I know not man?"[*] And the angel answering said to her: The power of the Most High shall overshadow thee.. And therefore also the Holy which shall be born of thee shall be called the Son of God." Then, according to the usual practice of the envoys of Jehovah, he wished to give her a sign confirming the truth of his words. "And behold, thy cousin Elizabeth, she also hath conceived a son in her old age; and this is the sixth month with her that is called barren. Because no word shall be impossible with God." Mary bends submissively to the divine decrees, and says to the celestial envoy, with the most sincere sentiments of humility: "Behold the handmaid of the Lord, be it done to me according to thy word." Then the angel disappeared, and the WORD was made flesh to dwell among us.[†] In this way it was that the angel of light treated

---

[*] Calvin, that proud and overbearing heresiarch, who condemned Servetus to be tied to the stake, when he himself was actually preaching tolerance, and cried down the morals of the Catholic clergy in the same sentence that declares his own infamous, has dared to calumniate the Virgin, by urging her interrogation to the angel as a proof of her incredulity. St. Augustin and St. Theophilactus have, by anticipation, answered him long since. "The Virgin doubts not," say these illustrious doctors; "she only inquired how the miracle was to be performed." St. John Chrysostom adds that this interrogation was the result of deep and respectful admiration, and not of vain curiosity.

[†] This mystery was accomplished on the 25th of March, on Friday evening, according to F. Drexelius.

L

THE ANNUNCIATION.

of our salvation with the new Eve, and that the transgression of the sinful Eve, who, with the infernal angel, had conspired our destruction, was gloriously repaired. Thus it was that a mere mortal was elevated to the incomparable dignity of mother of God, and that a virgin, and at the same time a mother, blended two states the most opposed in nature, by an unheard-of miracle. " Let us not enter further into this mystery," says St. John Chrysostom, " and let us not inquire how the Holy Ghost could operate this wonder in the Virgin; this divine generation is an abyss so profound that no human mind can sound its depths."*

We have adopted the opinion of those doctors and theologians who maintain that Joseph was legally the husband of Mary at the time of the incarnation; yet this opinion is strongly questioned, and among those who support the opinion that Mary was not then the wife but only the betrothed of Joseph, we find the name of the great St. John Chrysostom himself.† According to this illustrious authority, Mary was still living in the house of St. Joseph when the angel appeared to her. " For," says this renowned sacred orator, " a custom prevailed of old that those who were betrothed should come to dwell in the houses of their intended husbands; a custom still occasionally observed. We see that the sons-in-law of Lot lived with their intended wives in the house of their father-in-law."‡

Notwithstanding the deep veneration and respect due to the name of St. John Chrysostom, the Church inclines not to his opinion. The example of the sons-in-law of Lot, by which he endeavours to support his opinion, bears not in the

---

* St. John Chrysostom, Sermon 4.
† M. Descouture is mistaken in placing St. John Chrysostom among the supporters of the contrary opinion. This writer, generally accurate, has probably taken the matter on trust.
‡ St. John Chrysostom, Sermon 4.

THE ANNUNCIATION. 115

least on the question. The Scripture nowhere says that they lived with Lot, it rather inclines us to suppose the very contrary; for the patriarch was obliged *to quit his house* affrighted and alarmed, whilst the most dreadful commotion reigned in the city, *in order to warn his future sons-in-law* to fly at once from Sodom. Even in case that these young men, the intended husbands of Lot's daughters, had formed a portion of the family of this patriarch, whose flocks covered the hills and valleys of an entire province, we cannot infer, from the manners and customs of the times, that their position along the banks of the Jordan was other than that which Jacob held at a later period in Mesopotamia; namely, active and watchful servants *bearing on the plains the weight of the day, and chilled by the night breeze.* We onwhere see that they had their betrothed with them in their tents; the latter lived under the protecting hand of the patriarch, and the former stood in the relation of principal caretakers of his flock. In all this there is nothing that could clash with the manners of primitive Asia. Mary, an orphan, isolated and living under the roof of her affianced, would on the contrary, have held a very questionable position. A custom generally prevailing among the Hebrews could alone authorize such a supposition, and nowhere in their code do we find mention made of any such practice; on the contrary, we find a law expressly condemning it.† St. Chrysostom, holding the same opinion with the ancient theologians, tells us that God cast a dark veil, for a long time, over the divine maternity of Mary, in order to ward off a damaging suspicion; and another holy father adds, that Jesus Christ preferred appearing before the eyes of men

---

* Genesis xxiv., 40.
† Mischna, b. 3, *de Sponsalibus*. Bartenora, Maimonide, Surenusius, Selden, Uxor Hebraika.

as the son of a carpenter, than to confirm the truth of his incarnation to the prejudice of his mother's honour. But how reconcile this with that which would inevitably have happened in the supposition of mere espousals? If Joseph and Mary had been only affianced at the time of the incarnation of the WORD, their relation to each other must have been in no way changed four months later; for the Gospel tells us that Mary, after the annunciation, set out *in all haste* to visit St. Elizabeth, and that it was only at her return from the journey of Hebron, which occupied three months, that *she was known to be pregnant*, a phrase indicating a position visible to every eye. The marriage of Mary would not then be celebrated, as her pregnancy had been known, manifest, and undeniable. What would have been thought by both families? What would all Nazareth, hastening to witness the ceremony, have said? What vile reproaches the Virgin would have to encounter from a people who held female honour in such high repute, that a violation of it was invariably punished by death! The birth of the Messiah, that birth which was to be as unspotted as the *morning dew*, as David poetically expresses it, would it not have been stained and sullied? The Jews, and in particular the Jews of Nazareth, who manifested such hostility to Jesus Christ, and who designated him *the son of the carpenter*, would they not have bitterly reproached him with the irregularity of his birth? If they have not done so, no other reason can be assigned than that of having no pretext of that nature.

These, undoubtedly, are the reasons which have induced many illustrious theologians to maintain, that a true marriage existed between Joseph and Mary, notwithstanding the grounds of argument afforded the supporters of the adverse opinion by the words of St. Matthew—words which, though apparently admitting the interpretation of there being no real marriage, yet determine not the meaning sufficiently precise, so as to remove the difficulty.* Moreover, the disputation has never turned on the principal point; married or only affianced, no Christian has ever called in question, that the mother of God was a Virgin most blessed and pure. The Mussulmans themselves have never entertained a doubt of her being such.†

* The verse on which doctors disagree is this: *Christi autem generatio sic erat: cum esset desponsata mater ejus Maria Joseph, antequam convenirent, inventa est in utero habens de Spiritu Sancto.* Those who confine themselves to these words are of opinion, that the Virgin was only affianced, because the Greek word for the Hebrew expression of St. Matthew means *desponderi*, to be promised, a different word from that which signifies being married, and which can be translated into the Latin word *nubere*. Another reason they urge is this, that St. Joseph had not as yet brought to his house the Blessed Virgin, and this circumstance they prove by that passage of the 20th verse: *Noli timere accipere Mariam conjugem tuam; quod enim in ea natum est de Spiritu Sancto est*, translated by them thus: Fear not to take Mary for your wife, for that which is conceived in her is conceived by the operation of the Holy Ghost. But to translate the passage in this way, the words should have been *in conjugem tuam*. The contrary opinion, maintained by the holy fathers, by the greater number of interpreters, and by almost every theologian, is founded on the second chapter of St. Luke, where, notwithstanding that the Virgin had been already married, the evangelist makes use of the term *espoused; ut profiteretur cum Maria desponsata sibi uxore pregnante*, that he may be enrolled with Mary his espoused wife, who was with child. Again, in the 19th verse of the first chapter of St. Matthew, St. Joseph is called her husband, and not her spouse. When St. Matthew calls the Blessed Virgin *sponsa*, affianced bride, it must not be inferred that she had not contracted marriage, but as a holy father remarks, that her intercourse with her husband was such, as if she had been only an affianced bride.

† "The purity of the Blessed Virgin was so fully recognised by the Mussulmans that Abou-Isaac, ambassador of the caliph at the court of the Greek emperor, in a conference held with the patriarch and many Greek bishops on the subject of religion, and when the bishops in the heat of argument, reproached the Mussulmans with a great many things said by Mussulmans themselves against Aischah, the wife and widow of their prophet, and which raised troubles and contentions amongst them, made answer, that such differences should excite no surprise, as the Christians themselves were divided on the subject of the glorious Mary, mother of Jesus, called the mine and source of all purity; *Genab ismet mealo kan affet*."—*D'Herbelot, Bibliothéque Orien.,* b. 2, p. 620.

CHAPTER IX.
THE VISITATION.

MARY, meantime, informed by the angel of the miraculous pregnancy of Elizabeth, resolved on going to offer her congratulations to her venerable relative. Not that she wished, as heretics have rashly asserted, to have ocular proof of the reality of an event, which was beyond the control of the ordinary laws of nature; for she was well aware that nothing is impossible to God, and could not, moreover, suppose, that the envoy of heaven should be a bearer from the MOST HIGH of words of deceit and falsehood. She set out, then, not to ascertain the fact, but because she was certain of the fact: she set out in all haste, because charity, as St. Ambrose says, admits neither of stoppage nor delay; kind and benevolent as she was during her life, she was desirous of imparting to those dear relatives, who held out a protecting hand to her during the days of her infancy, and treated her as their child, some of that holiness, and those celestial favours, which, like unexhausted sources of limpid waters, gushed up in her soul, since she had conceived in her chaste womb the Creator of the universe. With the consent of St. Joseph, whose heart and soul beat in unison with hers, Mary departed from Nazareth, in that season when the flowers are in full bloom, and directed her steps towards the mountains of Judea, where dwelt Zachary, the priest of Aaron. The Scripture, generally omitting entering into any lengthened detail of circumstances, makes no mention as to whether or not the Virgin was accompanied by any one during this journey. Some writers have thence concluded that she travelled alone, an inference by no means

THE VISITATION.

probable, as the distance from Nazareth to the town of Ain* cannot be passed over within five days; and as, moreover, it is necessary to journey through a part of Galilee, hostile Samaria, and almost the entire lands of Juda. Again the country is overhung on every side with mountains, cut up by torrents, and overspread by deserts,† the roads, in later times repaired by the Romans, were so cut up from the heavy trampling of camels, and so covered over with large round stones, that the traveller's life was endangered at every step. At night, no more suitable place of rest offered than a confined nook in a caravansary, boasting neither of provisions nor of furniture, except a plain rush mat can be designated such ;‡ for the gradual decrease of primitive hospitality had marked out the different phases of civilization, then rather in an advanced state among the Hebrews. Under such circumstances, how can it be supposed, that a man so old and experienced as Joseph, would have wantonly exposed a wife, young, lovely, tender, a stranger to the world, and as confiding as innocent, to those many dangers and various inconveniences, which a solitary journey offered? Such a supposition would falsify the history of God's people and the manners of Asia :§ a Jewish woman

---

* Zachary lived at Ain, or Aen, two leagues to the south of Jerusalem. St. Helen erected a church on the site of his house.

† Although Judea was more populous then than now, yet there were many parts of it so arid as to defy cultivation. The gospel makes mention of deserts, removed but a short distance from the towns, where Jesus Christ retired to pray.

‡ There are no inns in any part of Syria and Palestine, says M. de Volney; but a large building called a caravansary, or a place of refuge for travellers, is erected outside the towns and the greater part of the villages. These buildings consist of four wings, surrounding a square court-yard; they are without either provisions or furniture.

§ "No person travels alone in Syria; people proceed always in large numbers and in caravans. Such a precaution is necessary in a country so exposed to the attacks of the Arabs as Syria and Palestine are."—*Volney's Travels in Syria.*

was never allowed to proceed such a long distance from home, without a large escort.

If St. Joseph, as Father Croiset thinks, had been unable to accompany Mary, it is probable that she was accompanied by some of her relatives whom, with their husbands and domestics, piety attracted to the holy city; and that hence she proceeded on her way under a faithful safeguard. Whenever necessity required her absence from home, we always find her accompanied by her relatives, whether she proceeded to Jerusalem, to be present at the solemn festivities, or followed, at a more advanced state of life, in company with the holy women, Jesus, in the course of his preaching:—in her mournful march to Calvary, she is not even alone.

Having arrived at the sacerdotal city, where lived the family of the Levite, Mary, without taking a moment's rest, proceeded at once to the house of Zachary. Elizabeth, informed by one of her servants of the coming of her cousin, met her with every manifestation of joy and gladness.

THE VISITATION.

At her approach the young Virgin made a profound obeisance, and laying her hand on her heart, said: "*Peace be with you,*" hastening at the same time to present her with the customary salutation.* Elizabeth recoiled a step or two. The animated and pleasing expression of her countenance gave place to that of deep awe; her features assumed each moment a ruddier glow, and it became quite apparent that something unusual and marvellous was passing within her. The simple expression of greeting pronounced by the Virgin in a low and soft voice had altogether disconcerted her relative. Suddenly the spirit of prophecy descended on Elizabeth, and she cried out: "*Blessed art thou amongst women, and blessed is the fruit of thy womb.* And whence comes this happiness to me," she adds, "that the mother of my Lord should visit me? For, behold, as soon as the voice of thy salutation sounded in my ears, the infant in my womb leaped for joy. And blessed art thou that hast believed, because those things shall be accomplished that were spoken to thee by the Lord." The response of Mary was that sublime, sudden outpouring of the MAGNIFICAT, the principal canticle of the New Testament, and the most beautiful passage in the Holy Scriptures:—

"My soul doth magnify the Lord, and my spirit is ravished with joy in God my Saviour.

"Because he hath regarded the humility of his handmaid; for behold from henceforth I shall be called blessed during the course of all ages. Because HE who is mighty hath done great things in me, and holy is his name.

"And his mercy is from generation to generation, to them that fear him.

---

* The forms of salutation which Christ frequently made use of, are still practised in the East.

"He hath showed might in his arm; he hath scattered the proud in the conceit of their hearts.

"He hath pulled down the mighty from their throne, and hath exalted the humble.

"He hath filled the hungry with good things, and the rich he hath sent empty away.

"He hath been mindful of his mercy, and hath taken Israel his servant under his protection.

"According to the promise which he hath made to our fathers, to Abraham, and to his seed for ever."

It was thus that the Virgin, through a supernatural light, beheld at a glance those ancient prophecies and their perfect fulfilment, she herself a thousand times more enlightened and more privileged than all the prophets together. "During this celebrated interview between, and mutual congratulations of, Mary and Elizabeth, both," as St. Ambrose says, "prophesied by means of the Spirit with which they were filled, and through the merit of their children."

The Virgin remained three months in the country of the Hethites, and continued during this prolonged visit at a place not distant from the town of Ain, at the end of a shady and fertile valley, where stood the country seat of Zachary.* Here it was that the daughter of David, she herself a prophetess, and gifted with talents not inferior to those of the illustrious head of her race, could contemplate at leisure the starry heavens, the deep sounding forests, and the vast expanse of sea, whose billows rolled on as far as the eye could reach, and broke angrily and sometimes flowed smoothly on the echoing shore of Syria.

---

* "This country seat was situated a short distance from Ain, at the bottom of a delightful and fertile valley, now a garden belonging to the village of St. Jean. A church was erected on this spot in honour of the visitation, but is now merely a heap of ruins."—*Voyages de Jesus Christ*, p. 4.

Viewing nature's works so perfectly finished in every detail, so harmoniously arranged in every part, everything calculated to excite admiration and wonder, from the formation of the flower and the contrivance of the wing of the tiny insect to those wandering globes which burn in space, to dissipate the horrors of night and darkness, the Virgin's profound admiration of the wonderful works of the Creator was such as sometimes to cause her to shed tears.

How grand, thought the daughter of the prophet, how grand and great must he be, who issues orders to the morning star, who points out to the aurora the particular point of the heavens where he is to rise, who commands the thunder, and to whom the flashing lightning submissively says : " Here I am !" How grand is he ! but his goodness equals his power. He it is who has infused wisdom into the heart of man, and has endowed the brute with instinct ; he it is who has provided for the incessant wants of all his creatures ; who brings out the young of the ostrich in the sand, and who watches over the behemoth when sleeping amidst the reeds under the shade of the willows of the torrent ; he it is who provides the raven with food when her young cry towards God, and hungry, fly here and through the country. Then, in imitation of the psalmist, the Blessed Virgin calls on all nature to unite with her in praising and blessing the Creator.

In her excursions through the mountains, she on whom pious writers have bestowed the euphonious name of *Flower of the Earth*, loved to contemplate these simple flowers of the field to which she was compared by Solomon in his mysterious canticle. One day, say the learned of Persia, who have preserved this tradition, the glorious Virgin Mary laid her hand on the stem of a flower called by the Arabs Arthenita, and immediately, by the touch of her Virgin hand, a delicious perfume was communicated to the plant which it ever afterwards retained.* From a tradition among the Christians of the East, a spring towards which the mother of Jesus frequently directed her steps, and of whose murmuring sounds and gushing waters she was enamoured, has also received a peculiar name. This spring, called *Nephtoa* at the time of Josue, bears to-day the name of Mary.†

To the rear of the delightful *villa* of the Hebrew pontiff, one of these gardens, called *paradise* among the Persians, extended along, tastefully laid out, its plan and arrangement being borrowed by the captives of Israel from the people of Cyrus and Semiramis. There were seen the most beautiful trees of Palestine; and the knots of flowers carelesly spread along in the glades, the delicious perfume of the orange trees, and the silent and stealthy course of the streams under the pendent branches of the willows, rendered it a delightful and charming shade. Here it was, that the delicate attentions of Mary often diverted the mind of Elizabeth from being taken up with apprehensions regarding an event which, though looked forward to with joy and gladness, yet, from her advanced years, might prove fatal to her life. Of what a religious turn must the conversation of these saintly women be! One young, cheerful, and as complete a stranger to evil as Eve had been when she came forth fresh from the hands of the Lord; the other full of days, rich in her long experience of sublunary things; both deeply inclined to piety and the special objects of Jehovah's love; one bearing in her womb—a womb so long barren—

---

* "This is the plant called by us the 'Sweet Cyclamen.'"—*D'Herbelot Bibli. Or.*, b. 2.

† This spring sends forth such an abundance of water as to fertilize the whole valley. Tradition hands down that Mary occasionally visited it, and hence the change of the name of *Nephtoa* to that of the *Fountain of the Virgin*.

a son who was to be a *prophet, and more than a prophet;* the other, the blessed germ of the MOST HIGH, the leader and liberator of Israel.

In those delightful evenings of Summer, when the moon was shedding its silvery light on the foilage, the repast of this opulent family was laid under a large spreading fig tree, or under the green branches of the vine.* It consisted of lamb fattened on the spicy herbage of the mountains, a quarter of kid, fish hooked by the Sidonian fishermen, a comb of wild honey taken from the hollows of the old oak; then—in green fruit baskets interwoven with the leaves of the palm—of the dates of Jericho which were often laid on even Cæsar's table, the apricots of Armenia, the pistachios of Aleppo, and melons from the banks of the Nile. The wine of the hills of Engaddi, which the high priest's steward preserved in stone jars,† circulated around it in rich cups, filled by happy and contented-looking waiters.

Mary, practising frugality in the lap of abundance as well as in the state of mediocrity, contented herself with a little fruit, cheese, and a cup of water from the spring of Nephtoa. Her temperance was not the effect of necessity, but rather that of choice.‡

Some, in order to extol Mary's profound humility, which indeed required no such aid, have pretended that, during her stay with Elizabeth, she fulfilled the duties of a servant, and almost those of a slave.

---

* "The Hebrews willingly partook of their repast in gardens under the trees and vines; such a choice is only natural in warm climates, where the cool fresh air is so much to be desired."—*Fleury's Manners of the Israelites,* p. 101.

† "The Jews established in Yemen still make use of these jars."—*Niebuhr, Voy. in Arabia.*

‡ "Her abstinence did not arise from any self-imposed restriction; it proceeded rather from a customary practice of not making use of meats."—*F. Valverde's Life of Jesus Christ,* b. 1, p. 60.

THE VISITATION.

Such an assertion is altogether groundless. Elizabeth would never have allowed that a woman whom she herself had proclaimed the mother of God, and whom she extolled high above the other daughters of Sion, should subject herself to such degradation. The blessed wife of Zachary could not be in want of either servants or slaves. Christians, Jews, and Arabians are unanimous in their avowal as to the distinguished position of this family, and the illustrious birth of St. John the Baptist casts discredit even on that of Jesus Christ, as being born of parents less distinguished, and as living in the ordinary way in which people of the most humble condition live.*

The attentions which the amiable and sweet Virgin paid Elizabeth could not be considered either laborious or slavish; attentions they were, delicate and anticipating every want; attentions such as she would have paid to her mother, had heaven spared her: and often, indeed, she thought she beheld again the authors of her existence in the persons of that affectionate, devoted, and venerable pair, who entertained for her a paternal love, and who, from their very first interview, when her greatness and glory were so marvelously

---

* "Zachary was descended from Abdias, father of the eighth sacerdotal family. These old families were few, many of them being located in Persia, after the captivity. Elizabeth was descended from Aaron and from David."— *Father Valverde's Life of Jesus Christ*, b. 1, p. 63. "The Jews ranked St. John the Baptist above Jesus Christ, as he had spent his life in the desert, and had been the son of a High Priest. On the contrary, Jesus Christ, born of a poor woman, appeared to them an ordinary man."—*St. John Chrysostom on St. Matthew, Sermon* 12.

"The Mussulmans held St. John the Baptist in the highest esteem; they called him *Jahia ben Zacaria*, John, son of Zachary.

"Saadi, in his *Gulistan*, makes mention of the sepulchre of St. John the Baptist, honoured in the temple of Damascus; he prayed there, and relates that a king of the Arabs made a pilgrimage to his shrine. The Caliph Abdalmalek wished to purchase this church from the Christians, and it was only after the refusal of four thousand *dinars* or pistols of gold that he seized on it by force."—*D'Herbelot, Bibli. Or.*, b. 2.

THE VISITATION.

revealed, manifested towards her feelings of admiration and respect, which Mary endeavoured but in vain to resign every pretension to. Zachary, who doubted the word of even an angel, entertained not the slightest doubt of the immaculate purity of Mary; if we are to believe an Eastern tradition adopted by a great many learned persons,* he defended in after times, in the temple of Jerusalem, the fruitful virginity of Mary, and sealed with his blood this bold avowal.

We can easily understand, say the fathers, the many and great blessings which the visit of the Virgin brought down on the sacerdotal family who had so affectionately welcomed and entertained her. If the Lord so blessed Obededom and all his, as to render a king jealous at his having possession for three months of the ark of the covenant, what graces and favours from on high must not the three months' sojourn of her, of whom the ark of the old law was but a figure, bring down on Zachary and all his household! The purity for which the life of St. John was so remarkable was, according to St. Ambrose, the effect of that unction and grace infused into his soul by the presence of the Virgin.

Whether or not the Virgin assisted at the *accouchement* of Elizabeth, we cannot with exactness determine. Origen, St. Ambrose, and other respectable authorities, both ancient and modern, have pronounced in the affirmative, an

* This tradition, supported by the names of Origen, St. Basil, St. Gregory of Nyssa, and St. Cyril, hands down that Mary, after having brought forth the Saviour, took her place in the temple in that part assigned to the virgins, from which the priests wished to remove her; but that Zachary strenuously opposed their intentions, by maintaining that she was always a virgin, in consequence of which he met with his death at the hands of the priests. However plausible this opinion may appear, we must allow that the fact appears to us very doubtful, and that Zachary, the father of St. John the Baptist, has been confounded with another Zachary, son of Barachias, slain, according to the gospel, between the temple and the altar. Yet, the Arabs have preserved this tradition, and have added, moreover, that Zachary was placed in the trunk of a fir tree, and sawed asunder together with the tree.—*See Herb.*

opinion indeed very probable; for it would appear rather extraordinary that after having remained so long with her relative, Mary should suddenly leave her at the very moment of danger, and that without the slightest plea which could give a colour to such an unseasonable and hasty departure.

The theologians who have embraced the opinion contrary to that of Origen and St. Ambrose, argue principally from the passage of St. Luke, which makes no mention of the *accouchement* of Elizabeth, until after recounting the return of the Virgin into Galilee. We think it well to make a few reflections on that line of argument. We have carefully examined the gospel of that apostle, and that exact inquiry has fully convinced us that the argument deduced from the passage of St. Luke is by no means conclusive, for St. Luke occasionally in his narrative inverts the order of facts, as can be shewn by citing other passages in his gospel. Thus, after having related the preaching of St. John the Baptist, and having told us of his imprisonment, he makes mention in the verse following, of the baptism of Jesus Christ, though there can be no question of doubt that the baptism of Christ preceded the imprisonment and tragical death of the precursor. Again, in giving an account of the adoration of the shepherds, St. Luke enlarges on the wonderful things related by them regarding their journey to the stable at Bethlehem, on the astonishment caused by such a recital; then leading us back to the suspended scene of the adoration of the shepherds, he speaks of their departure from the stable.

Weighing well, then, the arguments on both sides, we fully adopt the opinion of St. Ambrose, the probability of which strikes us at first sight.

Together with the argument deduced from St. Luke, other

reasons are assigned as inducing Mary to depart from the house of Elizabeth previous to her *accouchement*; virgins absented themselves, it is said, on occasions of that nature; yes, that we can easily understand; but Mary, in the eyes of her relatives, was married, and what is more, was pregnant; her virginity was a secret confined to herself, and so could not then be urged as a plea for her leaving. The argument drawn from the retired and solitary habits of the Virgin appears to us equally inconclusive. To say that the noise and rejoicings which would necessarily attend the birth of the precursor of Jesus Christ frightened her away, like a scared young dove, is so futile, as scarcely to require an answer. Mary could well reconcile her little taste for the world or its concerns with that exquisite feeling of propriety attributed to her by the fathers, and with a tender solicitude for the niece of her mother; she could remain under the roof of the High Priest until Elizabeth was out of danger; and then, withdrawing from the admiration which she invariably elicited, could leave the mountains of Judea, after having embraced and blessed the new Elias.*

A religious writer remarks that the blessed daughter of Joachim, when visiting her cousin, made every possible haste, but that on her return she proceeded at a very slow pace; perhaps, like the sea bird, she had a presentiment of the storm.

---

* Father Valverde is equally of opinion that the Blessed Virgin did not take leave of her relatives until she had embraced and blessed the precursor of the Messiah.

CHAPTER X.

THE VIRGIN MOTHER.

AFTER her return to Nazareth, Mary, without difficulty, entered upon her ordinary way of life, and resumed those humble occupations which she was obliged to supend in the elevated sphere which she had just quitted. She became again the young, active, and industrious housewife, who could find time for prayer, time for the reading of the sacred books; whose whole conversation was in heaven, and to whom might be applied these beautiful and sage words of the Psalmist: " All the glory of the king's daughter is within the interior of her house." In the meantime, she was advancing in her virginal pregnancy, and Joseph was beginning to assume a dark, gloomy appearance. A poignant uncertainty, a dolorous perplexity, tortured the upright and lofty soul of the patriarch. At first he had misgivings as to his visionary faculty, and thought it more equitable to doubt the testimony of his senses than the purity of a wife who had invariably appeared to him a prodigy of candour and sanctity. He asked himself if it were possible that a woman so reserved, so chaste, and so fervent, a woman whose loveliness gave birth only to the most refined ideas and feelings, and whose every action, however simple, was stamped with the impress of heaven, could have stifled every sentiment of honour, and blast the reputation and life of a man who had received her under his roof as a vessel of sanctity. It could not be: it was a suggestion of hell; and Joseph rejected the thought as blasphemous. But Mary's state became more and more visible; "*she was known to be pregnant,*" says the gospel; meaning that all Nazareth had information of it, and that the relatives of Joseph, not knowing the chaste tie by which he and Mary were united, offered him, in the innocence of their hearts, their congratulations; congratulations cruel indeed to him, but which he must receive with an open air, and with a countenance unchanged, but which, like a clap of thunder, flashed conviction on his mind. What is he then to do? Is he to retain an adulterous wife? That would be to transgress against the law, and to defame himself in his own eyes, for Solomon had said: "He who keeps an adulterous wife is a fool and a madman." Is he to repudiate her without assigning the true reason? But Mary, being pregnant, would be defamed by the mere fact of repudiation; for it never would be believed that a man fearing God, a man of austere and unaffected manners, could repudiate, without the most urgent reasons, a mother and child at the same time. How get out of this dilemma? on the one hand there was dishonour, and on the other death. Joseph dare not decide either way, but remained plunged in the deepest dejection.

Then it was that the Virgin had reason to rejoice at having given her hand to a poor artisan; had she been married to another, her memory would have been branded with infamy, and she would have met with a tragical death; for the Jews carried to excess the fanaticism of honour, and the resentments of jealousy, as the history of Dina, of Thamar, and of the illustrious Mariamne prove. "*Jealousy is as inexorable as death,*" said Solomon, who was well acquainted with the people subject to his sway, "*and the husband pardons not on the day of his vengeance.*"

The fraternal tie by which Joseph was united to his young wife prevented, indeed, the outbreaks of passion and the ravings of jealousy; but there remained the honour of an Israelite; there remained the tortures of a father, and the cruel deception of a man who sees his dearest treasure changed into whatever is most vile and unclean; there remained in fine, the awful and severe voice of Jehovah, crying out by the mouth of his prophet-legislator: "*Let the adulterous wife die the death.*" And Joseph floated in uncertainty amidst a thousand opposing projects, and he would have given a thousand lives could another Daniel arise, and say to him: " This woman is innocent and pure ;" but there is no prophet to re-assure him, and Mary herself utters not a word.

The Eternal, from his starry throne on high, cast down a look of complacency on this just man, whom he had put to this severe trial, before elevating him to the unheard-of honour of representing him on earth; and the angels, their eyes fixed on the holy house of Nazareth, were anxiously awaiting the result of that inward struggle, in which humanity, duty, and the loftiest feelings of the mind were engaged. At last, an idea struck the patriarch, and that of a nature so generous, as to place him almost on a level with the queen of angels. He formed the resolution of sacrificing his honour, his all, the esteem gained by a life unsullied, the means which provided him with his daily bread, the air of his native land, so consoling to breathe when the hour of dissolution is drawing nigh; everything was to be sacrificed to preserve the reputation of a spouse, who sought not even to justify herself, and against whom appearances were so very strong. One way only remained of saving Mary's character, for to enter into any explanations on the matter would lead to a fatal issue. That way Joseph determined to adopt—self-exile, to quit his home and lay his bones in the land of the stranger, to take on his own head all the odium attending his flight. There are sacrifices as glorious as triumphs and sufferings, the patient endurance of which, heaven rewards no less munificently than martyrdom; the hidden sacrifices of the spouse of the Virgin was one of that nature. To reconcile duty with humanity, he accepted, by anticipation, the degrading epithets of, heartless spouse, cruel father, unfeeling and unfaithful man; he accepted the contempt of all his friends, the deadly hatred of Mary's relatives, and resolved to tear off, with his own hand, the crown of his fair name, and cast it at the feet of her, against whom he never directed the least suspicion either by word or look, so great was the love which he entertained for her.

St. John Chrysostom never tires of giving expression to his admiration of the handsome and noble conduct of St. Joseph. "It is necessary," says this great saint, "that when the gracious favour of the Lord is nigh, there should already appear many marks of the highest perfection possible. As when the sun is about rising, the East is coloured with a clear bright light, although the first rays of day have not ascended above the horizon. In like manner, Jesus Christ, when about coming forth from the Virgin's womb, enlightened the world, although he was not yet born. And for this reason it was, that the prophets, before even the divine birth, leaped for joy in the bosom of their mothers; for this it was that the women prophesied, and Joseph manifested a virtue more than human."

We have adopted in this matter the opinion of St. John Chrysostom, in preference to that of St. Bernard, who thinks that Joseph himself penetrated the mystery of the birth of Jesus Christ, and that, seeing Mary pregnant, he did not in the least doubt, on account of the deep veneration in which she was held by him, that she must be the miraculous Virgin of Isaias. "He believed it," says the apostle of the Crusades, "and it was through a sentiment of humility and respect, similar to that which, in after times, induced St. Peter to say, *Depart from me, Lord, for I am a sinner,* that St. Joseph, who was no less humble than St. Peter, thought to depart from the Virgin, fully knowing that she was bearing in her womb the Saviour of man."

This interpretation, a very pious one, indeed, and one worthy of him who has been honoured with the title of the *Devout Chaplain of Mary,* is, however, more in accordance with the ascetic ideas of the middle ages, than with the manners of the ancient Hebrews, and cannot stand the test of a careful inquiry into the text. The words of the evangelist are so clear, that no little difficulty would be experienced in rendering their meaning otherwise than what they ostensibly bear. It was not that instinctive movement of religious affright, by which we are held at a distance from a sacred object, that suggested to Joseph the idea of abandoning Mary; no—a feeling of compassion and duty dictated that line of proceeding; his conscience would not allow him to throw a veil over a fault deserving death, over a woman whom he believed criminal; and being just, good, and charitable, he would not defame her.

In the hypothesis of St. Bernard, the words of the angel would convey a false impression, a thing impossible. "Fear not," said the ambassador of the Most High; "guard this woman under your roof; that which she has conceived is of the Holy Ghost." Does Joseph protest his unworthiness at the moment that he is informed that Mary is bearing in her womb the author of nature itself? Does he make known to the angel the doubts with which his mind was filled, and which must be then more pressing than ever; and does he demand that this cup of honour presented by the celestial envoy should pass from him to a more deserving mortal? No, the whirlwinds of the soul are appeased, and he falls into that delicious and profound calm which succeeds the violence of the tempest.

It is objected that the oracles regarding the Messiah were as familiarly known to Joseph as to all the other Hebrews; that he must be aware that the time of the Messiah was near at hand, and that, from Mary's great sanctity, he ought at once understand, that she was bearing in her womb the Saviour of the world. The knowledge of the prophecies regarding the mystery of the redemption was not so easily acquired as we may imagine. Whether it was, that the allegorical descriptions of the glorious reign of the Emmanuel of Isaias had led the synagogue into error, or that the ambitious ideas of the Jews could not prevent them from referring everything to temporal blessings, it has always happened, that the Hebrew people, *that stiff-necked nation*, had been thrown into a wrong path, and had no desire of being led out of it. The envoy of God, the desired of nations, must be a law-giver, a warrior, a monarch as illustrious and renowned as Solomon. The apostles themselves for a long time looked down with contempt on the humble and peaceful mission *of the poor King who passed on without either noise or commotion;* even in view of the deicide city into which their master entered to find death, they were filled with golden visions, and flattered themselves with kingdoms yet to come. And it was with no little difficulty that our Lord led them back to consider matters in a spiritual light, and rectified their ideas, always prone to enter into the narrow circle of material and palpable benefits, towards which they were led by the ambitious reveries of the Scribes and the traditionary Pharisees.

If then the apostles, these divine founders of Christianity, experienced so much difficulty in divesting themselves of the prejudices of their early days; if those who lived in the midst of miracles, and in the continual companionship of the Messiah, were unable to understand the nature of his mission, how could Joseph of himself, and without aid from on high, have done so? The badge of the artisan could little accord with the purple of the kings of Juda, and that which was least expected was the birth of the Messiah from among the people. Besides, Gallilee was the very last country which would be looked to for such an event: "Read the Scriptures," said the Scribes to the disciples of Christ, "and you shall see that nothing can be expected from Galilee." Moreover, the prophets had designated Bethlehem of Juda, *Bethlehem the house of bread*, as the place of the birth of the Messiah, and the Rabbin commentators, outstripping even the prophets, have distinctly pointed out even that portion of the town in which he was to be born:* but Joseph's humility would not allow him to think that his poor roof was to afford shelter to such greatness and grandeur, and from Mary's silence he could infer nothing.

With regard to the project of sending back the Virgin to her family through *pure respect*, as those learned theologians who have adopted the opinion of St. Bernard are inclined to suppose, the thing would have been altogether impracticable among a people so jealous about everything connected with female honour. Mary was an orphan, and therefore depending on her relatives, all of whom were not of a pacific turn of mind, and some of whom had not approved of the union of their young relation with the obscure and unknown Nazarean. It is by no means probable that they would be satisfied with Joseph's reasons, and would have admitted, without more ample information, that the Virgin was preg-

---

* " Whence is he (the Messiah)? From the regal town of Bethlehem of Juda. Where do his parents reside (parents of the Messiah)? In the quarter *Birat-Harba* of Bethlehem of Juda."—*Talmud of Jerusalem.*

nant with the *royal Messiah*. On the contrary, everything leads us to think that they would have dragged the husband before the tribunal of the elders, to compel him to assign reasons for the manner in which he had acted; for there was question not merely of a simple divorce, but there was question of the condition of the child which Mary was bearing, of a young woman illustriously descended, but unhappily married.

Hence would have resulted two important and serious facts; either Joseph would have maintained perfect silence, and in that case would be obliged to take back his wife, and would be enjoined never again to separate from her; * or, he would have affirmed on oath that the child which Mary was bearing was not his, and in that case the child disowned would be incapable ever afterwards of holding any employment; his birth, sullied in its source, would be a perpetual obstacle to his entering the national assemblies, the public schools, the temple, and the synagogues; his posterity, inheritors of his shame, could not be admitted to the privileges of Hebrews until after the tenth generation; he would become an outcast, without home or rights, or country; and the decree which should brand his mother would have marked him and his children with the seal of reprobation. But it could not have been so: sooner than have such a stain of infamy on their genealogy, the fiery descendants of David would have stabbed the Virgin with their own hands. Such examples are not of rare occurrence, and even in our own days we have many instances of such tragical scenes in Judea as well as in Arabia.†

* Mosaical Inst., &c., v. 2, b. 7.
† Niebuhr relates that in a *cafe* of Yemen, an Arab, having inquired of one of his countrymen if he were not the father of a young and lovely woman, lately married to some member of her tribe The father, suspecting that the inquiry was made in a tone of irony, and thinking the honour of his family

Joseph was possessed of too much wisdom and humanity to adopt either alternative; and he knew from experience that to act generously was to act wisely. He resolved, then, to quit his native town, and take an eternal farewell of that cherished but suspected wife, who since their chaste union, had rendered his life so happy and delightful. Whilst preparing for this mournful separation, and during the disturbed slumbers of a restless night on his lonely bed, the angel of the Lord appeared to him in a dream. "Joseph, son of David," said the celestial envoy, "fear not to take unto thee Mary thy wife, for that which is conceived in her is of the holy Ghost. And she shall bring forth a son, and thou shalt call his name JESUS, for he shall save his people from their sins."

Joseph, on awaking, adored the inscrutable ways of Providence: the revelation of the angel had removed all his doubts. Seeing Mary in no other light than that of mother of the Redeemer to come, he retained her under his roof, and no longer thought of a separation from her.

compromised, cooly arose, ran to the house of his daughter, and without pronouncing a single word, stabbed her to the heart. Father de Geramb relates a similar occurrence that took place not long since at Bethlehem. The widow of a Catholic Bethlemite was attainted with suspicion, and, as usually happens, the suspicious charge was aggravated by malignant tongues. Not knowing how to escape the vengeance of her relatives, she fled for refuge to the convent of the fathers of the Holy Land, and placed herself under the sacred protection of the altar. Her place of refuge being discovered, the gates of the monastery were forced open, and the young woman was dragged, her hair all dishevelled, to a public place, amidst the uproar of the populace, and the suppliant tones of the religious, who demanded, in the name of a crucified God, pardon and mercy for the unhappy creature, who with tears in her eyes, strongly protested her innocence. In accents of despair, she appealed to her father and her brothers; she adjured them in the most touching strain to save her from a cruel death. They slowly advanced, each holding a poignard; the unhappy one trembled; a moment, and the three poignards were plunged into her breast, and the murderers, washing their hands in the blood of their daughter and sister, congratulated themselves in having wiped away the stain which the suspected guilt of this unhappy woman might have affixed to their family.

St. John Chrysostom inquires why the angel of the Lord appeared to Joseph in a dream, and not in a more manifest way, as he appeared to the shepherds, to Zachary, and to the Virgin? "Because," he says, in answering the question, "Joseph's faith was stronger, and he required no clearer revelation. But as the most sublime and the most extraordinary things were to be announced to the Virgin, things far more wonderful than had been announced to Zachary, it was deemed necessary that they should be declared in the clearest and least suspicious way. The pastors, as little enlightened, also required a very clear revelation. But Joseph, having already seen the pregnancy of Mary, *having conceived injurious suspicions of her*, and being but too ready to change his sadness into joy, had any one afforded him the slightest grounds, he unhesitatingly and at once received the revelation of the angel. . . . The ways of Providence are here marked by infinite wisdom, for they point out to us the excellence of Joseph's virtue, and render the evangelical history more credible, by representing him as agitated by the same feelings which every man would have experienced under similar circumstances."[*]

CHAPTER XI.

MARY AT BETHLEHEM.

MEANWHILE, the *impious empire* [†] had planted her eagles at the very extremities of the globe. The Romans had made themselves masters of the oriental world: Sarmatia, to the very interior of her deserts, trembled before them;

---

[*] St. John Chrysostom, Sermon 4. See also Father Valverde, in his Life of Jesus Christ, v. i., p. 114.
[†] This was the term which the Jews applied to the Roman empire.

and the peaceable Chinese, the most remote people of Asia, deputed an ambassador to Cæsar, to court his powerful friendship. Egypt and Syria were already subject to Roman sway; Judea even was become a tributary province, and its king, having purchased a capricious protection, was no more than a crowned slave. The time marked out was come: the oracles regarding the Messiah were about being accomplished; the power of Rome was at its apogee, as Balaam had foretold; and, according to the grand prophecy of Jacob, the sceptre was departed from Juda, for the phantom of royalty which still hovered over the holy city, was not even a national phantom. Then it was that an edict of Augustus Cæsar, was published in Judea, that a *census* should be taken of all the people subjected to his sceptre. This enrolling, much more complete than that which had taken place in the sixth consulship of the nephew of Julius Cæsar,* comprised not only persons, but even properties, and the very nature and description of such properties; it was the groundwork on which the tribute of slavery was to be laid. †

The Roman governors were charged, each in his own department, with the execution of the imperial edict. ‡ Sextius Saturninus, governor of Syria, first commenced

---

* "Augustus passed an edict on three successive occasions, that a general *census* of the provinces of the empire should be taken: the first, during the sixth consulship with M. Agrippa, in the year 28 before the Christian era: the second, under the consulship of C. Marius Censorinus and C. Asinus Gallus, in the year 9 before Christ; and the third and last, under the consulship of Sextus Pompeius Nepos and Sextus Apuleius Nepos, in the year 14 of the Christian era. St. Luke speaks of the second enrolling; the decree ordaining it was passed in the ninth year before Christ."—*Sueton. in Octav.*

† Augustus then engaged in a work, containing a description of the Roman empire, and of all the countries under his sway. Tacitus, Suetonius, and Dion Cassius make mention of this book, and from the way in which they have spoken of its contents, it must somewhat resemble our *Domesday-book*.

‡ Tertullian assures us, that Syria fell accidentally to Sextius Saturninus, as being president of it.

through Phœnicia and Syria, rich and populous cantons, and so requiring long and patient labour. That which was done a thousand years later in England, by order of William the Conqueror, in order to prepare the famous registry, known among the English as the Domesday-book, can alone give us an idea of the nature of that *census*.

After the execution of the orders of Cæsar, in the Roman province, as well as in the different kingdoms and tetrarchies tributaries to it, and about three years from the date of the decree,* the census opened at Bethlehem, just at the memorable time of the birth of the Redeemer. Cæsar and his agents were, without knowing it, the docile and blind instruments of Providence; the pride and ambition of the Romans came in aid of the prophecies: *Man proposes, but God disposes.*

It appears that, in conformity with an old custom, the Jews were enrolled by families and tribes. David being born at Bethlehem, his descendants considered this little town as their native place, and the cradle of their family; here it was, then, that they assembled to give in, conformably to the edict of Cæsar, their names and the nature and the particulars of their possessions.

The autumn was just closing; the torrents were roaring along the valleys; the northern blast was whilstling through the branches of the high firs, and the sky, lowering with heavy grayish clouds, indicated the approach of snow. On a

---

* The three years spent in this enrolling, put into execution by the Roman prefect, cannot present any difficulty; for less time would not suffice to prepare the census book of Syria, Cele-Syria, Phœnicia, and Judea. Joab spent nearly ten months, in taking down those who were in a condition to bear arms, from among the ten tribes; but the enrolment of Augustus, at the birth of Jesus Christ, comprehended many other details besides the enumeration of individuals. William the Conqueror spent six years at a work nearly similar, though the Domesday-book does not include Scotland, Ireland, or his Gallic dominions.

heavy gloomy morning, in the year 748 of Rome,* a Nazarean might be seen engaged in hasty preparations for setting out on a journey, which, it would appear from the unpromising aspect of the day selected, could not admit of delay. A young woman cautiously sitting on a quiet and gentle ass—a beast still highly valued by the women of the East—appeared to be his companion for the journey, though far advanced in her pregnancy. To the saddle of the beautiful animal,† on which the young Galilean was sitting, a palm basket was tied, containing provisions for the journey: dates, figs, raisins, and barley biscuits; in it was also an earthen vessel of Ramla, for the purpose of drawing up water from a cistern or well. A leather bottle of Egyptian workmanship, was suspended from the other side. A traveller throwing over his shoulder a bag in which some clothes were packed, girded up his loins, enveloped himself in his goat hair cloak, and holding his crooked staff with one hand, seized with the other the bridle of the ass, on which the young woman was sitting. In this way they quitted their poor and now lonely home, and descended the narrow streets of Nazareth, accompanied by the blessings of their relatives and friends, wishing them a prosperous journey and a safe return, and crying out to them on all sides, *Peace be with you.* These travellers, setting out on their journey on a gloomy winter's morning, were no other than Joseph and Mary, the humble descendants of the princes of Judah, who were going, in obedience to a pagan and foreigner, to

---

* No date has ever been so much controverted as that of the birth of Jesus Christ. We have given the preference to that of the authors of the *Art of Verifying Dates*, which appears to us the most probable. It gives the 25th of December, 748 of Rome, as the time of the birth of our Lord, six years before the common era. According to Baronius, the day on which the Saviour was born fell on Friday.

† The asses of Palestine are remarkably beautiful.

inscribe their obscure names alongside the most illustrious names in the kingdom.

Painful, indeed, must this journey be to the Virgin, taking into account both the peculiar circumstances of her condition at the time, and the rigorous season of the year, together with the nature of the country through which she had to pass. But yet she makes no complaint. Though young, with a tender and delicate frame, yet her mind was strong and resolute, and her lofty soul could neither be puffed up by prosperity, nor daunted by adversity. Noble Mary! Joseph walking pensively by her side, was resolving in his mind the ancient oracles which gave promise, after the lapse of four thousand years, of a Saviour to the world. On his way towards Bethlehem, he was pondering on those words of Micheas: "And thou, BETHLEHEM Ephrata, art a little one among the thousands of Juda; out of thee shall He come forth, that is to be the ruler of Israel, and his going forth is from the beginning, from the days of eternity."* Then, casting a look on his poor unpretending equipage, and fixing a glance on his unassuming companion, whose simple attire was just suited to her condition, he began to reflect on the grand oracle of Isaias: "And he shall grow up as a tender plant before him, and as a root out of a thirsty ground: there is no beauty in him, nor comeliness......he appeared to us an object of contempt, and the most abject of men."† And the patriarch seemed to understand God's designs regarding his Christ.

After a fatiguing journey of five days, the travellers distinguished in the distance Bethlehem, the city of kings, seated on high, amidst smiling vineyards, olive groves, and clusters of oaks. Camels bearing women enveloped in purple

---

* Micheas, v. 2.
† Isaias liii., 2.

cloaks and wearing white veils; Arabian *nakas* forced on at full speed by young and gorgeously dressed cavaliers; old men riding beautiful white asses, and conversing in solemn tones, like the ancient judges of Israel; all were ascending to the town of David, where had already arrived, during the preceding days, a great number of Hebrews. Without the precincts of the town a square built edifice arose, surrounded with a green paling of olive trees; a Persian caravansary it might have been. Through the open gate a great number of servants and slaves were seen going from, and coming into, a large court-yard, and here was the inn. Joseph, quickening the pace of the animal on which the Virgin was seated, hurried on with the expectation of obtaining one of those narrow cells which belonged by right, to the first comer, and which of course could not be refused.*
But the caravansary was overcrowded with merchants and travellers, and not a vacant space remained; gold, perhaps, might have procured a place, for the porter was a Jew, and more, a Jew of Bethlehem; but no gold had Joseph to offer.

The patriarch, with a dejected mien, returns to Mary, who receives him with a smile of resignation, and then laying hold of the bridle of the poor animal which had almost fallen down through fatigue, he wanders up and down through the streets of the little town, hoping, but in vain, that some charitable Bethlemite, would offer him a night's lodging for the love of God. But no one there was to make such an offer. The night wind was blowing sharp and cold on the young Virgin. She made no complaint, but her countenance was becoming every moment more wan and

---

* "These cells consist merely of four naked walls. The keeper is obliged to give up the key, and procure a mat; the traveller must provide himself with everything else; he must bring his own bed, kitchen furniture, and even his provisions."--*Volney's Travels in Syria.*

pallid; she was scarcely able to support herself. Joseph in despair still persevered in his fruitless attempts; and more than once alas ! he saw the very door which had been rudely closed against him, opened for a richer applicant.

Self-interest, the ruling passion of the Hebrews, must have indeed hardened every heart, when the position of Mary could not excite the slightest pity in the breasts of those of her own country. Joseph and Mary, seeing themselves rejected by the whole world, and abandoning every hope of being able to procure a place of refuge in the city of their forefathers, departed from Bethlehem, without knowing whither to direct their steps. Accidentally they gained the open country, now glimmering with the faiding twilight, and resounding with the cries of the jackals roaming about in search of their prey.

To the south of, and not far distant from, the inhospitable town, the mouth of a gloomy cave, cut out of the rock, presented itself. This grotto, looking towards the north, and becoming narrower as you enter it, served as a common stable to the Bethlehemites, and sometimes as a place of refuge to the shepherds during stormy nights. Joseph and Mary returned thanks to heaven for having guided them even to this wild and savage place of shelter, and the wife, supported on the arm of the husband, took her seat at the end of the grotto, on a naked rock, a seat indeed narrow and inconvenient.

It was here, on that cold stone, at the very time when the stars were telling the midnight hour, that the innocent and immaculate virgin, without assistance and without pain, brought forth a Being, tender, patient, compassionate like herself; wise, mighty, powerful, and eternal as God: the *Schilo* of Jacob, the Messiah of the oracles, the Christ of Christians, he whom David called his Lord, and whom, veiling their faces with their wings, the angels adore in the highest heavens. The Redeemer of the human race, not provided even with a wicker cradle, as Moses had been, was lying in a manger, on a handful of damp straw, providentially forgotten by some camel driver of Egypt or Syria, setting off hurriedly before dawn. God had provided for the bed of his only Son in no other way than that by which he provides for the nests of the birds of the air.

"Ah! Mary," cries out St. Bernard, "cover over the splendour of this new sun, place him in a manger, envelope in mean swaddling clothes this infant-God; these swaddling clothes are our riches; the swaddling clothes of my Saviour are more precious than purple, and this manger is more glorious than the thrones of kings; the poverty of Jesus Christ is richer than all other treasures."

St. Basil, removing the veil thrown over the raptures of Mary, points her out to us as equally divided between the deep affectionate love of the mother, and the ecstatic adoration of the saint. "How can I call you?" cries out the daughter of the patriarchs, bending over her infant God; "a mortal? but can it be that I have conceived by the divine operation......a God? but you have a human body! Shall I offer you incense or present you with my milk? Shall I tend you as a mother, or as a slave? Shall I wait on you with my head bowed down to the earth?"

Thus it was that the predestined Virgin, verifying the prediction of Isaias, brought forth her first begotten Son, and thus it was that the WORD was made flesh, to repair everything and to suffer everything.

"And there were in the same country, shepherds watching and keeping the night-watches over their flocks. And behold, an angel of the Lord stood by them, and the brightness of God shone round about them, and they feared with a great fear. And the Angel said to them fear not; for behold, I bring you good tidings of great joy, that shall be to all the people. For this day is born to you a Saviour, who is Christ the Lord, in the city of David. And this shall be a sign unto you, you shall find the infant wrapped in swaddling clothes, and laid in a manger. And at the same instant a multitude of the heavenly army joined the angel, praising God, and saying: GLORY TO GOD IN THE HIGHEST HEAVENS, AND ON EARTH PEACE TO MEN OF GOOD WILL."*

---

* The village of the shepherds is situated in a delightful plain, distant about a quarter of a league from the town of Bethlehem, and at the end of the valley is pointed out the celebrated field where the shepherds watched their flocks during the night of our Lord's birth. According to many respectable authorities, both sacred and profane, the apparition of angels to the pastors was not the only prodigy by which the birth of an infant-God was signalized. It is related that, on that blessed night, the vines of Engaddi blossomed; that at

The wonderful apparition had disappeared, the celestial songs had ceased, but the shepherds, inclining forward over their knotty staffs, were still listening. When the fitful gusts of the night wind through the valley was the only noise heard, and when there remained in the heavens but one sole point, white and shining, which could present the appearance of an angel, the shepherds took counsel together and said: *Let us go over to Bethlehem*, and let us see what has come to pass. Then filling their baskets with

Rome the temple of Concord suddenly fell, and that the oracles of the demons became silent for ever. The birth of OUR LORD was a sentence of perpetual banishment to these Pagan divinities, who up to then had been allowed to utter their predictions.

Milton, in one of his early pieces, in a strain of true poetry, thus describes the departure of these pretended divinities on the night of the nativity :—

> "The oracles are dumb,
> No voice or hideous hum
> Runs through the arched roof in words deceiving.
> Apollo from his shrine
> Can no more divine,
> With hollow shriek the steep of Delphos leaving.
> No nightly trance or breathed spell,
> Inspires the pale-eyed priest from the prophetic cell.

> "The lonely mountains o'er,
> And the resounding shore,
> A voice of weeping heard, and loud lament,
> From haunted spring and dale,
> Edged with poplar pale,
> The parting genius is with sighing sent;
> With flower-inwoven tresses torn,
> The nymphs in twilight shade of tangled thickets mourn.

> "In consecrated earth,
> And on the holy hearth,
> The Lars and Lemures moan with midnight plaint:
> In urns and altars round,
> A drear and dying sound
> Affrights the Flamens at their service quaint:
> And the chill marble seems to sweat,
> While each peculiar power foregoes his wonted seat.

such little presents as their cottages could supply,* they left their flocks to the care of the angels of the solitude, and proceeded onwards by the clear and silvery light of the stars, to the little city of David. On their way a supernatural impulse induced them to enter the mean stable in which the Saviour had just been born. There they found the Messiah lying in his manger. The Virgin inclining over her newly born was paying her adoration to him, with the deepest reverence and the most profound humility; above them, Joseph was bowing down his venerable head before his adoptive Son, who was no other than God. A ray of the moon's pale but clear light entered the grotto and fell on the heavenly group; without everything was lulled to rest under the beautiful starry canopy of heaven.†

Here is the place, said the shepherds, and prostrating

> "Peor and Baalim
>   Forsake their temples' din,
> With that twice-battered God of Palestine;
>   And mooned Ashtaroth,
>   Heaven's queen and mother both,
> Now sits not girt with tapers holy shine,
> The Libyc Hammon shrinks his horn,
> In vain the Tyrian maids their wounded Thammuz mourn.

> "And sullen Moloch, fled,
>   Hath left in shadows dread
> His burning idol, all of blackest hue;
>   In vain with cymbals ring
>   They call the grisly king,
> In dismal dance about the furnace blue:
> The brutish gods of Nile as fast,
> Isis and Orus, and the dog Anubis, haste."

* "Chi le portava candidi agnellini,
   Chi latte, chi formagio et ch' una pelle;
   E lei (*la vierge*) di tutto un poco ne accettava,
   E del restante gli ringraziava."—*Cant. Ital.*

† "The Persians call the night of Christ's birth, *Sheb jaldai*, the clear and brilliant night, on account of the descent of the angels."—*D'Herb. Bibliothèque, Or.*, b. 2, p. 294.

themselves before the manger of the King of kings, they then offered to the poor and infant-God, the poor man's gift and the poor man's homage.

They then began to relate the apparition of the angels, the ravishing music sung by them, their words of hope, peace, and love; Joseph listened with admiration to their recital, exulting at the manifestation of heaven; and Mary, silently drinking in every word, engraved them indelibly on her heart. This duty over, and their mission terminated, the shepherds of Juda retired glorifying God, and making known through the mountains the wonders of that blessed night. Those who listened to them were seized with astonishment, and said to each other: Can this be possible? Have the times of Abraham again returned, that angels should visit shepherds?

These reports, circulated in the evening, along the skirts of the woods and in the depths of the ravines, while the camels were drinking together out of the distant and lonely spring, were perhaps the impelling motives which induced a tribe of the Arabs of the desert to deify the Virgin and the child. The lovely image of the Virgin, holding her son on her knees, was sculptured on one of the columns of Caaba, and solemnly placed among the three-hundred-and sixty divinities of the three Arabias. At the time of Mahomet it was still seen, as is attested by Arabian historians of celebrity.*

After the massacre of the holy innocents, that valiant tribe arose as one man, sent forth a lengthened cry of

---

* "El Azraki brings forward the ocular testimony of a great many respectable persons," says Burchardt, "in proof of a very remarkable fact, of which, I believe, no mention has been made up to this time; the fact is this, that the figure of the Virgin Mary with the young *Issa* (Jesus) on her knees, was sculptured as a divinity on one of the columns of the gate of Caaba.—*Burchardt's Travels in Arabia.*

vengeance, and without being intimidated by a superior force, made an attack on the son of Herod, vassal as he was, and under the protection of the Romans.* · This fact, curious and singular, though authentic, confirms the supernatural fact related by St. Luke, a fact which the sneering philosophers of the school of Voltaire, and the no less incredulous disciples of the doctrine of Pantheism, have ranked among fabulous occurrences. The whimsical devotion of these Arabs who, before the preaching of the gospel, blended idolatory with the true God, cannot be accounted for on other grounds, except that of the knowledge of the marvels of the blessed night of Christ's birth.

* This occurrence, confirmed by the relation of an Arabian historian, is mentioned in the Toldos, a very ancient Jewish book, and written in a strain of enmity against Christianity. It is there inserted, that Herod the Great and

MARY AT BETHLEHEM.

On the eight day after his birth, the Son of God was circumcised and called Jesus, conformably to the command of his Heavenly Father. As every other Israelite, he must have a god-father, but on whom that high honour devolved we know not. With regard to the ceremony of circumcision, which was always performed under the auspices of Elias, who, as the Hebrews say, was invisibly present at it,* it took place, according to St. Epiphanius, in the very grotto in which Jesus was born, and it is the opinion of St. Bernard, an opinion not without grounds of probability, that St. Joseph was the minister of it.

Men from the ranks of the people, docile to the call of the angels, had come to adore the infant-God in his poor crib, and to share with him their coarse bread and goat's milk; not long after, a miracle of greater import, and of far more depth, led to the very same crib the first of the Gentile converts; the shepherds of Juda had taken the initiative; it was now the turn of sages and kings.

About the time of the birth of Jesus Christ, the Chaldean *Magi*, deeply learned in the science of astronomy, discerned a star of the first magnitude, which, from its extraordinary course and other evident signs, they recognised as that star of Jacob, which long since foretold by Balaam, was to arise radient and beautiful over their horizon at the time of the parturition of a Virgin. Zerdascht, the restorer of magism, a man of great research and well versed in astronomy, and in the theology of the Hebrews,† announced under the

---
his son were engaged in a war against a tribe of the desert who *adored the image of Jesus and Mary his mother*. This tribe endeavoured to enter into an alliance with a great many towns of Palestine, and in particular with that of Hai. But, when the Jews place this event as occurring during the life of Herod, it must arise from the massacre of the innocents, as the old king survived the birth of our Lord only one year.

* Basnage, b. 7, chap. 10.
† Some have supposed that he was a disciple of Jeremiah; but chronology

immediate successors of Cyrus, and a short time after the rebuilding of the temple, that, from the ancient traditions of Iran, collected by Abulfarage, a divine infant, charged with a mission to change the face of the world, would be born in the most western parts of Asia, of a pure and spotless virgin. He moreover added, that a star unknown to their hemisphere would signalize so remarkable an event, and that, on its appearance, the Magi themselves would bear presents to the young King. Faithfully and religiously executing the wishes of Zoroaster, three of the most illustrious *Savans* of Babylon* no sooner remarked the star, than they struck up the sounding notes of departure. Leaving behind them the city of Seleucia with its stately edifices built of palm-tree ;† passing by Babylon, where the desert wind moaning over crumbling ruins seemed to be whispering to the silent waste the sinister oracles of the son of Amos, they leave the land of dates and enter upon the sandy way of Palestine.

The star of the Messiah moved on before them, like the

is opposed to such an opinion; it is far more probable that he was a disciple of Daniel.

* There is no unanimity of opinion regarding the country of the Magi; some think that they were from the interior of Arabia Felix; others that they were from India, an opinion by no means probable. The best authorities are in favour of Persia being their country, and indeed such appears to us to be the truest opinion. The names of Gaspur, Melchior, Balthasar, given to the Magi, are of Babylonian origin. Babylon, and after its fall, Seleucia, situated at no great distance from the former, were the native places of the most distinguished astronomers of antiquity. These cities were to the east of Jerusalem, and a twenty days' journey would bring one from the banks of the Euphrates to Bethlehem. Origen, a man of learning and research, tells us that the Magi were astrologers. Drexilius sneers at Origen for giving such an opinion, but in doing so he only betrays his own ignorance of the history of the ancient East, where astrology had the same signification as astronomy. Herbelot, the best authority on matters regarding the East, tells us that the Magi came from Persia.

† Strabo, b. 17.

pillar of fire which conducted the fugitive cohorts of Israel to the sandy shores of the Red Sea. This strange star, uncontrolled by those unchangeable laws which regulate the motions of the starry orbs, had no fixed regular movement; at one time it advanced at the head of the caravan, but invariably pursuing a direct course towards the West; at another time it continued stationary over the tents when pitched for the night, and seemed to balance itself softly on the bosom of the clouds, like the albatross floating in fields of air; at break of day it gave the signal for departure, as it had at night given the signal to halt.*

At length, the pinnacles of Jerusalem were distinguished in the distance, towering aloft in the middle of the misty and wild ridges of its mountains; the camels were quenching their thirst in a well by the way side, when a cry of surprise and alarm burst forth from the Magi; the star had just concealed itself in the upper regions, like some intelligent creature, who sees that danger is near.†

The Magi, disconcerted like the mariners of the olden times, when the murky clouds intercepted the view of the polar star, held immediate consultation. What meant the sudden disappearance of their shining guide? Were they at last at the term of their long and tedious journey, and were they now to pitch their tents for a prolonged

---

* See St. John Chrysostom on St. Matthew, Ser. 6. Chalcidius, a pagan philosopher, who lived about the end of the third century, makes mention of the star which conducted the wise men of the East to the cradle of Christ. Let us hear what St. Augustin, the doctor of doctors, has said with regard to it: "A new star made its appearance at the birth of him whose death was to darken the old sun. What, then, was this strange star which never before was beheld, and which, since, then, cannot be discovered in the firmament? Was it not the magnificent language of heaven, recounting the glory of God, and publishing the parturition of a Virgin?"

† "This cistern or well, lying on the road to Jerusalem, is even at this day called the *Cistern of the three kings* or of the *star*, in memory of that event."— *Voyages de J. C.*

stay? It was possible, and even probable, that the infant-King, to whom they came from the banks of the Tigris, to pay their adorations, would be found in Jerusalem. The *God of Heaven*, thought they, prolongs not unnecessarily his miracles, they cease when human agencies suffice, for such is the order of Providence. It matters little that the star has abandoned us, we can, without aid, easily find out the object of our search in the capital of his dominions. To find out the young Royal Messiah, we have only to enter into the principal street, which assuredly must be strewn with green branches, perfumed with rose-water, and lined with rich, gorgeous tapestry; the sound of the Jewish harps, the dancing bands, and the notes of exultation and joy will clearly point out the direction in which we are to proceed. Then quickening the pace of their animals, they passed the outer gate, which was guarded by a lofty tower deemed impregnable, and now entered, through a double file of foreign soldiers, the ancient Sion.

Jerusalem presented a dull aspect, its inhabitants, noiselessly engaged in their ordinary affairs, had neither joy nor gladness depicted in their countenance; here and there a knot of persons were assembled but only to view the strange travellers as they were passing on, whom, from their long white robes closely fitted by magnificent cinctures to their *bazubends*,* enriched with precious stones, and more particularly from the manly beauty of their features, they recognised as satraps of the great king. The Oriental travellers, inclining over the necks of their dromedaries, as they went along, inquired of the many spectators collected about them, where was the King of the Jews, who had been

---

* Antique bracelets, ornamented with diamonds and pearls, worn above the elbow by the satraps of the royal family; the king of Persia and his sons still wear the *bazubends.—See Morier's Travels in Persia and Armenia.*

lately born, and whose star they had seen in Babylon. The natives of Jerusalem looking at them with surprise, knew not what answer to return to so strange an inquiry. . . . A King of the Jews. . . . . . .What King? They knew only Herod, whom they held in utter abhorrence; and he had no son lately born. The Magi, equally amazed at finding that every Hebrew of whom they made inquiries protested total ignorance of the matter, and moreover not seeing the slightest indication of joy, ascended, their minds rather disquieted, the populous street which led to the ancient palace of David, and pitched their tents in its gloomy and dilapidated courts.

Meantime, the strange and extraordinary inquiries of the Magi originated a whispering rumour through the city; their words were soon conveyed to the palace by those salaried officials, who paid a servile devotion to the ruling powers. Herod paused; his expansive forehead, deeply furrowed and marked with lines of gloomy thought, darkened up like a lowering sky: *he was troubled within himself*, says the Scripture, *and all Jerusalem with him*.

The alarm which the king of the Jews experienced we can easily conceive, and his position will at once explain the grounds of it. Herod was neither the anointed of the Lord, nor the chosen one of the people; a laurel branch—plucked out of the idolatrous precincts of the capitol, formed his tributary crown;—that crown of slavery, interwoven with thorns, every leaf of which had been purchased by heaps of gold, extorted from the savings of the rich, and squeezed out of the indigence of the poor. Held in detestation by the great, whose heads were forfeited on the first suspicion; feared by his own, whose lives he consigned to a bloody tomb; abhorred by the priests, whose privileges he trampled under foot; hated by the people for his nondescript religion and foreign origin. To the deep-seated, active, and openly declared enmity of the nation, he could oppose only his courtiers, tradesmen, and the wealthy, but inconsiderable sect of Herodians, who were dazzled by his exterior splendour and magnificence. The friend of Cæsar was often braved to his face, by his unyielding subjects. The Pharisees, a crafty and powerful sect, had, with mockery and insult, refused him the oath of fealty; the Essens, formidable from their invincible courage in battle, followed the example of the Pharisees; and the young and fiery disciples of the doctors of the law were after hurling down by their avenging axes the gilt eagle erected by the king on the principal gate of the temple. On every side conspiracies were hatched against the prince's life; and whenever, designedly or accidentally, a false rumour was circulated through the remote provinces, the people seized with avidity the deceitful lure, so flattering to their antipathies, and lighted up at once, in every place, bonfires. . . . but Herod extinguished them in blood.

During these conflicting elements of civil discord, and when an insurrectionary fever was spreading silently through the army, and when revolt, like a ripe fruit, seemed to invite the hands and arms of unsettled minds, there arrived at Jerusalem strangers of high rank, who demanded openly and unhesitatingly the King of the Jews lately born, whose star they had seen. Herod becomes astounded, he makes inquiries, he collects his scattered thoughts; the predictions fatal to his race, industriously circulated by the Pharisees, the oracles of the *Seers*, to which hitherto he paid but very slight attention, now vividly flash on his memory. This warrior Messiah, this prophet descended from David, who was to march his victorious ensigns from the rising of the sun to the going down thereof, caused him uneasy thoughts.

It was not a GOD that made the old king reflect; no, it was a *prince* that made him uneasy. The longer he reflects the more is he convinced that this event, so completely subversive of his political designs, was only a part and parcel of a wide-spread conspiracy, tending to erect on the ruins of his power some secret and powerful rival. What! was it for this that the illustrious blood of the Machabees had been cooly shed? Was it for this that the different branches of their family had been lopped off, and everything giving opposition to his sway had been trampled under the iron hoofs of his despotic power? Was it for this that he destroyed his soul, ruined his honour, and lost his rest? Was it for this that the shadows of butchered victims flitted at night through his sleeping thoughts? For this! to smoothen the way for the family of David to ascend the throne! * That sceptre so dearly purchased, that sceptre still reeking with the blood of his family, must it only be a barren and cursed stalk, to be shivered to atoms on his tomb by the blast of death!...... Must he then pass, like some meteor of the nocturnal tempest, through that land whose ancient glory would be the theme of future historians and poets!........And this nation, who entertained for him hatred deep and deadly, with what love and sympathy would they surround the issue of their ancient kings! and this last reflection entered as bitterly as gall the gloomy and

---

* We cannot feel surprised at the alarm which a descendant of the family of David caused Herod. There were others besides Herod who persecuted that illustrious family, through hatred of their ancient rights and glorious hopes. Eusebius, after Hegesippus, mentions that after the conquest of Jerusalem, Vespasian gave orders that the posterity of David should be sought and destroyed. Trajan continued the persecution. Domitian led two descendants of this illustrious race, whose grandfather was the apostle St. Jude, to Rome. The emperor, learning that their whole property consisted of only thirty-nine acres of land, tilled by their own hands, sent them back to their own country, as he apprehended little from their poverty.

desolate heart of the widowed king; for in the midst of his bloody and violent deeds, he found his heart empty, and experienced the want of being loved; a strange want, indeed, in a nature so constituted as his, but yet a real one. His character was truly a strange one, formed of the most opposite traits. The most engaging and noble qualities he made subservient to his ambition—the most absorbing and cruel passion that can rack and lay waste the human mind.

"Let this child be what he may, a prophet of God, or an earthly prince, die he must," said Herod after a few moments' reflection. "He shall die, though with that weak spark should be extinguished all the glories which our *seers* predict of the future. It matters little that the Hebrews are reduced to slavery and wretchedness under my sway. Have they not repudiated the lustre of my reign, despised my name, and abjured my policy? And is it for this that I have shed my blood for them on twenty battle-fields, that I have provided food for them during a wasting famine, that I have decorated their city with superb palaces, and rebuilt the temple of Jehovah? Yet I am in their eyes Herod the stranger, Herod the proselyte, Herod the butcher!......... And shall another come to render them great and happy, and is my memory to be trampled under foot? No; hated I may be, but eclipsed by another I shall not, and if the star of my reign has been unpropitious, I will at least take care that it shall be the last star that shall appear above their horizon. But this son of David is perhaps only a puling child. Ah! whence this chicken-hearted pity? Athaliah, that incomparable woman, forgot, in the massacre of the seed-royal of the house of Judah, one only child in the cradle, and that child hurled her from her throne, and deprived her of life. But as for me, I will see that nothing shall be forgotten. But where can he be concealed—this King of the

Jews, *newly born*, whom the stars announced, and in search of whom these insolent Satraps approached even the very gate of my palace? Is it possible that he can be the *Schilo* foretold by Jacob? But perhaps all this is merely the reverie of some astrologer. No matter; I will make myself certain."

A few hours afterwards the doctors of the law and the high priests, assembled in council under the presidency of Herod, were listening to a question which appeared to them very strange, coming, as it did, from the mouth of such a prince: Where should the Messiah be born? An unanimous answer was immediately given: *In Bethlehem of Juda*. And the ancients of Israel, delighted at an opportunity being offered for disquieting the mind of the friend of the Romans, were not certainly slow in adding that the last week of Daniel being nearly expired, the time of the Messiah must be near at hand. Herod was not content with such indications, so little calculated to give him any certainty; where exactly to strike the blow he was desirous to know. He resolved, therefore, to interrogate the Magi, and to make out, if it were at all possible, the precise epoch of the birth of the child, to be calculated from the time of the appearance of the star. Too artful a politician to grant to the wise men of Iran a public audience, which might give consistency to the report, which it was of the most vital importance should be stifled, the king sent for them privately, and closely questioned them as to the time the star first appeared. "He made particular inquiries, not about the child, but about the star," says St. John Chrysostom, "that the utmost circumspection should be used with regard to the snare which he was laying." Informed of what he was desirous of knowing, the man of blood dismissed the strangers very courteously: "Go," said he, "go to Bethlehem, and diligently inquire after the child; and when you have found him, let me know, that I also may come and adore him."

But the Magi, like all persons of superior minds, like all men of reflective and thoughtful habits, were upright, sincere, and little prone to suspect evil designs in others. They could easily understand how a prince could act tyrannically and cruelly, but that he could act with duplicity they never for a moment supposed; for the first thing inculcated on the minds of the kings of Persia during their early years, was to tell the truth under all circumstances. They then implicitly believed the deceitful words of the Idumean, and passing underneath the splendid porticos of his palace, which vied in magnificence with those of the Great King, except that there was wanting among the brazen figures and vaulted arches the bronzed bell of the *suppliants*,* they quitted the *Betzetha*,† packed up their tents, and a second time traversed the holy city, on their way to the supposed place of the Messiah's birth. As they were slowly passing along the trophied walls of the new amphitheatre, the extraordinary decoration of which afforded an inexhaustible source of sarcasm and ridicule to the Pharisees, they again encountered King Herod, encompassed with a forest of Thracian and German lances, and taking the direction of Jericho. ‡

* "The kings of Persia administered justice in a manner altogether patriarchal. Over their heads was a bronzed bell, to which a chain was attached, hanging down along the wall of the palace. Every time the bell tolled the officers of the prince quitted their rooms, and introduced to the presence of the *Great King* those who had any complaints to make, and who sought justice at the hands of the prince himself. The justice sought was immediately rendered."—*Antar. Trad.*

† The quarter called *Betzetha*, or the new town, united by Herod to Jerusalem, lay to the north of the temple; it included the lower pool, the pool of Siloam, and the palace of Herod.

‡ We have followed the opinion of those writers who think that Herod set out for Jericho, where he was laid up with indisposition, at the same time that

The Persians departed from Jerusalem, by the gate of Damascus; then taking the way to the left, they got entangled in the hollow ravines, intersected by mounds, which they were obliged to clamber up. They were hardly an hour's journey from the capital of Judea, when a bright spot appeared above their heads, and like a falling star descended rapidly towards them. The star! our star! cried out the servants with transports of joy; the star! repeated their masters, equally overjoyed; and now assured that they had entered on the right way, they resumed their journey with renewed ardour.

They were preparing to enter the city of David, when the star, on a sudden, assumed a stationary position over an abandoned cave, having all the appearance of a rustic stable, and then falling lower, balanced itself, if I may use the expression, over the head of the infant-God. The sight of this now motionless star, its beautiful rays falling, in the form of a luminous sheaf, on the grotto hollowed out of the rock, filled the minds of the Magi with unshaken faith; and strong indeed must be their faith, to recognise the king-Messiah in a poor infant, suffering every privation, lodged in a place so wretched, lying in a manger, and his mother, though lovely and graceful in form, yet, presenting all the appearance of one who could boast of no illustrious parentage. God, wishing to upbraid the Jews for their hardness of heart, by the contrast of the holy eagerness and implicit faith of the Gentiles, allowed not the humble and mean appearance of the Holy Family to stagger the strong faith of the Magi.

the Magi were going towards Bethlehem; this accords exactly with the account given in the gospel: for had Herod been in Jerusalem at the time of the return of the Persians, they would in all probability have seen him before the admonition of the angel. The illness of Herod, by turning aside his attention from the Magi and the child, left the former at liberty to return in peace to their own country, and gave the Holy Family an opportunity of returning to Nazareth.

The Gentiles—worshippers of the sun, who, equally as the children of promise, were to be redeemed by the cross, entered the mean habitation of Christ with the same veneration as they entered their own temples erected on subterranean fires, and in which the starry spheres revolved;* according to the usage of their nation, they took up some of the dust of the floor, and sprinkled it on their heads, then taking off their rich sandals, they adored the new-born babe; for all the children of the East, at that time paid adoration to their gods, as also to their masters. Opening, then, their caskets of perfumed wood, which contained the presents des-

---

* "These spheres, formed of bronze, and as perfect as our hollow spheres, revolved with a great deal of noise at the rising of the sun. They are still seen at Oulam, where stands a Gheber temple."—*Rabbi Benja.*

tined for the Messiah, they drew forth the purest gold, collected in the environs of Nineveh the Great, and the rarest perfumes, taken in exchange from the Arabs of Yemen for fruits and pearls. These mysterious gifts were not, like the offerings of the Jews, of a carnal nature; the cradle of HIM who was to abolish the sacrifices of the synagogue must not be sprinkled with blood; moreover, the Magi immolated neither spotless lambs nor snow-white heifers; they therefore presented him with gold, as to an earthly prince, and with myrrh and frankincense, as to a God.

This was the final scene of splendour in which the Blessed Virgin figured. The first period of her life, like a delicious reverie of Ginnistan,* flowed sweetly on under cedar and gilded roofs, amidst sacred perfumes, melodious chaunts, and the enchanting music of lyres and harps; the second, replete with marvels and mysteries, had placed her almost on an equality with the inhabitants of heaven and the princesses of Asia; the third was about to open under far different auspices; it was to be a period of secret agonizing tortures, and insupportable pains and sorrows.

Meantime the Magi, having no inducement to prolong their stay in Judea, and eager to make known the prosper-

* There existed, say the Magi, at the foot of Mount Caucasus, and along the shores of the Caspian Sea, a race of beings, called Dives and Peris; the Dives were formidable giants, the Peris, peaceful sages; both proceeded from the hands of the Eternal, long before the creation of man. The Dives governed the world during seven thousand years; the Peris, who succeeded them, exercised the same authority during two thousand years. Both are equally called Ginn by the Arabs. The country in which the Peris dwelt was situated, according to the Magi, under the most beautiful sky possible; it was called Ginnistan; a perfect fairy land. All nature, the elements, everything creative was subject to their power. The fairies must have a natural taste for diamonds, and so the capital of Ginnistan was built of them. By a stroke of the wand, diamonds, rubies, gold, marbles, emeralds were moulded together, and piazzas formed of them. Water the most limpid flowed along the ever-cooling meads and evergreen groves.

ous issue of their adventurous search, made their arrangements to leave Bethlehem. They intended, according to promise, to seek out the king at his palace in Jericho, in order to make him acquainted with the place of the Messiah's birth; but an angel of the Lord admonished them in a dream, of the black and sanguinary designs of that perfidious prince, and intimated to them an order to change their route. The followers of Zoroaster returned thanks to HIM *who dwells in the sun,* tendered their obligations to their good genius for this nightly revelation, and meriting, by their perfect obedience, the gift of faith received at a later hour,[*] instead of going along the barren and dangerous shores of the cursed lake, whose dull and stagnant waters reflect the ruins of those towns that had been reproved and devoted to destruction, they turned their camels' heads in a contrary direction from the *great sea,* and crossed the flowery plains bathed by the Euphrates and the Bend-Emir, in their course through the delightful plains of Syria.

CHAPTER XII.

THE PURIFICATION.

FORTY days after the birth of the Redeemer, the Virgin repaired to Jerusalem, in obedience to a law which prescribed the purification of mothers and the redemption of the first-born. True, this law could not be binding on Mary; for what could there be in common between defilement and the chaste spouse of the Holy Ghost? Yet Mary, notwithstanding her great natural understanding and deep

---

[*] The Magi were baptized by St. Thomas, and it is believed that, while preaching the gospel in India, they suffered martyrdom.

penetration, entered into no discussion respecting the obligation of that law, so far as she was concerned; she paid it blind obedience. Far from publishing to the world the astounding miracle of her virginal maternity, she concealed it under a triple veil, and in a spirit of humility wished to be lost in the crowd; she remembered her duties as daughter of Sion, and with the performance of such duties she would not allow her prerogatives of celestial mother to interfere. *Mariam supra legem fecerat gratia*, says St. Augustine, *sub lege fecit humilitas.*

The very moment that Joseph and Mary entered the sacred enclosure, with the sicles of silver, as the price of redemption, and the pigeons, as a holocaust and sin-offering, a holy old man called Simeon,[*] to whom it was divinely revealed that he should not die until his eyes should be blessed with the sight of the anointed of the Lord, entered the porch, moved by the spirit of God. At seeing the Holy Family, the eye of the old man lit up with the fire of inspiration; recognising the royal Messiah under the mean of dress of a low born child, he took him from the arms of his mother, raised him up, and in transports of delight gazed on him again and again, whilst tears of joy trickled down his venerable cheeks. "Now, O Lord," cried out the holy old man, raising his bedewed countenance towards heaven, "now, dismiss thy servant in peace, according to your word, for my eyes have seen the Saviour which you have bestowed upon us, and which you have destined to be exposed to the view of all people, as a light to the Gentiles, and as the glory of Israel." Concluding these words, Simeon bestowed a solemn

---

[*] The Arabs call Simeon *Siddik*, he who verifies; because he bore testimony of the coming of the true Messiah, in the person of Jesus, Son of Mary, whom all the Mussulmans are obliged to believe as such."—*D'Herbelot, Bib. Or.*, b. 3, p. 266.

THE PURIFICATION. 167

blessing on Joseph and Mary, and then, after a few moments of sad, solemn silence, addressed Mary, adding that the child, born for the salvation and for the destruction of many, would be a stumbling-block to preserve man, and that sorrow, like the sharp edge of a sword, should enter the heart of his mother.

At this unexpected glimmer, which cast a sombre light over the grand destiny of Christ, the ignominies, the sufferings and the agonies of the cross revealed themselves all at once to the Blessed Virgin. Before the sinister expressions of Simeon, as before a stormy blast, she bent her head; and her heart, in which was passing a silent scene of martyrdom, experienced a thrill similar to that caused by the touch of red hot iron slowly entering the quick and bleeding flesh.* But Mary knew how to receive without a murmur everything coming from the hands of God; she laid her pale ashy lips on the chalice of vinegar and gall, she emptied it to the dregs, and suppressing her tears, said in a composed melancholy tone: "*Lord, thy will be done!*" "If it had been in her power," says St. Bonaventure, "she would have accepted of the torments and death of Christ, to be suffered in her own person; but in obedience to God, she made him the glorious offering of her Son's life, suppressing, though not without pain and difficulty, the tender emotions of the love she bore him."† At that moment a prophetess called Anna, daughter of Phanuel, of the tribe of Aser, happened to enter; this chaste widow resided continually in the temple, serving God night and day, in fasting and prayer. At sight of the divine child she raised her voice in the praise of the Lord, and spoke aloud of him to all those who were in expectation of the redemption of Israel.

"Not only," says St. Augustine on this subject, "angels, prophets, and shepherds publish aloud the birth of the Saviour, but the just and the old of Israel cry out that truth. Both sexes, young and old, give authority to this belief, confirmed by so many miracles. A virgin conceives, a barren women brings forth, a dumb speaks, Elizabeth prophesies, the Magi adore, an infant in the womb of his mother leaps with joy, a widow makes confession of this marvellous event, and the just are in expectation of it."

As Mary could not be allowed to enter the inner court of the temple, and since the child, on account of his sex, must be there offered to the Lord, Joseph himself carried

---

* "My sovereign," says St. Anselm, on this subject, "it is impossible to believe that you could have survived, for even a single moment, such pain and grief, had not God aided you."

† St. Bonaventure, in p. i., dist. 48, 9, 2.

him into the *Hall of the first-born*, asking himself the question, if the scenes at the entry of Jesus, which had just ended, should be renewed in the court of the Hebrew pontiffs. But nothing occurred in that privileged part of the temple that could be considered as betraying a knowledge of the infant-God. Everything remained cold and gloomy under the rising beam of *the young son of justice*. A priest, altogether unknown to Joseph, took, with an air of indifference, from the horny hands of a man of the people, a man looked upon by him *as the sweepings and refuse of the world*,* the timid birds required by the law, and deigned not even to to pay Christ the slight honour of a look. The love of gold—that disgraceful idol worshipped in secret, as long as a blush remains to mantle the cheek—the love of gold had changed into stone the narrow, selfish, and resentful † hearts of the greater number of the princes of the synagogue. Leaving virtues and privations to be monopolised by the mere Levites,‡ they passed by the indigent stretched on their hard thresholds, and turned aside their heads with an air of indifference from the poor and needy traveller, who lay mortally wounded on the mountain road; at heart, they had no love for God or man. And it was for this that our Lord, HE, the constituted priest of perfect charity, reproached them in a holy strain of biting sarcasm, in that sublime

---

* Prideaux's History of the Jews.

† "The Jewish doctors held then, as they hold even to-day, an appalling maxim; they hold that he who nourishes not his hatred, and takes not revenge, is unworthy the title of Rabbin."—*Basnage, b.* 6, p. 262.

‡ The luxury and wealth of the high priests of Jerusalem appear now incredible. They scoured the country on all sides and took away the tithes from every granary, which they exclusively appropriated to themselves, and consequently left the simple priests to live on nuts and figs. On remonstrating, the unhappy Levites were charged with insubordination and rebellion, and delivered up to the Romans. The governor, Felix, alone, in compliment to the high priests, cast forty of them into prison.—See Josephus, in his Antiqu. and Basnage, b. 1, chap. 4, p. 12b.

parable of the good Samaritan. For this also it was, as Malachy had foretold, that *God pronounced a curse on their blessings*, and averted his eyes from his temple, which he was soon to deliver up to the fire and sword of the Romans.

The presence of the Messiah, which at a later period fired the hearts of the disciples of Emmaus, even before they recognised him in the breaking of bread, glidded along over the soul of the Aaronides, as a beam of the vernal sun glimmers over the eternal snows of Ararat. That solemn moment, when the heavenly concerts, playing around God, suddenly ceased their melody; that solemn moment when the looks of the heavenly host were steadfastly fixed on one sole point of the universe; that moment passed on unnoticed before the darkened eyes of the priests and doctors. There was none to recognise *that pure and clean oblation to be offered up for ever*, as foretold by Malachy. The desired of nations, he, for whom the angels had prepared the way, the glorious Redeemer so long promised and so long expected, was there, corporally present, in his house of sanctity, and yet there was no one who entertained even a thought of receiving him with palm branches; and of crying out from the embattlements of the temple, or from the roofs of the houses, *Hosanna to the Son of David!* But a God subservient to their own private views, a God, a slave of the *Sanhedrim*,* a God covered with worn garment, and tinctured with the blood of Alexander, such a God only would these men receive!

And the infant-God who, whilst carried through the streets of Jerusalem, had recognised the sites of the redemption, was silently counting his executioners from among this imposing and gilded crowd: during the melody of the choirs

---

* Basnage, b. 6, chap. 26.

who were chaunting hymns of praise and thanksgiving to the Eternal, Christ distinguished, rising higher above them, the arrogant and sinister tones which, at a later period, were to cry out aloud, *Crucify him! Crucify him!* Accursed race of Aaron, where are you now? The avenging breath of the Crucified has scattered you like chaff through every part of the globe; swallowed up in the masses that you despised, you are not even recognised by the partners of your exile. But experiencing no uneasy feelings about the future, which, even then, was lowering over their heads, the Hebrew priests offered to the God who rejected them, the chosen victims of the rich and poor. One among them took the turtle doves from the hands of Joseph, ascended the steps of the altar of holocausts, and offered to the Lord that poor and unpretending sacrifice.

"And after Joseph and Mary had performed all things according to the law of the Lord," says St. Luke, "they returned into Galilee, to their city, Nazareth."*

---

* We have followed the opinion of St. Luke, that of St. John Chrysostom, and other authorities, in stating that the Holy Family set out for Nazareth after the purification. We cannot reconcile in any other way St. Matthew, who is silent regarding the wonderful events of the presentation in the temple, with St. Luke, who makes no mention of the innocents and the flight into Egypt. "How can both the evangelists," says St. John Chrysostom, "be reconciled, except the return to Nazareth preceded the flight into Egypt? For God did not order Joseph and Mary to go into Egypt before the purification, lest the law should be violated in the slightest tittle. But this duty performed, they returned of their own accord to Nazareth, where they received the order to fly into Egypt."

CHAPTER XIII.
THE FLIGHT INTO EGYPT.

JOSEPH and Mary had scarcely arrived in Lower Galilee, when they were forced to set out on a long and perilous journey, the term of which was to be the land of exile. One night an angel of the Lord appeared to Joseph during sleep: "Arise," said he, "and take the child and his mother, and fly into Egypt, and remain there until I shall tell thee to return, for Herod will seek the child to destroy him." Joseph, alarmed at these words, arises, adores the Lord, and hastens to awake Mary, who alongside the cradle of her child, was enjoying a slumber as light and refreshing as that of an angel. The young mother at once comprehended the necessity of this hasty and stealthy departure. She cast an agonizing look on her son, hastily collected whatever provisions, clothes, and garments might be required during the journey, and then, preceded by Joseph, and bearing Jesus in her arms, left her native town, now glittering with the silvery light of the moon and stars.

The prophecies of Simeon were now about being verified; scarcely born and still in his cradle, Jesus was diligently sought after by a persecuting tyrant, and his immaculate, youthful, and saintly mother was forced like a criminal to fly during night, having no companion but one old grayheaded man, who had no other means of defence against the lance of the Arab lying in ambush in the defiles of the mountains, or against the murderous pursuit of Herod's soldiers, except those of resignation and prayer. And it might well be said, that God himself abandoned this holy family to their fate, for in intimating to Joseph an order

to depart, the angel gave no assurance of protection during
the journey. The spouse of the Virgin fully understood that
the solemn moment of Christ's manifestation not as yet being
come, God willed not that he should be preserved from the
snares of Herod, through any other means save those re-
sulting from human prudence and natural foresight. On
Joseph then devolved all the care and anxiety attending
this difficult enterprise; on him, a poor and unsophisticated
old man as he was, devolved the duty of subverting the plans,
unravelling the plots, and eluding the suspicious vigilance
of a jealous and artful tyrant, commanding the services of
his emissaries, such as an Eastern despot can do. What
was he to do, and what part was he to take, in case of any
fatal encounter on the way? The sudden, unexpected departure of the Magi had awakened the suspicions of Herod,
and these suspicions were confirmed by the words of Anna
and of Simeon; disguised inquiries and secret searches
had already commenced, and no one could tell where the
sanguinary prince, who was profusely flinging gold into
the red hands of the assassin would stop. The more Joseph
reflects, the more vividly is presented to his mind some appalling deed, the vague terror of which freezes the blood in
his veins. As to Mary, she is stricken with the paleness
and silence of death. She now and then casts a look, expressive of fear and alarm, into the crevices of the valleys,
the opening of the forests, or along the solitary windings of
the rocky and difficult path, which had been selected by
Joseph as the safest, and as the one the most remote from
human habitations. The moon shed down her soft and
silvery light on this silent journey, stealthily undertaken
under cover of the azure drapery of a beautiful Oriental
night. "The season was yet cold;"[*] says St. Bonaventure,

[*] About the middle of February, the season is cold in the interior of the

"and in their journey through Palestine, the Holy Family were forced to select the wildest and least frequented roads. Where can they procure a place of shelter during the night? Where shall they find a secure spot during the day to take a few moments' repose from the fatigues of their weary journey? Where shall they partake of their frugal repast, so necessary to support their strength nearly exhausted, and their spirits nigh spent?"*

Tradition is altogether silent regarding the greater part of this sad and perilous journey. It must, indeed be long and weary, obliged, as they were, to direct their steps across the mountains, taking advantage of the early hours of morning, and often, also, waiting for the rising moon to set out again. Whilst journeying through Galilee, its deep caverns, with their hitherto unexplored windings, calculated to screen them from every prying eye, offered them a place of repose and rest. But these grottos, notwithstanding their peculiar formation, so contrived as to afford security, yet had their dangers! for numerous depredatory bands, who, for a long time, had held in check all the forces of the kingdom, and who were now emboldened by the illness of Herod to appear again abroad,† selected them as the most secure hiding-places. Fear of entering, unknowingly, one of these haunts of assassins, made Joseph more than once hesitate before accepting the protection which these hidden caves offered.

---

mountains; the temperature, according to M. de Volney, being about the same degree as that of France; on the contrary, the plains of Syria, at that season, enjoy the heats of summer.—See note in the beginning of the 4th chapter.

* St. Bonaventure's Life of Christ.

† These armed hands, sometimes two or three thousand strong, were commanded by experienced leaders, who allowed not a moment's respite to Herod and the Romans. Some of them, influenced by political motives, carried on a factious war, others were merely a band of assassins, who carried poinards concealed under their dress, and murdered whomever they pleased, even in the very streets of Jerusalem.

At last, after a thousand perils, a thousand inconveniences of every sort, the Holy Family gained the environs of Jerusalem. Here, their precautions and uneasiness increased from the proximity of danger; the fugitives dared not approach the towns, nor even the populous hamlets, as they were filled with detectives and informers, who had an eye on every stranger that might arrive. They, therefore, followed the beds of the torrents, plunged into the paths the least frequented, and moved along stealthily under the drooping foliage of the trees, not daring, even for a moment, to swerve from the path, though their provisions were now exhausted, and though suffering almost the extreme of fear, hunger, and cold. They had now passed Anathot, and were proceeding by Ramla, in their descent to the plains of Syria; eager to remove themselves from so dangerous a neighbourhood, they were borrowing some hours of the night, when they perceived, emerging from a dark gloomy ravine, a body of armed men, who at once obstructed their passage. He who appeared the leader of this band of robbers stepped out from the group, for the purpose of scrutinizing the wayfarers. Joseph and Mary stopped suddenly, and looked on each other, alarm and affright depicted on their countenances; Jesus was sleeping. The brigand, whose object was blood or gold, fixed a look of amazement both on that unarmed old man, so strikingly resembling a patriarch of the days of old, and on that muffled woman, who, from the agonizing way in which she pressed him to her bosom, seemed desirous of hiding her infant in the very centre of her heart. "They are poor," said the bandit to himself, "and travelling by night, like fugitives!" It might be that he, even he, had, too, a child in the cradle; it might be, that the atmosphere of gentleness and pity, surrounding Jesus and Mary, exerted its peculiar influence on his wild, unbridled soul. He immediately lowered the point of his lance, and extending to Joseph the hand of friendship, offered him for the night whatever shelter his fortress—a fortress suspended from an angle of the rock, like the ærie of some bird of prey—might afford. This offer, loyally made, was accepted in the same spirit of confidence and trust, and the very den of a robber, like the tent of the Arab,* became a place of refuge and protection.

* The site traditionally assigned to this scene, and where are still seen the ruin of the robber's den, still continues a place of evil fame. During the crusades, the Franks, well acquainted with this tradition, had installed a leader of banditti as a feudal lord; it, however, seldom happened, says Father Nau, that a lord of any influence or weight became a highway robber; but the crusades are better known in history than Father Nau. To this legend, having every appearance of authenticity, there is added a story, for the truth of which

On the morrow, about mid-day, the Holy Family rested in the interior of a large grove of palm-trees, maples, and wild fig-trees, which extended to a distance not far from Ramla;* a plot of amaranths, daffodils, and *anemonies*, received the Sovereign of heaven and earth; the heats of summer were reigning in the valley, and the warbling of birds, the perfumes of plants, the shady branches of fig-trees, and the noise of running waters murmuring in the distance, were shedding their soothing influences on the slumbers of Christ. After a short stay, every moment of which was counted, the travellers pursued their journey. We know not the reasons which induced them to direct their steps towards Bethlehem; tradition has preserved the remembrance of their route, and the Christians have raised an altar in the cave where Mary concealed herself and her child,† whilst Joseph was going up to the town, for the purpose either of obtaining information of the departure of a caravan, or to barter the slow mule of the blessed Virgin for a camel, essentially necessary for the journey through the desert. Be the motive what it might, that attracted Joseph and Mary into the crater of the volcano, one thing is certain, that they remained there only a few hours, and that they reached without delay a maratime port of the Philistines, in order to secure a place in the first caravan setting out for Egypt.

If we see no reason to dissent from the learned calcula-

we do not vouch, that the bandit who sheltered Joseph and Mary was the identical good thief pardoned by Christ on the Cross.

* " The site to which tradition assigned one of the stages of the Holy Family's journey is a delightful spot; there are seen, even on this day, the ruins of a monastery."—*Journey from Paris to Jerusalem.*

† This cave is called the *Grotto of the Virgin's Milk*, for a belief is there current that whilst the Virgin was suckling the infant Jesus, some drops of the milk fell on the rock.

tions of chronologists, who make no allowance for any interval of rest during this long and tedious journey, both Joseph and Mary must have fallen in with a caravan ready for immediate departure over the coasts of Syria; and this is the more likely, as the vernal equinox was near at hand, and as every one wished to anticipate the season when the *simoom* exercises its power over the desert, and renders its sandy sea as treacherous as the billows themselves.* Apart from the great uneasiness arising from the pursuit set on foot by Herod, the second stage of the Holy family's journey equalled the first, in fatigue, and pain, and insecurity. In setting out from Gaza, its crumbling towers echoing the dying sounds of the waves, the travellers saw before them only immense wastes of sand almost blasting the eye, and a frightful solitude ploughed up by the parching wind of the desert, and over which hung threatening an angry sky. No vegetation, if we except some stunted heath springing up here and there on this isolated waste; no water, except the salty spring, from which the Virgin and Joseph, though wearied and poor, and unprotected, could not drink, until the rich traders, with their servants and camels, had first quaffed of it, and then there remained of the scanty and muddy wave scarcely as much as would fill the hollow of the hand. The farther they removed from the frontier of Syria, the greater was their thirst, and the fewer were the springs. At one time they perceived in the distance, in the midst of these boundless wastes, a large lake, as blue and clear as the lake of Tiberias; The heavens were reflected in its limpid waters; in which also was mirrored a

* The Arabs call the parched wind of the desert *simoom*, or poison. It may be well compared to the heat issuing from the mouth of an oven when the bread is drawing. Those winds are most frequent during the fifty days before and after the equinoxes.—*Volney's Travels in Syria.*

solitary date tree; a cry of joy broke forth at this discovery; the paces of the camels were quickened; and Mary, like the flower of Saron, crushed by the rain, raised her languishing head. The happy lake was just reached; they were already, in imagination, quaffing its waters; when, O misery! a mocking demon transported it some leagues further on; and in its place nothing could be seen except the burning sand.* Night coming on, the caravan halted; the camels were unyoked, and tied to stakes fixed deep in the sand; the traders, after partaking of their repast, consisting of dates and milk, surrendered themselves up to sleep under their respective tents, and there remained until the moon appeared above the horizon. The servants, with the most needy portion of the travellers, among which may be classed the Son of God, his Divine Mother, and Joseph, were reclining on a sort of rush mat extended on the ground, having no covering but that of the sky, while the cold dew of night was falling on their bodies and limbs, now wearied and bruised with heat and travel.† From time to time a cry of alarm was heard; it proceeded from the Arabs of the desert roaming about the sleeping caravan, under the false and deceptive glimmer of the stars; a flight of arrows, accompanied with the suffering cries of the wounded, announced their departure. Then the youthful Virgin, who surrounded her Son as a rampart, raised towards heaven

* This phenomenon is known by the name of *mirage*. During the expedition of the French into Egypt, in the year 1798, the soldiers, in their march through the desert, were often tantalized by this cruel illusion. After the soil has become heated by the presence of the sun, the prospect seems bounded by a general inundation; everything about is reflected in the midst of a sheet of water; on approaching, however, the deceptive inundation recedes, and the reflected image vanishes, to be succeeded by another, as some more distant object comes in sight.

† "Though the days in that region are close and warm, almost to suffocation, the nights are extremely cold.—*Vol. Sav.*

her eyes moist with tears, and her countenance wan and pale from fright, for she had fears for his life.

When the moon was shedding down her silvery light on this silent and dreary waste, barren even of the slightest shrub, the tents were struck. The leader of the caravan consulted the polar star, and then was resumed the painful journey, with all its well-known inconveniences, sufferings, and terrors.

At length they reached the outskirts of this illusory and solitary region: Egypt, that cradle of arts and sciences, of light and darkness, now opened on the travellers' view, with its obelisks of red granite, its temples with pinnacles of shining metal,[*] its colossal pyramids, its villages, scattered around like islands, and its providential river, banked with reeds and covered with boats. This country appeared richer, more populous, and more of a trading character than Judea; but it was the land of exile! On the other side of the desert lay their home, and on that were fixed the hearts and affections of the exiles!

After a journey of a hundred and forty leagues,[†] the fugitives reached Heliopolis, the native City of Moses,[‡] where a colony had been founded by their nation. In that city a temple, constructed on the plan of the holy house had been raised to Jehovah; the decorations of that Egyptian temple were scarcely inferior to those of the

---

[*] On the dome of the sanctuary of the principal temple there was an immense sheet of polished metal, in which the light was beautifully reflected. Something similar was placed on the top of a light-house at Alexandria, which reflected the different vessels coming into port, long before they could be perceived in the horizon."—*Eastern Correspondence.*

[†] See Barad., vol. i., chap. 8. The author of "The Travels of Jesus Christ" calculates only a hundred leagues; probably not taking into account the circuitous nature of the route.

[‡] "Moses ut accepi a grandioribus, natu Ægyptiis, Heliopolitanus erat.—*Josephus contra Appionem.*

temple of Jerusalem; a massive bronze lamp, suspended from the vaulted ceiling, instead of the celebrated chandelier with the seven branches, marked the inferiority of one to the other. At the gate of this city—a city containing a large population, of which the greater part were idolatrous Egyptians and Arabs—there grew a majestic and shady tree to which the Arabs of Yemen, established along the banks of the Nile, paid adoration in their own peculiar way.* At the approach of the Holy family, the idolized tree bent its leafy branches gracefully and slowly, as if to offer the *salem* to the youthful Master of nature, carried in Mary's arms.† And if we are to believe Palladius and many other pious writers, at the very moment that the divine travellers passed under the granite arches of the principal gate of Heliopolis all the idols of a contiguous temple tumbled headlong to the ground.‡

Joseph and Mary merely passed through the city, and thence directed their course to Matarich, a smiling village overshadowed by sycamores, and containing a spring of

---

* The Arabs, who had by degrees forgotten the God of Abraham, at that time paid adoration to a great number of idols, one more fantastical than another. The date tree, says Azraki, had adoration paid to it by the tribe of Khozua, and a rock was adored by Beni Thekif; a large tree called *zat arouat* was adored by the Koresich, &c. The Persians contemptuously styled the Arabs worshippers of stones.

† This particular circumstance has been gleaned from Sozomen, and it requires more than ordinary courage to attach importance to such a matter in this scoffing age; and yet it can scarcely be deemed miraculous. It is a certain fact that there grows in Arabia a tree which bends its branches at the approach of man. Niebuhr, who cannot be suspected of credulity, has discovered a tree of that kind in Yemen, and the Arabs, who name it the *hospitable tree*, hold it in such high veneration, that they will not permit even a leaf of it to be plucked. If this *mimosa*, by a natural phenomenon, lowers its branches at the approach of man, particularly must this be the case when a God approaches.

‡ Palladius is not the only person who makes mention of this miracle; Dorotheus, martyr; Sozomen, St. Anselm, St. Bonaventure, Sira, Denis the Carthusian; Testat, Ludolphus Barradius, &c., equally attest it.

water, the only sweet one in all Egypt; here, in a dwelling something in the form of a bee-hive, the fugitive family breathed in peace, far from Herod, who was then in a paroxysm of fury, spilling the blood of the innocents." *

According to many illustrious and respectable authorities, † whose opinions are founded on tradition, and whose assertions offer nothing improbable, the Holy Family remained seven years in Egypt; even at this day we find traces of their sojourn. The well where Mary used to wash the little clothes of the Infant, ‡ the bushy hill where she exposed them to be dried by the sun, the sycamore, under the shade of which she loved to sit with her Son on her knees, § are, after the lapse of eighteen centuries, still pointed out by the pilgrims of Europe and Asia who are thoroughly acquainted with the route, and even the descendants of the Pharaos have shown them honour. Every site has its own

---

* This evangelical fact is proved not only by Scripture, but even by Jews and Pagans.—(Macrobe.—Origen *against Celsus*. Toldos Huldr., p. 12, 14, 20. See, also, the erudite History of the New Testament, by M. Abbé James.)

† See Trombell, in his Life of the Blessed Virgin, Jacharias, Anselm, Eusebius, St. Thomas.

‡ "This well is still called *Mary's Well;* an old tradition hands down that the Blessed Virgin bathed the infant Jesus in it. In the early ages of Christianity the faithful erected a church on the site; and in latter times the Mussulmans built a mosque there, and the followers of both persuasions met together at *Mary's Fountain,* to be healed from their various diseases. The fountain yet remains; the pilgrimages to it still continue, but no traces of either church or mosque can now be discovered."—*Savary, vol.* 1, *p.* 122.

§ "At no great distance from the fountain, we were introduced into an inclosure planted with trees; a Mussulman, who acted as guide, made us stop before a sycamore, saying to us at the same time: 'This is the tree of Jesus and Mary.' Vansleb, *curé* of Fontainbleau, mentions that the ancient sycamore had fallen down from age in the year 1056; the gray friars of Cairo have piously preserved in their sacristy the remains of that celebrated tree; in the garden there is seen only a naked trunk, undoubtedly that of the tree of which we speak. General Kléber, after the victory at Heliopolis, felt a desire to visit, as a pilgrim, the tree of the Holy Family; he wrote his name on the bark of one of the branches, now defaced either by time or some jealous hand."—*Letters from the East.*

appropriate legend of bygone times,* like the moss clinging to the damp walls of a monastic ruin.

At Nazareth, Mary's life had indeed been one of labour and of toil, and one removed little above want; but then she experienced none of those restless nights, nor those horrible fears, nor those many and hard privations which indigence draws in its train; at Heliopolis she was sunk in the lowest depths of poverty, and experienced misery under its various aspects. The gold of the Persians was now exhausted, † so she must endeavour to render available other resources—not an easy matter in a strange country, and among people divided into national and hereditary bodies, from whom a stranger could expect only a disdainful and contemptuous refusal. The son of David and of Zorobabel becomes a mere labourer, and the daughter of royalty is obliged to work during a part of the night, to make up for the miserable and scanty hire received by her husband. As they were poor, observed St. Basil, they must lead a life of pain and labour to procure the means of existence.......... Alas! had they always even the necessaries of life? Often, says Landolfe of Saxony, did the child Jesus, when oppressed by hunger, demand food of his mother, but she could only give him her tears!

* We insert here one of those legends of the East, as related by the Count of Englure, an old French baron; we give it in the plain *naive* style of the good old times. "When our Lady, mother of God, had passed the deserts and arrived at this spot, she laid our Lord on the ground, and went through the country in search of some water, but was not able to procure any; so she returned in a sad and pensive mood to her dear child, who lay extended on the sand; but alongside him she beheld, to her surprise, a spring of good and wholesome water. She was greatly overjoyed, and at once gave thanks to our Lord. On that spot she again laid down her dear Son to sleep, and then washed his clothes in that very spring, and placed them out to dry," &c.

† F. Gibieuf thinks that the *Magi* presented the Messiah with only a small quantity of gold; this offering, he says, was something like what vassals presented to their sovereign, as a recognition of his being Lord paramount, and not for the purpose of enriching him. A judicious remark.

An angel of the Lord comes to put an end to these excruciating pangs, so courageously and patiently endured. Joseph was informed in a dream of the death of Herod. " Arise," said the angel, " and take the child and his mother, and return into the land of Israel, for they are dead that sought the life of the child."

Joseph arose, took the child and his mother, and returned to the land of Israel.

"But hearing that Archelaus reigned in Judea in the room of Herod his father, he was afraid to go thither; and being warned in sleep, retired into the quarters of Galilee."

Thus was fulfilled the oracle of the Lord, *ex Ægypto vocavi filium meum.* * I have called my son out of Egypt.

CHAPTER XIV.

THE RETURN FROM EGYPT.

AH! sad indeed is exile, and sweet it is to breathe one's native air! The bread of the stranger, like that of the murderer, *is unpalatable to the mouth*, and bitter to the heart; the streams of a foreign land but ill recall the sports of our childhood; the warbling of its birds is wanting in melody, and its varied sites possess not that peculiar and attractive charm, like the sweet spots of our native home!

What must have been the joy of Mary and Joseph on again beholding the dear old land Chanaan, its bold outlines, its gentle undulations, the unity, harmony, and variety of all its parts, beautifully and strikingly contrasting with the monotonous splendours of Egypt. In the one, a hardy and

---

* Oseas xi. 1. Matt. ii. 15.

rural population, of a martial turn of mind, frank and open in their bearing, and possessed of worship pure and undefiled; in the other, slaves divided into *castes*, addicted to pillage, mixing up the most infamous practices with their worship, and exhausting all their resources in erecting temples to the god Apis, to crocodiles, &c. ! To be able to conceive the dear and holy impressions made on the minds of Joseph and Mary, on again beholding the land of Jehovah, and particularly their own sweet town of Nazareth, rising to view at the end of a confined and shady valley, with all the natural grace and beauty of a flower* of the field, we must be impressed with those deep feelings of religion which animated them, and have as deep and passionate an attachment for home, as the children of Abraham had then.

Many were the greetings, great the amazement, eager the questions, emulous the welcomes which attended the Holy Family, as they entered their humble home after such a lengthened absence. But desolation and renewed sorrow and bitterness soon took the place of all this welcome and joy. The home of the poor and Holy Family, untenanted for some time, was now hardly habitable; the roof shattered and almost fallen in, with tufts of long rank grass growing on it here and there, allowed the winter's wind and the pelting rains of the equinoxes to enter;† the lower apartment was cold, damp, and mouldy; wild pigeons built their nests in the mysterious and sanctified little cell where the WORD was made flesh; the brambles, with their dun and prickly stems, were creeping along the little threshold; everything,

---

* According to Dr. Clarke, the word *Nazareth* means a *flower* in the Hebrew.

† "The rainy season in Judea comes on about the time of the equinoxes, and particularly during the Autumnal one. That is also the season of the trades winds, which are accompanied with showers of hail."—*Volney's Travels in Syria.*

in fine, in that antique dwelling, already marked with signs of decay, presented that ruinous aspect which, like the seal of the owner's absence, is impressed on abandoned edifices. The house must be immediately repaired; the furniture, either lost or unfit for use, must be replaced; a debt, perhaps, contracted in Egypt at the time of their return, must be discharged. How is all this to be done? Where are the means? There are none, except the sale in perpetuity of their hereditary farm. Of everything possessed by Joseph and Mary previous to their long journey into Egypt, there remained now only the ruinous house of Nazareth, the workshop of Joseph, and the arms of himself and his cherished spouse. But they had Jesus too—young as he was, the child took up the hatchet, and tripped along with his old father into every village likely to give employment;[*] nor was his mother wanting in giving that aid and assistance which her age and strength would permit. Their money had long since been spent, but by dint of privations, late watching, and persevering exertion, they might be able to procure the chief necessaries of life. Jesus, Mary, and Joseph then entered upon a life of toil and hardship, and those noble souls, who could command legions of angels, demanded of God only their daily bread.

Man has not been led into the knowledge of the interior life of that Blessed Family, surnamed the *Earthly Trinity;* it is concealed from our eyes like a stream of water running through the long, luxuriant grass; like the Holy of Holies surrounded by clouds of perfumes, and covered with a double veil, we cannot behold it. Yet, as in closely studying, in

---

[*] St. Justin Martyr—*Dialogue with Tryphon*—mentions that Jesus Christ assisted his father in making yokes and ploughs. Godescard, b. 14, p. 436, in his *Life of the Blessed Virgin*, says, "A very ancient writer assures us, that at his time yokes were pointed out as made by our Saviour's hands."

examining one by one, and under every aspect, the evangelical facts, the certain knowledge of one thing will afford us a clue to the meaning of another, so the public life of Jesus Christ is a brilliant reflection of his hidden life, and of that of the Blessed Virgin. We shall then endeavour to fill up that gap with all that moderation, and all that conscientious application, which so grave and important a subject demands.

Jesus, as the Master and source of every science, needed not the teachings of man; but as he was pleased to conceal his dazzling lights under an earthly covering, and to appear in everything like other men, he disdained not the lessons of his pious mother in his early childhood.[*] Indeed, it is generally believed that Jesus Christ received the rudiments of education from Mary, and theologians there are that say that he received no further instruction than that instilled into his youthful mind by her. The Jews, holding a different opinion, maintain, on the contrary, that a celebrated Rabbin,[†] then teaching at Nazareth, perfected what Mary begun. But, despite this assertion of the Jews, the education of Jesus was not the work of the Rabbins; for it is well known that he was neither a zealot nor a traditionist, and that he reprobated

---

[*] According to F. Gibieuf, in his work on *The Grandeurs of the Virgin*, approved by the Theological Faculty of Paris, and by many other French bishops, Jesus received the rudiments of his early education from his mother. "She spoke to him of God," says this theologian, "as we speak to little children; she told him to adore and love God: that God was his Father, and her words entered his mind by degrees, and took root there; and when he grew older, and was able to prattle, she herself sung and taught him to sing the hymns which had been composed in praise of God. *O holy and blessed school,*" he cries out, "*where Mary taught and Jesus learned.*" *The Life and Greatness of the Virgin*, b. 2, chap. 10.

[†] The Jews say that he learned under Josue, son of Perachia, who had studied under Akiba. This assertion is, however, altogether inaccurate; for Akiba, the most illustrious man among the Jews, lived in the reign of the emperor Adrian, more than a hundred years after the death of Herod and Jesus Christ.

that narrow-minded, interested, and cavilling spirit which pervaded the synagogue. Moreover, St. John decides the question, in saying in his Gospel, that the Jews looked on Jesus as an unlettered man.* He, whose mission it was to alter the opinions and creeds of the world, could learn nothing from man, and so his learning must be his own work; it was a vigorous plant, inhaling the free air through every pore, and watered only by the dew of heaven. Christ, like the cedars, towers aloft of his own innate force, indebted only to nature for his beauty and majesty. Nature was, indeed, his book; and from that he invariably drew his affecting morality and his sublime parables. Jesus was endowed with a deep and reflective mind, which required an extensive area to expand itself; confined during the day to manual labour, which engaged every moment of his time, he indemnified himself in the evening for all those toilsome and servile duties, by becoming a legislator and prophet in presence of the starry heavens. Standing on an elevated mound, whence might be seen the mountains and extensive woodlands of Chanaan, he poured forth his whole soul before the Author of nature, whose envoy, Son, and equal he was. These entertainments, alone with God, during the silence of night—that time of reflection and thought—were frequent practices of Jesus Christ; the Gospel furnishes us with many examples of such practices. The WORD incarnate was, no doubt, willing to teach his own how to separate the pure gold of prayer from that monstrous alloy of ostentation and hypocrisy, which the Pharisees of his time were such adepts in mingling.

The Virgin, never importunate nor exacting, gave not the slightest opposition to that inclination for solitude, now

* " The Jews wondered, saying: How doth this man know letters, having never learned?"—*John* vii. 15.

become habitual to her Son. She well knew that Jesus was then sounding the lowest depths of that immeasurable abyss, opened under the feet of the human race, and that the redemption of the world would be the fruit of these solitary meditations. Appreciating the working of that powerful spirit falling back on itself, and looking forward to that glorious future, which every moment was bringing nearer, Mary already beheld heaven opened, death conquered, and the Messiah rallying the people of every tribe and tongue to his standard......But, gloomy as a shroud, the prophecy of the old man of the temple flashes suddenly on her mind, and at once destroys the glorious and enchanting perspective; a thrill of horror runs through the veins of the poor mother, and her heart, in which the love of Jesus had so large a part, is broken into a thousand agonizing fragments. A secret voice whispers her: there must be an expiation by blood; Christ must die! Then laying aside those humble and unpretending engagements, to the performance of which her indigence condemned her, * the daughter of David went in search of her son; she should see him, to be assured that he was yet hers, and that he was still living.

On seeing her, Jesus lowered his pensive eye, which had been just contemplating the starry heavens; his youthful brow, marked by traces of deep thought, was once more the smooth and polished brow of childhood. Her boding fears flowing back on her heart, Mary then counselled rest and repose after such late watching; it was necessary, she said, that his strength should be recruited against to-morrow, for the journey would be attended with difficulty and pain....

---

* Tertullian, in the third century, said that Mary gained her bread by manual labour; and Celsus, in the thirteenth century, reproached the Christians with the fact, that Mary lived by the labour of her hands.

The Son of God silently followed his mother, according to the flesh, for he loved, *and was submissive to her.*

St. Bernard no less admires the dignity of the Blessed Virgin, than the submissive manner of our Lord. " That God," says the apostle of the Crusades, " that God, to whom the angels are subject, and whom the principalities and powers obey, was subject to Mary. Admire whichever you please, either the astounding humility of the Son, or the eminent dignity of the mother; but, as for me, I am amazed at both; both are miracles in my eyes. That God should obey a woman, is humility unheard of; that a woman should command God, is a degree of glory never before attained."

When Jesus was entering on boyhood, an extraordinary incident occurred, which quite upset the mind of the Blessed Virgin. Joseph and Mary, religious observers of the law of their fathers, regularly paid a visit to Jerusalem every year at the paschal time. The journey, privately and stealthily made whilst the son of the enemy of God enjoyed the throne of the Machabees, was attended with less difficulty during the exile of Archelaus, and whilst the Romans were in occupation of the kingdom. When Christ had attained his twelfth year, his parents, free from all that disquietude and uneasiness caused by Herod, conducted him to Jerusalem. They set out in company with others from Nazareth; but on the way the Hebrew pilgrims divided themselves into small parties, according to their respective ages and sex, or according to their respective ties of friendship or relationship. *

---

* St. Epiphanius and St. Bernard mention, that during these journeys the men proceeded in separate bodies from the women, and that Joseph and the Blessed Virgin belonged to different parties—a cause of uneasiness to them on first missing Jesus, whom they did not again see until the travellers met together in the evening.—See also Aelrede.

THE RETURN FROM EGYPT. 191

The Virgin was immediately accompanied by Mary of Cleophas, sister of Joseph; by another Mary designated in the Gospel as *altera Maria;* Salome, wife of Zebedee, come from Bethsaida, together with her husband and children; Joanna, wife of Chus; and by a party of Nazareans, connected with her by ties of relationship and friendship. At a short distance in their rear, Joseph followed them, in serious conversation with Zebedee the fisherman, and the ancients of his tribe. Jesus walked in the middle of the youthful Galileans, called his brethren in the Gospel, from the peculiar idiom of the Hebrew language, but really, and in language not figurative, his nearest relatives.

In this youthful party, in advance of the others, one could recognise James, son of Zebedee, impetuous as the lake of Tiberias during a storm; John, younger even than Jesus, his lovely figure alongside that of his brother almost personifying the Lamb of Isaias, peacefully reclining with the lion of the Jordan. Walking by the side of the fishermen of Bethsaida, were the four sons of Alpheus, called by Jesus at a later period, *Boanerges* (sons of thunder)— James, afterwards bishop of Jerusalem, an austere and grave young man, with long hair, pale visage, and a reserved and mortified appearance. Annoyed at having the Nazarean one of his party, and recognising him only as the son of a carpenter, he assumed towards him a disagreeable air of superiority. The virtues and faults inherent to his country formed his character; a resolution not to be shaken, inclinations of a good and religious tendency, but with these he manifested a thorough contempt for everything not deriving its origin from Abraham, and had no small opinion of himself. Jude, Simon, and Joseph, the remaining sons of Alpheus, were young men of rough exterior, simple and brave, and already on the threshold of manhood, they looked down on Jesus as their inferior in every way, and we can infer from the Gospel, that they experienced in after time some difficulty in laying aside that inherent feeling.* And Jesus?—Jesus affected nothing, neither devotion, nor austerity, nor wisdom, nor knowledge, because he possessed all these things in their greatest plenitude; and what we know not, is generally what we most affect.

To see him simply but neatly attired like an essen, his long auburn hair parted evenly on his bronzed brow, and floating in graceful ringlets over his shoulders, one would have taken him for David at the moment when Samuel beheld him approaching, diminutive, timid, attired as a simple shepherd, to receive the holy unction. The hazel, soft eye of Christ† was, however, lighted up with a greater fire of expression than the poetical and prophetic eye of his illustrious ancestor. Something indescribably divine and penetrating beamed from it, which laid open the very thoughts, and entered the inmost depths of the soul; but Jesus then veiled the lustre of his gaze, as Moses veiled his shining brow when coming out of the tabernacle. Speaking in a serious tone, but yet suited to his years, he proceeded on with his young relatives according to the flesh, whom he intended as his apostles in after times; under their rough exterior he clearly beheld and fully appreciated the weight and value of those unpolished gems, which were, at a later period, to glisten with a vivid and bright glare. Nor was he disappointed in his expectations. These men, like the

---

* See St. John Chrysostom, Sermon 44.

† See Nicephorus, in his History of the Church, vol. i., p. 125. His portrait of our Lord, drawn from what has been handed down by tradition, is the most authentic now remaining. The Rev. M. Walsh, a late writer, draws our attention to a very curious medal discovered in the fifteenth century. One side represents the *profile* of our Lord, with his hair parted on the forehead, according to the custom of the Nazareans, and flowing over his shoulders, &c.

rest of their nation, indulged in gilded dreams of the magnificence and power of the Messiah; but yet, at his call, divesting themselves of all their national and religious prejudices, they adopted a calumniated creed, the principles and promises of which, like the maledictions of the old law, spoke only of sufferings to be endured, and persecutions to be contended with. They leagued themselves to him by chains so strong, that neither the princes of the world, nor cold, nor nakedness, nor hunger, nor the sword, could separate them from his love; they walked in his ways, manfully crushing down the thorns which the world were sowing under their feet, and allowed themselves to be treated as the refuse of mankind. They were ashamed neither of the Son of Man, nor of his Gospel, *nor of the folly of the Cross!* And why so? Because it is only impostors who have cause to blush and be ashamed, and the apostles preached but the sentiments of their inmost convictions. Whatever could render their testimony sacred and worthy of belief in the eyes of men, that they bestowed on it; they abandoned everything, they suffered everything, they pardoned everything, and sealed with their blood the Gospel of their Divine Master.*

But at the time of which we are now speaking, these heroic virtues had not even blown, and the young Galileans little thought that a day would come when they would willingly lay down their lives in support of the divinity of the companion of their travels.

At the end of the fourth day's journey, they reached the holy city, into which an immense concourse of foreign Jews was flowing. The family of Joseph and Mary met together, to eat of the paschal lamb, immolated by the priests in the

---

* Pascal has said: "I willingly believe every history, the truth of which has been sealed with blood."

porch of the temple, between the hours of prayer;[*] to it were added unleaven bread, bitter legumes, and whatever else was required by this ancient rite.

The festival days over, the relatives of Christ assembled together, and proceeded on their homeward journey. As they returned in the same order in which they had come, Joseph and Mary did not perceive at first that Jesus was missing. Mary thought that he was either with Joseph or in the company of the Jameses; and Joseph believed that he was with Mary or with his young cousins. In the evening the different parties met, and Mary searched for Jesus, but to no purpose, among the various parties of travellers arriving in succession at the caravansary. No one could tell what had become of the Redeemer. The grief of his parents cannot be described. "Oh, heaven's deposit, God's envoy!" murmured Joseph, in a sad tone. "Oh, my son!" sighed forth the poor mother, tears trickling down her cheeks. They sought for him during the night, they sought for him during the day, inquiring for him on the way, calling out for him in the woods, thrusting their eyes into the precipices; now fearing for his life; now for his liberty; and knowing not what to do, were he lost. They returned to Jerusalem, ran to the houses of their friends; and wearied with running here and there through every quarter of that large city, they at last entered the temple. Under the portico, where were seated the doctors of the law, a child was both astonishing and delighting the ancients of Israel, by the depth of his learning, and the propriety of his answers to the most difficult questions proposed to him. A circle was formed about him and his precocity of intellect and extent of information astounded all who heard him. "He is either Daniel or an angel," cries out one not far re-

[*] "From twelve or one o'clock to sunset."—*Basnage, vol.* 5, *b.* vii., *chap.* 11.

THE RETURN FROM EGYPT. 195

moved from the disconsolate Virgin. "He is Jesus," said the mother, advancing, at the same time, towards the doctors. Then approaching the Messiah with an expression of the tenderest emotion, tincturing, if I be allowed the expression, the fading reflections of sorrow: "My son," she sweetly said, "why hast thou done so to us? Behold thy father and I have sought thee sorrowing."

The child was absorbed in the God; the answer was cutting and mysterious. "Why is it that you have sought me? did you not know that I must be taken up with the concerns of my Father?" Joseph and Mary observed perfect silence; they understood not at first the Messiah's answer.

Jesus arose and followed them to Narareth; his perfect submission to their will soon effaced this passing cloud. "But his mother kept all these things in her heart, and Jesus advanced in wisdom and age before God and before men."

CHAPTER XV.

MARY AT THE PREACHING OF JESUS.

THERE are two worlds in history, said one of the finest characters of our day, one beyond, and the other, at this side of the cross. The primeval world, falling into decrepitude at the time of the regenerating mission of Jesus Christ, presented a strange spectacle indeed, verifying the truth of the saying, that the ridiculous is closely allied to the sublime and terrible. Arabia and Gaul, after having retained for centuries the primitive idea of the unity of God, paid adoration to the acacia and the oak;* India deified the Ganges, and offered up human victims of Sakti, the goddess of death;† Egypt rendered pious worship to the garlick, the lotus, and to nearly all the bulbous plants;‡ the inhabitants of newly discovered America adored tigers, vultures, roaring winds, and foaming cataracts;§ and, last of all, the Greeks and Romans, according to their own admission, crowded their temples with demons;‖ and polished, and refined, and

---

* "The pagan Gauls of the sixth and seventh century worshipped the oak; they lighted up fires before these trees, and called out to them in a strain of invocation, as if they had been endowed with understanding. The huge stones contiguous to these trees shared the honour paid the latter."—*Ecclesiastical History of Brittany, seventh century.*

† See a picture of India, by Buckingham.

‡ The satire of Juvenal is well known : "O sanctas gentes, quibus hæc nascuntur in hortis numina."—*Sat.* 15, b. 10.

§ See Garcil. b. 1, chap. 2 and 12.

‖ Porphyry, well acquainted with all the mysteries of polytheism, assures us that demons were the objects of pagan worship, "They are," he says, "impure, deceitful, and evil spirits, who wish to be considered gods, and to receive adoration from man. They must be appeased lest they should inflict harm. Some, gay and sportive, are content with spectacles and public shows; the sullen humour of others must have the odour of fat, and so receive bloody sacrifices."

enlightened as they were, they yet deified vice in its most hideous and revolting forms, and peopled their Olympus with robbers, adulterers, and assassins.

Their manners were in perfect keeping with their creeds; corruption, descending like a foaming and devastating torrent from the seven imperial hills, inundated all the provinces. Judea, corrupted equally as the others by the contagion of vice, fell into depravity with a frightful rapidity; her religion no longer rested on fundamental dogmas, but on a rabble of base and fetid parasites, and on the idle fancies of her Rabbins, enthroned on the chair of Moses.*

In the midst of such frightful aberrations of the human intellect, what then became of proud reason —that queen of intelligences, who takes the very limits of the universe within her scope, and places the gods on the bed of Procrustes? Where did she then hold her empire? Where had she planted her standard, when on every side a breach was made on her bulwarks? Had she been able at any time to reconquer, without foreign aid, the land wrested from her grasp, why not have done so then?.....But she felt that the torrent would surmount her feeble efforts: and impotent to restrain it, she contented herself with merely noting its ravings. Resting for support on her handmaid, philosophy, she mourned over the inanimate remains of socialism, whose fall she had not power to prevent—Christianity comes on apace, saying to the dead: "Arise, and walk"... ..And it was done according to his word.

---

* The Jews hold that the oral law, and not the written law, was the foundation of the alliance entered into with them on Mount Sinai. They destroyed the latter to give place to the former, and had subjected religion to tradition. This corruption had arrived to such a pitch at the time of our Lord, that he reproached them, as we see in St. Mark, with destroying the word of God by their traditions. But matters are even worse in our own day. The sacred text is compared to water, and the *Mischna* or the *Talmud* to the rarest wine; again, the written law is salt, but the *Talmud* is cinnamon, pepper, &c.

From that day, a new race, healed from every evil, cleansed in the sacred pond from every defilement, rallied around the Cross which the Son of Mary had hoisted over a regenerated world, as the trophy of God over hell.

This glorious revelation, which enthroned charity and placed in her train every other virtue; this ever memorable event, which changed the face of the world, and the efficacy of which shall be felt even to the consummation of ages, had Nazareth as its starting point.

From the hollow of that nameless rock, humble Christianity flowed, "a hidden source, a drop of water scarcely perceptible; a drop which would not be sufficient to quench the thirst of a pair of sparrows, and which a single ray of the sun would dry up; but which to-day, like the great ocean of spirits, has filled every abyss with human wisdom, and has bathed in its inexhausted waters the past, the present, and the future."*

We are unacquainted with the means by which that great event was prepared, which had so mighty an influence on the history of modern times. After his manifestation in the temple, the Son of God spent a hidden and retired life with his mother and adopted father. This epoch, lost to the world, was, assuredy, the one during which the Virgin enjoyed the greatest happiness:—that portion of human life is, certainly, not the happiest, which flows on with clatter and noise, like a winter's torrent; but rather that which resembles a stream, gliding stealthily and noiselessly along through the grassy meadow. Mary, deprived of all the enjoyments of luxury, and all the pleasures of ease, but residing with her Son, toiling for him, studying his tastes, seeing him at every hour, making a daily offering of herself to him, be-

---

* Lamartine's Travels in the East.

coming the lowest, the humblest, the most docile of his disciples, and subjecting her understanding to the superior and divine understanding of her Son; Mary must then have been a happy mother indeed! If at any time, whilst Jesus was expounding the hidden meaning of the prophecies, a passage presented itself which spoke of the sufferings to be endured, a dark cloud overspread the chaste brow of the Vigin, but soon her sweet and lovely countenance gradually regained its former serenity; the storm as yet was howling only in the distance, and their bark was moored in a calm and secure harbour. Her Son was there; she hung on his looks—his words—his slightest gestures. How eager she was to serve him, her Son! What a source of happiness it was to her, to remain up during entire nights spinning and knitting his working dress, his holiday garments, and particularly that seamless robe—*chef d'œuvre* of skill and patience, which at a later period!......but then the *Lord had not as yet anointed his Christ, but with the oil of gladness.* As follower of the bridegroom, the wise Virgin of the Gospel "*left the morrow to provide for itself;*" and the peace of God, which surpasses all other things, reigned in her heart and soul."

Jesus possessed all the treasures of wisdom and knowledge; the plenitude of the Divinity resided corporally in him; he was the brightness and glory of his Heavenly Father; but, inasmuch as he was man, he owed no small debt to Mary; she it was, who instilled into his tender mind the humble virtues inherent to human nature, and formed his tastes simple and poetical. That sweetness of disposition and affableness of manner, which he could well combine with the firmness of the legislator and prophet; that compassionate mercy, which tempered the indignation of an irritated God, perfected the just, and supported the sinner; that all-bountiful tenderness *naively* exercised towards children, whom he was pleased to caress and bless during his heavenly mission; a thousand imperceptible traits—a thousand reflections, half drowned in the great floods of light which constituted the mortal life of Jesus Christ, all bore the impress of Mary.

That Christ repaid his mother's fondest love by a return of deep and lasting gratitude, we cannot, for a moment, doubt. To her he was indebted for his being—for his existence; and the blood which was flowing in his veins—the blood which he was to shed on the cross, in expiation of the sins of the world, was derived from Mary, and from Mary alone. All those sacred and fond feelings, implanted by nature in the minds of children towards the authors of their being, were centered by Jesus in the sole person of the Virgin. To her, whom he as a son and as a God loved, he was indebted for his earthly existence. It was only once that the Divinity, which confers every benefit, and receives nothing in return, saw itself called to exercise gratitude—that virtue of great minds and magnanimous dispositions—towards its creature; and that of Jesus for Mary was augmented, in proportion to the many sacrifices, privations, and labours, which she had suffered for love of him. If, then, we might have observed in the Gospel, that Christ sometimes spoke to his divine mother less as her Son than her Lord, that arose not from any want of affection or indifference, but from a desire to break off any earthly ties that might interfere with the promotion of his Father's glory, to whose interests he made everything else subservient, and before whose power and grandeur all other things, he thought, should sink into insignificance. The Virgin knew too well the nature of her Son's mission, to feel at an occasional word of severity from him; she knew that the young Galilean, whom she nourished with her milk, was destined for a legislator, and the transformation appeared tardy of coming; human nature ere long granted what divine nature refused.

When Jesus had attained his twenty-ninth year, the angel of death was in the act of decimating the Holy Family. Joseph, that patriarch of primitive manners, whose submissive faith and simplicity of heart recalled to mind the times of Abraham; Joseph, on whom the Holy Ghost himself had bestowed the lovely name of *Just*, sweetly slept in the bosom of the Lord, between his adopted Son and his immaculate spouse. Jesus and Mary, deeply afflicted, remained up during the night along-side his cold remains; the midnight blast was the sole accompaniment to the lamentations of the miserable family. The Nabals of Galilee died and were laid out in greater state, though they had not, on the other side of the tomb, the glorious hopes of the Nazarean carpenter.

The funeral of the son of David, like his means, was on an humble scale; but Mary shed copious tears on his coffin, and her Son walked as chief mourner in the poor procession. What emperor ever received such funeral obsequies?

The time for preaching the Gospel had, at last, arrived, and HE who was destined by God from all eternity as its High Priest and Apostle, quitted Nazareth, and repaired to the banks of the Jordan, where John was then baptizing. The parting adieu between the Virgin and her Son must, indeed, have been a sad and solemn scene. The public life of Jesus was about to commence: alone, unfriended, unknown, without any other resources except those furnished by his patience, his courage, his miraculous gifts, never employed for his own personal advantage, he commenced an assault on an order of things, *not strong enough to give him resistance, but strong enough to cause his death.**

* Lamartine's Travels in the East.

The Virgin could not suppress a thrill of horror, on seeing Jesus launched out on the stormy sea of the Judaical world, in which so many and such illustrious prophets had been wrecked. She well knew the indomitable pride of the Pharisees, the bigoted and revengeful fanaticism of the synagogue, the sanguinary disposition of Herod Antipater; and more than all, she was fully acquainted with the oracles regarding the Messiah, which spoke of sufferings and ignominy!....This first parting, only the prelude of a more cruel separation, afflicted the soul of the Virgin not the less that she knew her Son was God. She parted from him with a bruised heart, and when the sound of his footsteps died away in the distance, and when she found that she was alone—all alone—in that house where she had passed so many delightful hours, in the company of her Son and her spouse—hiding her face in her veil, she stood silent and pensive, like a statue of grief on a mausoleum.

Christ prolonged his stay: the Virgin learned that he ascended the high and barren mountains bordering on Jericho, to prepare himself for the great work of the world's redemption, by fasting, watching, and prayer. What must her sufferings have been, on thinking that Jesus was straying in a wild and desolate region, where the eagle could scarcely pick up a bit of moss for its nest, where paths wound along the brink of precipices so deep as to cause dizziness! What must be her agony when the tempest howled without! Where was Jesus, and what was he doing, alone and unprotected on the mountain? In case his foot slipped on the brink of some abyss, who was there to hold out to him a helping hand? If, after his long fast—a fast so little proportioned to the strength of his constitution—he should faint on the way, who was to offer him aid and assistance? These forty days appeared to Mary forty centuries; her maternal anxiety converted every minute into an age. But Jesus returned to Nazareth with his disciples, and his presence infused a soothing calm into the afflicted heart of his mother.

At that time it was that the marriage of Cana in Galilee took place. Jesus, Mary, and Joseph were invited by the bridegroom and bride, who were relatives of the Blessed Virgin.* All accepted the kind invitation; and the Virgin, ever good and kind, went a day or two before the others, in order to assist in the preparations for the marriage feast, at which national customs required a certain degree of splendour.

But the party was large, and the family poor; the bridegroom had not calculated aright, and the measures of wine were nearly empty, when our Lord, who wished to raise marriage to the rank of sacred things, by honouring it with his presence, entered the banqueting hall, followed by Peter, Andrew, Philip, and Nathaniel, four young fishermen, whom he had impressed with a high opinion of his character and mission. The wine unexpectedly failed in the middle of the feast, and Mary, being the first to notice it, turned towards Jesus, who happened to be sitting near her, and said to him in a voice of meaning: "*They have no wine.*"

Jesus answered in a low and solemn tone: "Woman, what is that to me and to thee? My hour is not yet come."†

---

* "An Eastern tradition, received by the Mahometans from the Christians, hands down that St. John the Evangelist was the bridegroom at the marriage of Cana, but that after witnessing the performance of the miracle of Jesus Christ, he immediately left his bride, and followed him."—*D'Herbelot, Bibliothèque Orientale, vol. 2.*

† The answer of our Lord to his mother must, we should think, be given *aside;* we can infer so from the Gospel. At first it was impossible that Jesus Christ should give this enigmatical answer in a loud tone, for had he done so, the guests, not understanding the nature of it, would have charged him with

The Virgin, wishing to save her relatives from a humiliation which would have filled them with shame, did not take that answer in the light of a refusal; she thought that, if the hour of manifestation was not yet come, Christ, despite his harsh expression, would anticipate it in consideration of her; and, penetrated with that faith which removes mountains, she sweetly said to the servants: "Do whatever he shall tell you."

Now there were placed there six water-pots of stone, used for the purpose of purifications: Jesus ordered them to be filled up to the brim with water from a neighbouring well; and this water was changed into most delicious wine.

harshness towards his mother. Again, we see that the servants, in attending to what the Blessed Virgin had said to them, were ignorant of the apparent refusal.

Thus it was that the first miracle of God was performed at the request of his divine mother, and that the decrees of heaven bowed to her merciful intercession.

The miracle of Cana was, ere long, followed by many others, which stamped the high and providential mission of the Redeemer with the seal of the Divinity. At his voice the winds were hushed, human infirmities disappeared, the demons were flung back into their gloomy kingdom, the dead arose from their coffined graves, and in that small spot of land which he pressed with his sacred feet, all the evils, both of soul and body, were healed.* Persons came to him from Sidon, from Tyre, from Idumea, from Arabia; and multitudes of people flocking around him, and obstructing his passage, impressed warm kisses on the fringe of his garment, and in tones of humble supplication, demanded of him health and life, things which God alone could bestow.

Mary, whom our Lord had not yet thought it well to associate with his laborious and wandering life, listened to these extraordinary recitals with joy, yet blended with fear; with admiration, though attended with disquietude. Her fears were well grounded; for, if the people followed the Messiah, loading him with blessings, the Pharisees, the Scribes, and the high priests of the synagogue began to be scandalized, good souls as they were, at the conduct of the Son of God. He remits sins!—blasphemy—He console and convert sinners!—folly. He heal the sick on the Sabbath day—crying and daring impiety. His doctrine falls from his lips like beneficent dew, not as the pelting hail; then, in nothing does he resemble the ancient prophets! He preach humility! pardon of injuries! volun-

---

* A Mussulman poet has described, in a delightful strain of poetry, the empire which Jesus Christ exercised over the diseases of the soul.—See *Herbelot.*

tary poverty! alms to be bestowed for God's sake alone, and without being made known to men! universal charity! Hah! ....All this is very strange, and more, it is very dangerous, said the *arrieros* of the synagogue. Hypocrisy cannot be attacked without giving offence to the Pharisees; avarice and usury cannot be cried down without making enemies of the doctors of the law: again, the preaching up of eternal life will not be endured by the Sadducees. These men, with different views, different creeds, and different political interests, gave a truce to their secret antipathies in hatred of the Galilean. They rose up as one man to blacken his reputation, and pressed forward to effect his destruction; every word of his was a snare, every whisper a treason, every expression of satisfaction an insulting mockery.

Some openly branded him an impostor, a heretic, a Samaritan; others gently insinuated that he was drunk; but the greatest number consisted of the envious of the lowest grade. Impotent to produce anything great or good, but ever forward in the work of slander and calumny.

Wearied of the eulogiums passed on Jesus, and unable to deny the miracles wrought by him, they divide the honour of them between himself and Satan: "If he expels the devils," said they, "it is by means of Beelzebub, the prince of devils." *In Beelzebub principe dæmoniorum ejicit dæmoria.** These vague rumours alarmed Mary, and the peculiar character of the place was ill calculated to reassure her.

* Methnevi Manevi, speaking of the envious but unavailing hatred of the Jews against Jesus Christ, says: The moon shines, and the dog bays; but the baying of the dog prevents not the moon from shining. The sweepings are thrown into the running stream; but they merely float on the surface, without either discolouring or arresting its course. The Messiah raises the dead, and the Jews, swollen with rage, bite their nails and pluck out their beard.—*Herbelot.*

Of all the towns of Galilee, Nazareth was the most incredulous, and the least open to the word of God; of all the families of Nazareth, the family of Jesus Christ, it appears, was the least inclined to receive him as the royal Messiah. As the divine parturition of the Virgin had not been revealed to her relatives, and as the miracles by which the infancy of the Lord had been rendered illustrious, had taken place in a distant country, they saw in the supposed son of Joseph only a young unlettered Israelite, brought up among them, supported like themselves, worse housed, worse clad, and so living from day to day by the work of his hands, as to leave him in a position no better than persons of the lowest grade. Christ, wishing to ennoble poverty by taking it for his inheritance, rendered himself subject to the ievitable results of the ill-favoured position which he had chosen. "*His brethren,*" says St. John, "did not believe in him." The fame of the miracles which attended the preaching of the Gospel amazed, but did not convince, the stiff-necked Nazareans. Learning that Jesus was greeted, through all Galilee, with the dangerous title of Son of David, and that crowds of two or three thousand persons pressed around him, to catch his words; they feared that such large assemblies would give offence to Herod Antipater, and that the descendants of the kings of Juda would experience uneasiness of mind on account of the young prophet. With this feeling upon them, they gave out that Jesus was mad, and swore that they would lead him back to Nazareth, under a strong escort. Carefully concealing from Mary this family conspiracy, they brought her with them to Caphernaum, that her name might be a passport to get near Jesus.

The Messiah was teaching in the synagogue, surrounded by a crowd of attentive and respectful hearers, when the

Nazareans arrived. Pompously unfolding an authority which they were desirous should appear important in the eyes of the multitude, as St. John Chrysostom remarks, they gravely intimated to the Redeemer, that his brethren and his mother were without seeking for him. But Jesus, reading the secret thoughts of his relatives according to the flesh, and laying hold of this circumstance for the purpose of enlarging the confined limits of the old law, by solemnly adopting, and without any exception of persons, all the great human family—gave this admirable answer to the indiscreet message of his relatives: "Who is my mother, and who are my brethren?" Then looking round on his disciples: "My mother and my brethren," said he, aloud, "are those who hear the word of God, and practise it." After that severe rebuke, fully understood by the sons of Alpheus, "the Son of God," says St. John Chrysostom, "*proceeded to pay His mother every honour which decency required of him.*"

After having saluted his mother, and having remained some time with her by the sea-shore, the Redeemer ascended a bark, whence he preached to the multitude. The Virgin, though lost in the crowd, was listening with deep attention, and in religious silence, to the parable of the sower. The Nazareans, fixed in amazement at the irresistible eloquence and dignified appearance of Jesus Christ, inquired in tones of surprise if he were indeed the Son of Mary.

As the snake of the American savannahs becomes fascinated by the tones of music in the depths of the forest, so were they by the thrilling tones of the Redeemer. They came with the celerity of fear, the eloquence of egotism, the arrogance of superiority, to withdraw Christ from his perilous mission; and now they quailed before his look, and could not utter even a single word in his presence. Such we can easily infer from the text of St. Mark, who, after making known to us their hostile intentions, is entirely silent with regard to any attempt on their part to speak to their Redeemer.

Some time having elapsed, Jesus returned to Nazareth, and great then was the joy of the Blessed Virgin. To see her Son sitting down on the same matted seat on which he sat during his childhood, to eat the bread which he broke in blessing it, to conduct him secretly to the sick bed of some indigent creature, who received at his hands the blessing of health, with an injunction of observing inviolable silence regarding the miraculous cure; to see him, powerful in word and work—him, who had been so long a man of silence and patient labour. Ah! the cup of her joyful existence was full even to overflowing. But the Lord was pleased soon to pour a few drops of gall into it. On the Sabbath-day, the Son and mother returned together to the synagogue; a great concourse of people were there assembled to see and hear Jesus; but the eagerness of the Nazareans was not characterized by that confidence in, and respectful attention to him, which he had so frequently experienced elsewhere. They were then scandalized by anticipation at whatever the Son of Man was to say or do, and fully disposed to stone him if an opportunity presented itself.

There are countries that entertain hostile feelings towards everything redounding to their glory and honour; not even the grass growing on the graves of those they envy will they spare.

Meantime, one of the ancients handed the Redeemer of men the book of the Prophet Isaias, and Jesus, opening it, read, in an unaffected yet dignified manner, the following passage: " The Spirit of the Lord is upon me, because the Lord hath anointed me; he hath sent me to preach the

Gospel to the poor; to heal the contrite of heart; to preach release to the captives, and deliverance to them that are shut up; to announce to the blind the recovery of sight, and to publish the favourable year of the Lord."

Having closed the book, he returned it and sat down; the whole synagogue had their eyes fixed on him. Then the Man-God, speaking with that impassionate, yet natural eloquence, which had made so strong an impression on his hearers, entered into an explanation of the prophecy, and expounded it, not as a disciple of the synagogue, but as the master of the synagogue itself. A suppressed burst of applause ran through the whole assembly; some stood amazed at the force and beauty of his language, others, faithful to their system of envenomed slander, said in a loud tone of voice: "Is not this person the son of Joseph?" And Jesus, searching into their false hearts, and reading their very thoughts, made answer in these words, now proverbial among us: "A prophet is not without honour, save in his own country, and in his own house, and among his own." Aware of their intention to require from him the performance of miracles, similar to those of which Capharnaum had been the theatre, he plainly tells them that their incredulity had rendered them unworthy of them, and that, to obtain what they required, they must solicit them with a firm faith. Hence, making allusion to the propagation of his Gospel, and to that wild olive tree engrafted on the ancient trunk of the synagogue: "Verily I say to you, that there had been a great many widows in Israel at the time of Elias, when the heavens were closed for three years and six months, and when a great famine was on the land, and yet Elias was not sent to the house of any of them, but to the house of a woman of Serepta in the country of the Sidonians. There had been even many afflicted with leprosy in Israel, at the time of the prophet Eliseus, and yet only Naaman was cured, who was of Syria."

These last words fell on the assembly like a lighted torch on dry stubble; wounded in their national pride, in their hereditary resentments, in their traditional hopes, they were fired with resentment. *They rose up in a tumultuous body, drove Jesus out of the city, and conducted him to the highest peak of the mountain, on which it was built, in order to preciptate him from it.*

Sitting with women of inferior rank, on a trellised seat, the Vigin had observed, with anxiety and alarm, the increasing progress of the storm. Reading the sinister designs of the Nazareans, in their haggard looks and furious gestures, she hesitated not to brave every danger, in opening a passage to where he Son was standing. But her strength was unequal to her courage. These Jews, who had been always nimble of foot when the shedding of blood was in question, were running on, and Mary, trembling like an aspen leaf, and scarcely able to support her failing strength, walked at a distance after them, like one in a dreamy state. She beholds Jesus on the very top of a rugged rock overhanging a frightful precipice; she hears in the distance the cries of death; her feet can no longer support her; a mist passes over her eyes; she breathes forth a long moaning sigh, and then falls senseless on the hill. *

Meantime, the wolves madly running on in pursuit of the

---

* Between the rugged hill, from which the Jews intended to cast down Jesus Christ, and the town of Nazareth, " we observed," says F. Geramb, " the ruins of a monastery and also those of a church, which had been erected by St. Helena, and dedicated to the Blessed Virgin, under the name of our Lady *del Tremore*. According to some, Mary had already gained this point, when the Jews were dragging her Son towards the summit of the mountain, in order to preciptate him from it. Others think that hearing of the murderous intentions of the enraged populace, she ran in all haste, but arrived too late: seized with affright, *she could go no further*.

Lamb, had been foiled in their attempt; the hour of sacrifice had not yet sounded for the Son of Man, and his blood belonged to others superior to them. Striking this murderous band with blindness, Jesus passed through the midst of his enemies without being recognised, and regained the road of Capharnaum, where his mother, Mary of Cleophas, and the sons of Alpheus, joined him.

At that time it was that the Blessed Virgin, after having been baptized by Jesus himself, on the banks of the Jordan, as we learn from Euthine,* broke through her lonely habits to follow her Son in his travels. She had piously and faithfully ministered to him during three years, both in a foreign soil, and in the land of her fathers; she had toiled for him, wept over him, suffered for him; she had adored him morning and evening whilst yet crying in his cradle, as we learn from Albertus Magnus; and now it was only natural that, attaching herself to his declining fortunes, she should abandon the peaceable roof in which she had lived, to walk in his blessed footsteps, during his preaching among the Hebrews.

In the midst of the agitations of this life of pain and anxiety, she was, as she had ever been, the same admirable, delightful creature, loving Jesus with more than maternal tenderness, loving him with an excessive love—a love carried to the farthest limits of adoration; yet she never allowed her maternal tenderness to interfere with the brief and precious moments of the Redeemer's mission: she never spoke to him of her fatigues, of her apprehensions, of her dismal forebodings, nor of her personal wants. Mary was not merely a blessed dove, hiding herself in the crevices of a rock, a pure virgin, nourishing with her milk, and fond-

* According to this writer, our Lord baptized only the Blessed Virgin and St. Peter.

ling in her arms a celestial guest; she was more, she was a strong resolute woman, whom the Lord was pleased to place successively in every stage of life, that he might leave to the daughters of Eve an example to follow, and a model to copy after.

It might not have been deemed proper, that the mother of God should, unattended, have followed Jesus and his apostles across Judea: so Mary of Cleophas, mother of James, of Simon, of Joseph, and of Jude, commonly called the brethren of the Lord; Salome, mother of the sons of Zebedee, for whom the Lord entertained a particular affection; Susanna, wife of one of the tetrarch's officers, and some wealthy Galileans, who became poor for Christ's sake, accompanied Mary. One of them, a young and rich Jewess, of illustrious descent and of surpassing beauty, was particularly attentive to the divine mother of *her Master*. This woman, whose heart, mighty, but tempest-tossed, like the billows of the Egean sea, had burned with a thousand impure fires in the face of the world, and had braved public opinion with mockery and disdain, was now come, submissive and penitent, to lay her haughty head at the feet of Jesus Christ, and to demand of him the cure of the diseases of her soul; and the chaste love of the Lord had absorbed all the criminal amours, all the wordly attachments of the lady of Magdalum. She had trampled under foot her pearly necklaces, and her gold and jewelled chains; sold her *chateau*, delightfully situated among the rose-laurels which border the beautiful sea of Galilee, and now, without other ornament, except a serge dress, and her long silken hair, with which she had wiped the feet of the Lord, the youthful patrician, rich in alms and good works, and clothed in new virtues, shed copious tears of repentance on the compassionate and pure bosom of Mary. The immaculate Virgin took to her arms, and pressed to her heart, the great sinner, and cultivated in that rich, but long neglected soil, the flowers, which were, for ever after to blossom for heaven alone.

After many sufferings, many anxieties, now too tedious to enumerate, the Virgin entered Jerusalem, the fatal city, in the suite of Jesus Christ, to celebrate the pasch, which he was to make for the last time with his disciples. She beheld the inhabitants of the city of kings coming out in crowds to meet the Son of David, who, mounted like the youthful princes of her race in the olden times, was receiving, with benignity, the unaffected honours which the multitude, all eagerness to catch a glimpse of the prophet, were freely offering him; for Jesus Christ never refused the humble testimonies of gratitude and love presented him by creatures. However slight might have been those pledges of gratitude and affection, they were received by the Divine Goodness at the very moment when they were springing fresh from the heart.

Magdalene, alternately surveying *her Master* and that multitude of people who were making the air resound with their *Hosannas*, wept in silence. Mary's eyes were also moist, but she was looking towards the North-west, in the direction of Calvary.

CHAPTER XVI.

MARY ON CALVARY.

THE olive branches which the Hebrew children had cast under the feet of Christ, lay still strewn with their verdant tufts along the road of Bethania; the echoes of the

valley of cedars* were yet faintly murmuring the dying
notes of joy and gladness, with which the daughter of Sion
had greeted the *poor king*, when Jerusalem became fixed in
silent amazement at an event as novel as it was unprecedented, and fraught with consequences of sad and mighty
import.

The high priests, the Scribes, and Pharisees (thanks to
gold and domestic treachery), had just laid hold of the great
guilty one, who endangered, as they said, both their state
and religion. If the extraordinary proceedings to which
they had recourse be taken as a test, a very dangerous man
indeed we must pronounce him. For the more effectual
seizure of his person,† an extraordinary fast was announced,
alms were bestowed, though not without ostentation, and
for his capture unbounded thanks were returned to *him* who
has declared, that he " abhors the wicked who shed innocent
blood." But the high priests, the learned doctors, and the
Pharisees, enjoyed the first honours, as well as places, under
the Roman governor, who laid his *fasces* heavily on them,
and for whom they, in return, entertained the most inveter-
ate hatred. They were, in truth, *extremely conscientious*
Jews, who would not tolerate the use of the *holy name* in
the cursing of parents by children; very *scrupulous* men,
indeed, who would leave their neighbour in the bottom of
the well, lest by extracting him they might violate the Sabbath; men of *rare probity*, who would plunder none except
the uncircumcised; in fine, men of *inviolate purity*, who were
most careful in not entering the judgment hall on the eve of
a festival, and who, while extorting an unjust sentence,
would take a thousand precautions against being sullied
by contact with the Roman toga.

* The ancient name of the Valley of Josaphat.
† We find this anecdote in the *Toldos*, published by Huldric, pp. 56 and 60.

The boisterous and seditious tones in which they cried out for the punishment of this *great criminal ;* the means to which they had recourse to gain over both the people, whom they ordinarily held in pity and contempt, and the Roman soldiers, for whom they usually entertained no other fellings save those of hatred and aversion, would lead one to think that he was the sworn enemy both of God and man.

The sooner to rid the country of him, no means were left untried, which malice could invent, or hatred suggest.

With unprecedented boldness they trampled on every law, and violated all the ordinary usages of the Israelites.

They constituted themselves his accusers, witnesses, and, by anticipation, even his judges. His executioners, too, they would become, were it not that, in order to fix a stain on his memory, and to deprive him of honour no less than life, they preferred his undergoing an ignominious punishment lately introduced among them, and one which was reserved for the most abandoned wretches.

Thanks to their instigations, never was child of man treated with such refined cruelty, and cold barbarity. Every species of insult and violence was he forced to endure, and like the lamb preparing for the sacrifice, against all these indignities and outrages he made no complaint, he offered no remonstrance.

They placed on his head a crown of thorns, and the wounds caused by their sharp points were many and painful. After divesting him of his under garment, they laid on his shoulders a purple rag; in his hand placed a reed for a sceptre; and then greeted with bitter sarcasms and genuflexions of derision this mockery of royalty. His whole frame, bleeding from the recent scourging, presented the appearance of one vast wound, and on his sweet and affable countenance, now sullied by filthy spittle, were fixed, here and there, black

patches of blood, which flowed from his sacred forehead, and which, from the position of the hands, bound behind his back, he was unable to wipe off.

The high priests, the Scribes, and Pharisees, with heart-felt satisfaction gloated on this scene of blood; for pity appeared to them in no other light than that of degeneracy of soul.*

* M. Salvador, author of the *Mosaical Institution*, in order to exculpate his co-religionists, charges the Roman soldiers with the unheard-of outrages which Jesus received in the judgment hall; but it is quite evident that the Romans acted only through the instigations of the enemies of Jesus Christ. See, on this point, the testimony of St. John Chrysostom: "The Jews are they who themselves condemned Jesus to death, though they may excuse themselves by making use of the name of Pilate. *They wished that his blood should fall on themselves and their children.* They alone were the persons who insulted him— who bound him—who led him to Pilate, and who caused him to be treated so cruelly by the soldiers. Pilate had given no orders to that effect.—*Serm.* 77. *on St. Matt.*

But who was this unhappy man that was subjected to such unheard-of torture? Was he a midnight incendiary, surprised in the act of casting a lighted torch into the Holy of Holies? Was he a remorseless assassin, arrested in his mountain den, or a traitor, preaching revolt through Asia, and inflaming the minds of the populace against Cæsar? No, he was nothing of all this; he was neither an assassin nor rebel; his crimes were of a blacker—a deeper die, more glaring, more unpardonable.

To exhort mankind to fraternal love, and lead all to a glorious state of immortality, was his aim and sole object. He enforced sublime virtues, of which, in his own person, he afforded an example; he loaded Judea with benefits.

This culprit, on whom so many bad passions were glutted, was the descendant of David, Solomon, and Ezechias—Jesus, the great Galilean prophet, who had traversed the popular rejoicings only to reach Golgotha. When the high priests and Pharisees had vilified him before the eyes of the populace, so as to remove every idea they might have conceived of his divinity, the Sabbath pressing on, they take their victim, previously sent back to them, though reluctantly, by Pilate; and after having loaded his yet bleeding and lacerated shoulders with the heavy weight of his cross, they urge on with the shafts of their spears his tardy and mournful march towards Calvary, the place destined for his crucifixion.

Crowds of spectators lined the streets, and encumbered the public ways. Some in high tones of defiance testified a brutal joy, and cried out "anathema" to the Son of God; others took pity on the sad fate of this young prophet, who had, as they well knew, been basely betrayed and sold for no other crime than that of universal philanthropy. But these marks of barren sympathy were scarcely perceptible. The well-disposed mourned in silence; those who were indebted to him for their support in the desert, by the miraculous multiplication of the five loaves; those who felt grateful to him, as being to them the source of health and life; those who were linked to him by the strong ties of love and affection, could scarcely be recognised in the crowd; and not a voice was raised to protest against the inhuman sentence. The apostle who had previously expressed such ardent professions of love, was now after basely denying him! The rest, with one single exception, had cowardly fled.

As he was descending the long line of street which leads to the Judiciary Gate, a woman conspicuous for beauty of person, and for that affable sweetness of demeanour which truly stamps nobleness of origin, rushes through the crowd. She appeared wholly absorbed in silent and inexpressible sorrow. Poignant indeed must be her grief, and great her sufferings, so pallid was her appearance. The look which she fixed on the frightful wounds of the Saviour was so expressive of inward grief and holy sadness, that the women of Jerusalem, on beholding her, were unable to restrain their tears or withhold their expressions of sympathy. "Ah! the poor mother!" said they, in low and faltering tones.

She glided through the populace, who, moved by an instinct of pity and sympathy, fell back to open for her a passage.

Some of the Pharisees, more hardened than the others, were with opprobrious epithets upbraiding Jesus, now bathed in sweat, and expiring under the heavy load of the cross; but she hears them not: the foreign soldiery who surrounded her Son were threatening him with menacing gestures, but she sees them not; but when their spears, the points directed towards her breast, were interposed between her and Jesus, then did there flash from her large and fixed eyes a ray of brightness which revealed the blood of David, and her glowing and inspired countenance assumed such an expression of mournful grandeur and cold contempt of death, that the soldiers, abashed, slowly lowered their arms before the heroic and holy woman. Though wild and truculent in disposition, consequent on military service, the recollection of a mother's claims was not extinct.

Mary directed her faltering steps towards the Saviour — she fixes an agonizing look upon this dejected form, who bleeding and half naked, was trailing along under the crushing burden. She looks on that imposing, compassionate, and sweet countenance, which she feared sullying with the breath of her chaste lips, but which, now blue, livid, covered with blood and filthy spittle, scarcely retained the image of the Creator. She mournfully passes her hand across her brow, as if to ascertain whether or not she were under the influence of some frightful hallucination. Not a groan did she send forth that might solace her oppressed heart; no gesture of despair escaped her, which might lead the bystanders into the secret of her agony.

Once it was thought she was dying; and died indeed she would have a thousand times during this solemn and heartrending pause, if he who " tempers the wind to the shorn lamb," had not by his divine power aided and supported her.

Jesus soon recognises, at some paces distant, this silent and motionless figure, and inclining towards her his head, bent under the burden of the cross, he pronounces the name of mother. * At this word, which sounded in her ears like

---

* Tradition, confirmed by the authority of St. Boniface and St. Anselm, hands down that Jesus Christ saluted his mother by these words : *Salve Mater.* As we again find the holy Virgin at the foot of the cross, this tradition of the fathers seems very probable. " Faith does not destroy these traditions," says Chateaubriand, " they indicate how deeply engraven in the memory of men has been the wonderful and sublime history of the passion. Eighteen cen-

a funeral knell, a poignant grief transpierces the heart of the holy Virgin: a pallid hue overspreads her countenance: she totters: then reeling, she falls headlong on the uneven pavement, already tinged with the traces of blood, which flowed from the wounds of Jesus in his passage.

A young Galilean of a sad and dejected mien, accompanied by a young woman bathed in tears, opened for themselves a passage to where Mary lay prostrate. Thanks to their timely aid, the dolorous Virgin regained the use of her

turies have now flown by; persecutions without end; revolutions without number have not effaced or hidden the traces of a mother who comes to mourn over her son." In memory of the swoon of the Blessed Virgin, there has been erected a church, which was consecrated under the name of Notre Dame du Spasme. "It was here," says Abbe Gerambe, "that Mary, rudely repulsed by the soldiers, met her Son, bearing with difficulty the ignominious wood on which he was to die."

mental faculties, and the consciousness of this physical and moral martyrdom, to which, according to the fathers, no scene recorded in the annals of the martyrs could bear a resemblance.

That John and Magdalene used every exertion to remove her whom they loved and cherished as a mother, from the scene of blood and death which was preparing on Golgotha, there is little doubt: but their earnest entreaties were unavailing: and arising with a strong effort, Mary begins, under a burning sun, the ascent of Calvary's steepest point. This was the shortest and most direct path, and the one through which Jesus had been conducted. *

They had now arrived at the sad term of this mournful pilgrimage. They were now treading the fatal and consecrated ground where the Lamb of God was to satisfy the justice of an offended Deity, by taking the place of all other victims, and charging himself with all our miseries. Here was to be consummated that great sacrifice, the efficacy of which was to be felt in all times, past, present, and future. This little rocky platform was the renovated altar, where was to flow in torrents the blood of Christ, to wash away the sins of the world, and blot out for ever the handwriting of sin and death, which gave us over at our birth to the angels of darkness.

But what has become of the holy victim? Where have his executioners concealed him from the desolate and searching looks of his mother? Mary casts a look of disquietude on the naked mountain. She sees the populace in a state of joyous expectation—the crosses extended on the ground—

---

* " This road, which formerly led to Calvary, and through which the Saviour passed, no longer exists. On the spot are now erected houses, and in the centre there is a large column, which marks the ninth station. Turkish fanaticism has been pleased to cover it over with filth, in order to turn aside the Christians."—*Gerambe, p.* 363.

and the workmen with an air of indifference excavating the ground which was to receive the three instruments of punishment. But where was Jesus then? He makes his appearance, but in what a plight! Stripped even of his under garment, not a shred left to cover his naked flesh and bleeding wounds. Oh! he so pure and chaste! His executioners, ignominiously trailing him along, exposed him for a short time to the derision of the populace. Then the just man was extended on the cross—the bed of glory offered him as the testimony of man's gratitude for his immense love!

Oh! what a dismal spectacle to those who loved him! Mary was borne a few paces distant from this scene, into a grotto naturally formed in the mountain, and there she remains standing upright, cold and white as marble.* Immediately there was heard without a low murmuring sound, like to that of the bees of *Engaddi*, when expelled by the herdsmen of Israel from the hollows of their oaks. Then was there raised on high, in the midst of this dull monotonous sound, a storm of hooting, shouts of derision, and frightful bursts of laughter.

The rabble of every nation were always remarkable for instincts of ferocity; but with regard to this scene, they fell far short of the Hebrews.

During an interval of profound silence, caused undoubtedly by some fresh scene of barbarity, which attracted the attention of the multitude, there was heard the sound of a hammer—a heavy monotonous sound, falling, as it appeared, on wood and mangled flesh. Magdalene, shuddering, presses

---

* "Near the place where the executioners nailed Jesus to the cross, there is a chapel, dedicated to the MOTHER OF SORROWS. Here it was that the Blessed Virgin retired, during the sanguinary preparations for the punishment of her Son."—*Gerambe, p.* 151.

more closely against Mary. The disciple well beloved by Jesus, through an instinctive feeling, assumes an erect position against the grotto.

Again was heard a second stroke, heavier and more stunning than the first. It was followed by two or three others falling at equal intervals, and then all was hushed. "See," was the observation of one of the Roman soldiers to his companion, "they have nailed him to the cross." John and Magdalene interchanged a look of desolation and woe: they were impressed by a feeling similar to that which a person experiences, who, in the midst of a nocturnal tempest, hears the cries of the shipwrecked mariners coming over the wide waste of waters, and then die away one by one in the depths of the sea.

But Mary! a cold perspiration suffuses her whole frame; a convulsive trembling agitates her limbs; she, too, poor, feeble, desolate woman, then felt all the pangs of a crucifixion; for never did confessor extended on a rack—never did a martyr in the midst of flames, experience either in soul or body such excruciating tortures.

Soon is heard the friction of the cords on the pulleys. The cross is slowly raised aloft; and the Son of Man, his face turned towards those regions of the West, which were long in expectation of the light, was hoisted as a standard to the view of infidel nations: so it was written! Then did the reprobate rabble send forth a hoarse and lengthened roar of brutal joy: "Hail! King of the Jews!" "If God loves him, let him deliver him." "If thou art the Son of God, Nazarene, descend." And the robber crucified on his left, in the very rattles of death, also cursed him.

Jesus supporting with calm and majestic dignity his grand character of Prophet and of God-Saviour, sealed in silence with his blood the great doctrines of the New Law. In the midst of the ignominious punishment which he endured in the sight of the whole city, he made no complaint, he uttered no reproach: he casts on this misguided people a look of tender mercy; and seeking to soften divine justice in favour of his executioners—" O my Father," he utters with his dying voice and failing breath, "pardon them; for they know not what they do." And yet, after eighteen centuries, the Father has not yet pardoned them, and they still drag on a miserable existence through the whole earth, and through the whole earth the slave is forced to stoop to get a view of them.*

The Virgin leaves the temporary asylum where she had taken refuge, and with bended head moves on towards the place of punishment. Some paces from the tree of infamy, the rude soldiers were casting lots for the seamless garment, which she had spun and woven with her own hands,† and were contending in tones of violence about the division of the sacred garments which had wrought so many miracles.

A slight convulsive pang passes over the countenance of Mary. She recalled to mind the time when, enriched by the love of Jesus alone, and exempt from her present disquietude, she worked during the evening by his side the tissue of this holiday garment, and the thought as a dart transpierced her heart; for the light in which was presented the happiness of days past, only rendered darker the view of her present misery. She raises her eyes to heaven, to seek, as she was wont, the strength of patient endurance, and her look met that of the crucified God. At this frightful vision, her tottering feet became fixed to the earth. She stands mute and petrified; and so intense was her horror

---

* De la Mennais.
† There is an old tradition that the Blessed Virgin herself had worked the garment of her Son.

and so frightful the shock, that everything she experienced hitherto appeared to her only as a disturbed dream—a fearful but passing vision. The cross absorbed every other consideration.* Jesus, fixing on her a tender and mysterious look, seemed to say to her, as on the eve he said to his apostles: My mother, the hour is come.

What hour? An hour the most memorable, and most pregnant with astounding events, since the creation of the universe—the hour in which the Son of God was to triumph over the world, death, hell, and divine justice itself—the hour in which the prophecies were to be fulfilled, the sacrifices to be abolished, and the human race to be redeemed.

And the Virgin thought she saw passing in review before her eyes the patriarchs, the just kings, the inspired prophets of God, bowing down before Christ as the sheaves of the sons of Jacob before the wonderful sheaf of Joseph. And she thought she beheld Moses and Aaron placing at the foot of the new tree of life the ark of the covenant, the ephod, the golden censor, and the almond-rod—the symbols of the Hebrew priesthood, whose mission was then to cease. And then appeared David placing his prophetic harp by the side of the sword of Phinees, the sacred knife of Abraham, and the brazen serpent.

Priests and victims, rites and ceremonies, types and symbols, grouped about the cross, were awaiting their consummation; and the book with the seven seals of brass lay opened at the feet of the High Priest, according to the order of Melchisedech.

The old world retiring, as wave follows slowly on wave,

---

* The fathers and great doctors of the Church place the sufferings of the Blessed Virgin on Calvary above those of all the martyrs. "The Virgin exceeds all the other martyrs, as much as the sun exceeds the stars," says St. Basil; and St. Anselm adds: "The cruelty inflicted on the bodies of the martyrs was alight in comparison of your suffering."—*De ex Virg.*, v.

gives places to other images. Mary thought she beheld all the nations of the earth awaiting at the foot of the cross to receive the Gospel. Ethiopia and the isles afar off extend their hands towards the Messiah; the desert beginning to rejoice, *blossoms like the rose;* the knowledge of God fills the earth; and a thousand voices seem to repeat, in a thousand different tongues, Christ has conquered, blessed be his name! The noble and generous woman, giving a truce to the poignant sorrows which transfixed her, sympathetically joins in the triumph of the law of grace, of the great social regeneration; but this pleasing vision soon passes away, and sorrow again prevails; like Rachel, Mary bewails her first born, and would not be consoled.

Now all nature is in suffering, and seems to participate in the sorrow of Mary.

The day declines apace, and the waning light casts a mournful tint on the grand and sterile landscape, well assorted to the crime of which it was the theatre. Each instant the darkness becomes thicker; the dew begins to fall through the sudden cessation of heat; the eagles with hoarse cries ascend to their aerie on high; the jackals howl along the side of Cedron; and Calvary, already so forbidden and wild in its aspect, assumes the appearance of a huge black stony *catafalque*. The people, vividly impressed by so extraordinary an event, became still and silent from fear; but sòme isolated and boisterous tones were yet heard—the voices of the Pharisees and high priests cursing Christ.

Soon through the dark veil which covered the face of nature, stars appeared, and like funereal torches glimmering around a coffin, shed on the theatre of the deicide an alarming and greenish light, which gave to the masses of spectators curiously grouped on the sides of Gihon, the appearance of an assembly of demons and spectres. They looked on each other with dismay ; they became pallid with affright.

In vain did the Scribes and Pharisees, now too deeply plunged in the waters of crime to regain the shore, endeavour to attribute this prodigy to natural causes. The longer the sun witholds its light, the less conclusive appears their reasoning. The old men, shaking their hoary heads, affirmed that no such eclipse was ever before seen ; and the learned among them, those versed in the science of the Chaldeans, supported on their side, that no eclipse of that nature was foretold, nor *could* it take place from the position which the moon held.[*]

During this universal alarm, Jesus was engaged with the faithful friends who were ranged around the cross, in this his hour of ignominy and suffering. Affected by the courage of John, and the deep sorrow which this young and loving disciple openly manifested, he wished to leave him a pledge of his divine love. The goods of this world he could not bequeath him, for even a stone whereon to lay his head he had not, and now he was about to receive the charity of a tomb. Of all things there remained to him only his mother ! That mother who had never forsaken him, and whose expressive looks, now fixed on his, seemed to say : " You are my all, you are my father, mother, spouse, son, my God, my life, my treasure ; in losing you, everything is lost, and no

---

[*] Phlegon relates that in the 202nd Olympiad, corresponding with the 33rd of our era, the most extraordinary eclipse of the sun that had ever taken place, had been observed, and that in mid-day the stars appeared in the heavens ; but astronomical observations not pointing out an eclipse in that year, force us to acknowledge that the cause of such universal darkness was entirely supernatural. (M. Roselly de Gorgues *Christ Devant.* b. *Siecle*, p. 367.) " We observed," says St. Denis the Areopagite (who was at that time in Heliopolis,) " that the moon unexpectedly passed between the sun and the earth, although the time of this *conjunction* was not in accordance with the laws of nature, by which the planets are ruled."—*Seventh Epistle to Polycarpe.*

longer have I father, spouse, child. *Nunc orbor patre, viduor sponso, desolor prole omnia perdo.*" He solemnly bequeaths her to his well-beloved disciple, as a pledge of the heavenly inheritance which he reserved for him in the kingdom of his Father. Fully aware of the extent of the love which these holy souls bore him, he in his adorable goodness prevented the frightful loneliness which his death would cause, and wished to strengthen both these unprotected boughs, by entwining their separate branches.

By means of this arrangement, which gave an additional interest in her life, the Virgin was given to understand that to follow her Son to the tomb was not yet granted to her, and that she had not yet arrived at the term of her earthly pilgrimage. She conformed to the decrees of heaven, through love for us, adopted by her in the person of the apostle.

The sacrifice of Mary was closely allied to the sacrifice of Jesus Christ. He willingly consented to die for us—she to live for us! The manner in which Jesus bequeathed Mary to the young fisherman of Bethsaida was simple and dignified, as were all the acts of his mortal life. "Woman, behold your son;" and to the well-beloved disciple: "behold your mother."

If in speaking to Mary he refrained from using a more tender name, the great power and influence of that name it was that caused the omission, as he did not wish to open and cause to bleed anew the wounds but recently closed.

After this, Jesus knowing that all things were accomplished, that the Scriptures might be fulfilled, said: "I thirst!" "Now there was a vessel set there full of vinegar, and they putting a sponge full of vinegar about hyssop, put it to his mouth. Infamous to the last! Jesus having taken the vinegar, says: "All is finished." Then, desirous of proving to the world that he died, not by the power of death, but by a formal act of his own will, he sent forth a loud cry, and bowing down his head, he expired!

At that moment the Idols of paganism tottered on their marble pedestals; the star of Moses, which was to glimmer only for a limited time, sunk below the horizon, and the glorious sun of the Gospel, destined to enlighten the world from pole to pole, and to continue as long as the world should exist, arose in all its splendour and brightness. But the indignity and outrage offered to his Son required on the part of God prodigies and marvels; and the lightnings of heaven were not long withheld. To the supernatural darkness, now clearing away, succeeded an alarming quaking of the earth, which subverted twenty towns in Asia.*

* Pliny and Strabo mention this earthquake. It was so violent, according to these writers, that it was felt even in Italy.

At the same time, the veil of the temple was rent, the rocks were cleft assunder,* and many bodies of the saints, which had long lain in the sleep of death, arose and came into the holy city, where they spread a fresh alarm among the affrighted citizens. Then it was, that a wonderful reaction operated in favour of Jesus. The centurion and the soldiers who presided at the execution simultaneously cried out, that the Nazarene Prophet was certainly more than man; and the immense concourse of people, who had upbraided Christ agonizing with every species of insult and derision, descended the mountain, striking their breasts, and repeating in tones of alarm: He was truly the Son of God! *Vere Filius Dei erat iste!*

In the midst of these piteous cries of the people, who fled without knowing whither, and whilst Golgotha (its flanks all rent) tottered on its old foundation, there was seen by the pale light which shed a sickly lustre on this scene of horror, a woman standing erect and immoveable in the midst of these convulsions and throes of nature. This lone woman seemed altogether unmoved by the universal alarm; with her hands

---

* Addison relates that an English traveller, a professed Deist, visiting Jerusalem, endeavoured to turn into ridicule the explanations given by Catholics respecting the sacred places; but the cleft in the rock disconcerted him not a little; and after examining it carefully, "I begin to be a Christian," said he to a friend who accompanied him. "Natural philosophy has been long the matter of my study; and from philosophical observations, I feel quite convinced that the clefts in the rock could not be produced by an ordinary and natural earthquake. A natural shock would assuredly have split the rock asunder, but then the clefts would be in a far different way. The opening in the rock would follow the course of the veins; but here, in this particular instance, it is quite the reverse. The rock is split transversely; the cleft crosses the veins in an extraordinary and supernatural manner. I then evidently see, that it is the pure effect of a miracle, as it could not be caused by nature or art. And it is for this reason," he adds, "that I return thanks to God for conducting me here to contemplate this monument of his marvellous power—a monument which proves, in the clearest light, the divinity of Jesus Christ."—*Of the Christian Religion, vol. 2, p. 120.*

joined in the attitude of prayer, she appeared wholly absorbed in the contemplation of the crucified Prophet. The women of Jerusalem renewed their tears, and in tones of pity, say " Poor Mother!"

CHAPTER XVII.

THE DEATH OF MARY.

THE sky once more appeared serene, and the signs of the anger of heaven had no longer any terrors for the Jews who had just shed the blood of the Redeemer. Like all blood-thirsty animals, the executioners of Christ were, for a moment, deprived of their brutal instincts at the hour of danger. Alarmed at first at what they had done, they feared lest the rocks torn from Calvary's Mount should crush them in their fall, and lest the earth should open and hurl them alive into the gloomy depths of *Scheol ;* but their remorse vanished with their fears, and seeing the heavens becoming again clear and bright, they lapsed into their wonted revengeful and malevolent dispositions.

Not being able to deny the prodigies which an immense concourse of people had seen with their eyes, and of which the gaping sides of the mountains, the scarcely closed tombs of the dead, and the torn shreds of the veil of the temple were still a standing proof, they attributed them to the power of magic, and maintained that Jesus, who stilled the winds and calmed the billows, by merely holding out his hand, was no other than a son of Belial, who had fascinated the people, and brought the elements under subjection by the influence of the name of the God of Israel, whom he had taken away by surpise from the Holy of Holies.* And the populace allowed this ridiculous story to be pawned on them by their leaders; for there is no calumny, however absurd, which will not find credulous ears to listen to it, and docile tongues to give it circulation. Yet a careful watch, selected from the satellites of the high priest, remained up at night to guard the tomb, for Jesus had announced that on the third day he would arise glorious, and the princes of the synagague affected fear that his disciples would steal him away at night.

The third day had just dawned, and the East was faintly glimmering, when several women of Galilee, bringing gum, myrrh, cinnamon, and other aromatic perfumes for the purpose of embalming Jesus after the manner of the kings of Juda, † made their appearance on the mount of punishment, on their way to the garden where the body of Jesus was deposited. Tradition hands down that Mary was among these holy women. Her dejected mien resembled a fine ruin laid waste by the tempestuous blast of adversity; but her countenance, though expressive of excessive grief and sorrow, yet indicated expectation and hope. Jerusalem, the deicide, enveloped in the mists of morning, was still asleep; the flowers were opening their leaves yet heavy with dew; the birds were gaily warbling on the moist branches of the wild fig-tree; all nature seemed to grow young, and the wild aspect of that desolate region was putting on an appearance of joy and gladness, which it had never before worn, and which seemed to indicate some mystery which had been entrusted to its keeping.

All on a sudden, in the midst of this smiling scene, the

---

* See Basnage, b. 6, ch. 27 and 28.

† It is clear that they intended to embalm Jesus not in the ordinary way, as Nicodemus had already wrapped the body in cloths of myrrh.

earth quakes, and the stone laid against the door of the monument rolls back, as if impelled by some powerful arm; the guards, half dead with fear, are felled to the earth, and the women, who had not deserted Jesus when hanging on the cross, even they recoil, apprehensive of seeing renewed the alarming wonders which attended the death of the Son of Man.

But an angel, his garments as white as the driven snow, and his benign countenance as resplendent as lightning, is seen sitting on the stone of the sepulchre, and words of assurance and hope flow from his lips. "Fear not," he says to the faithful followers of Jesus Christ, "for I know that you seek Jesus who was crucified. He is not here, for he is risen, as he said. Come and see the place where the Lord was laid." Whilst the pious Galileans were entering the tomb, and expressing their surprise on seeing the shroud and the perfumed linen cloths, Mary, motionless from the sudden shock caused by such joyful intelligence, was leaning against an old olive tree, at a short distance from them. A young man, dressed in the garb of a gardiner, was speaking to her in a low tone of voice; this young man was the *first born among the dead*, Jesus Christ, the glorious conqueror of hell. * What occurred during this solemn interview we know not; but that Mary, whose resolute soul had experienced more than mortal sorrow, then felt a degree of joy too much for mortals to endure, we can readily imagine.

---

* St. Ambrose, who lived in the fourth century, says that the Virgin was the first who had the happiness of seeing Jesus after his resurrection; and the poet Sedulius, who flourished a little after the time of St. Ambrose, has consigned this tradition to verse. Both speak of the fact as a belief generally received among the Christians of their times. The Arabian historians have also preserved this tradition: Ismael, son of Ali, mentions that Jesus descended from heaven to console Mary, his mother, who mourned for his loss. An altar was erected on the spot where this interview had taken place.

Our Lord, during the forty days succeeding his resurrection, frequently appeared to his apostles, and spoke to them of the things of heaven and of the regeneration which he was about to operate among men, by means of baptism. Pious authors have supposed that the Virgin was particularly favoured during these consolatory apparitions, and that she then received a foretaste of the happiness of the elect. The bitter waters of her affliction were changed into sources of grace, and the Redeemer *nourished her with that hidden bread reserved by him for those who practise patience as ordained by his holy word.*

At last the hour had come when the divine decrees summoned back Christ to heaven; his mission of redemption was fulfilled, and the apostles, fully convinced of his divinity by the miracle of his resurrection, had received from him the necessary instructions for the conversion of the Gentiles to the Gospel.

On the fortieth day, at noon, he set out with them from Jerusalem, and directed his steps towards the heights of Bethania. That particular way was not taken through mere accident; no, for in that direction lay the mount crowned with olives, where the Redeemer, slipping away from the multitude, had often prayed to his Father, whilst the stars were glittering in the heavens; in that direction the celebrated garden was situated, where his soul, wrestling against the first pangs of agony, had been sad even to death; there, he had found the bitter chalice at which he turned aside his head; there he had bowed down his beautiful face covered with a sweat of blood—bowed it down to that very ground which was soon to be trampled by the feet of assassins. It was but meet that his glory should begin in those very places where his generous sufferings had commenced, and that those fields, those woods and shady groves, which had so often witnessed his meditations and prayers, should receive the last impression of his feet before his ascension into heaven.

Having arrived at the summit of that high mountain, from which could be distinctly seen the Dead Sea, the deep confined waters of the Jordan, and the gigantic palm-trees of the plains of Jericho, the Redeemer stood in an open space, a few paces removed from the olive grove which, afterwards, during the seige of Jerusalem, had been cut down by the Romans. There, after taking a parting look of his mother, his apostles, and the hundred and twenty disciples who were to bear testimony to the illustrious miracle of that solemn hour, *he raised his hands to heaven, blessed them, and whilst he blessed them, he departed from them, and was carried up to heaven.* This final act of the Redeemer worthily closed his divine mission; during his life, *he went about doing good;* on the cross he prayed for his executioners, and whilst ascending into heaven he gave his blessing to those humble friends who were to remain after him in the world. Whilst his hands were as yet extended over his prostrate disciples, they beheld him entering a bright cloud which concealed him from their eyes.

The ascension of our Lord was not attended by those dismal and terrific signs which in olden times had struck so much dismay into the minds of the people. The Mosaical law had been promulgated by the sound of trumpets, by claps of thunder and by vivid flashes of lightning; Elias had been taken up to heaven in a fiery chariot; but the Redeemer of the world was gently carried in a light cloud, with that sort of calm and serene majesty which accords so well with the genius of the Gospel and with the feeling character of its author.

And the angels, those benevolent spirits who rejoice at

man's happiness, figured also in that final scene which closed the grand drama of the redemption. Their heavenly melodies had announced to the shepherds the birth of a royal Messiah, their voices had proclaimed his resurrection from the dead; it was only meet that their words should confirm his glorious ascension.

Whilst the disciples had their eyes attentively fixed on Jesus as he was ascending into heaven, two young men, clothed in white garments, unexpectedly presented themselves before them, and thus addressed them: "Men of Galilee, why stand you looking up to heaven? This Jesus who is taken up from you into heaven, shall come in the same manner as you have seen him ascending."

At the voice of the angels, the apostles and the disciples lowered their dazzled eyes; but did the Virgin also lower hers? Was it not granted to her to see her Divine Son taking his place in all majesty, at the right hand of Jehovah, in light inaccessible? Was she indeed less favoured than St. Stephen and the well-beloved disciple? Such can hardly be presumed. She who had been morally crucified with Jesus on Calvary, deserved to be glorified with him; it was her right, she had dearly purchased it! Yes, Mary's mortal eyes must have been blessed with a view of that blessed and happy country which Jesus had just opened for us by his blood, and where he himself wipes away all tears from the eyes of the just;* then the pearly gates of the heavenly Jerusalem† were slowly closed on God the conqueror; and Mary, separated but only for a short time, from her adorable Son, is left alone in the world, like a severed branch.

Forty days after, we meet with her again in the *cœnaculum*, where, with the apostles, she received the Holy Ghost.

* Apocalypse xxi., 4. † Ib. xxi., 21.

Mary was the luminous pillar which guided the fist steps of the infant Church. To her it was, that the apostles paid homage for the many ears of corn which they plucked in the barren field of the synagogue, to store them up in the granaries of the father of the family. This tribute she gratefully accepted in the name of her Son, and wherever the poor, the unfortunate, and the sinning were found, there she was seen in the midst of them, for she invariably entertained a love of predilection for those on whom she could confer a benefit. To her the evangelists came for light and understanding; the apostles for unction, courage, and constancy; the afflicted for spiritual consolation; the new converts for strength to bear their cross in imitation of Jesus Christ, and to abandon everything to follow him; all parted from her leaving her their blessing. *The Sun of Justice* had set behind the bloody horizon of Golgotha; but the *star of the sea* was still reflecting her most lovely rays over a renovated world, and was shedding a soothing influence over the cradle of Christianity.

The Virgin remained in Jerusalem until the year 44 of Jesus Christ, when a violent persecution raised against the Christians forced her and the apostles to quit it. Her adopted son then conducted her to Ephesus, whither Magdalene was desirous to accompany her. These noble souls were united at the foot of the cross by chains of adamant, which death alone had severed, and which are now re-united in heaven.

Nothing has been handed down to us respecting Mary's stay at Ephesus; but the peculiar and pressing engagements of that period will easily account for the omission. After the resurrection of the Redeemer, the apostles, exclusively engaged in propagating the faith, deemed everything not directly connected and bound up with this all-absorbing question as of secondary importance. Full of their high mission, entirely devoted to the salvation of souls, they were so far forgetful of self, that only a few documents, and even these incomplete, of the evangelical labours which changed the face of the world, have been handed down to us. Their history may be well compared to a splendid but nearly effaced epitaph, which you cannot well decipher either above or below. That the mother of Jesus shared the lot of the apostles, we can easily conceive; the closing years of her life spent far from Jerusalem in a strange land, where no remarkable event signalized her stay, present to us only a smooth polished surface, which has left no lasting impression on the fleeting memory of man. However, the flourishing state of the Church of Ephesus, and the high eulogium which St. Paul passed on its piety, sufficiently indicate the fruitful labours of the Virgin, and that the blessings of heaven accompanied her wherever she went. *The rose of Jesse* exhaled a little of her perfume in the air, and this trace, slight though it be, throws a charming light on her passage.

The coast of Asia Minor, studded with opulent cities, enjoying a high state of cultivation, and kissed by a sea literally furrowed by numerous vessels, would, in the eyes of ordinary exiles, amply compensate for the high and rocky mountains of Palestine; but it may well be doubted that the Blessed Virgin thought so. The footsteps of the Man-God had not hallowed that delightful land, and the bones of her fathers were not there laid!.. ...

Many a time and oft, when sitting under a plane tree, on the shore of the beautiful Icarian Sea, its waves noiselessly breaking at the foot of the myrtle in a confined sandy bay, did Mary and Magdalene, as they followed with their eyes a Grecian galley directing its course towards Syria, call up the remembrance of the land that gave them birth! The immaculate snows of Libanus, the blue summits of Carmel, the limpid waters of Lake Tiberias became then the fond topic of conversation; the different sites of the absent country, rendered more beautiful by its distance, passed in review before them, and seemed a thousand times preferable to the smiling and voluptuous Iona, which bore the same resemblance to the land of Jehovah as the lyre of Anacreon had resembled the harp of David.

It was during her stay at Ephesus that Mary lost her faithful companion, who, like Ruth, had quitted her country and her home to follow her beyond the seas; Magdalene breathed her last, and Mary mourned her as Jesus had wept for Lazarus.*

Of all these affectionate and parental ties, there now remained to the Virgin only St. John—the amiable and well-beloved disciple bequeathed to her by her dying Son; she accompanied him, it is thought, during his missionary career, and there can be no doubt that, to his frequent interviews with her, we may, in some measure, ascribe that high and sublime knowledge which he unfolds in his gospel.

Aided by the lights of her whom the holy fathers have compared to the golden chandelier with the seven branches, the young fisherman of Bethsaida entered more deeply than

* In some Greek writers of the seventh and following centuries we read, that after the ascension of Jesus Christ, Mary Magdalene accompanied the Blessed Virgin and St. John to Ephesus: that she there died and was interred. Such also is the opinion of Modestus, patriarch of Jerusalem, who flourished in the year 920; of St. Gregory of Tours, and of St. Guillebaud. The last-named writer, in his description of his journey to Jerusalem, says that he saw the tomb of Mary Magdalene at Ephesus. The Emperor Leon, the philosopher, removed the remains of the saint from Ephesus to Constantinople, and deposited them in the church of St. Lazarus, in the year 890. Another tradition, supported by the learned, hands down that St. Mary Magdalene ended her days in Provence; we have adopted the contrary opinion, as the more probable, but leave the question undecided.

any other of the evangelists into the incomprehensible mystery of the uncreated essence of the Word, and took a flight so bold into the mystical heights of heaven, that compared with him, the other evangelists, all-perfect, and all-inspired as they are, only skim the earth.*

Meantime, the sowers of Christ had sown the good grain of God's word through every part of the Roman world; the evangelical seed was springing up in green and verdant blades, and the workmen of the Lord of the heritage laboured with holy ardour in the sacred soil. Mary judged that her mission on earth was fulfilled, and that the Church could henceforward support herself of her own innate strength. Then, like a wearied reaper seeking the shade and rest at noon, she began to sigh after the delightful shades of the tree of life, planted near the throne of the Lord, and for those limpid and sanctifying streams by which it is watered.† He who sounds the inmost depths of the soul, surprised this longing desire in Mary's heart, and the angel who sits at his right descended to acquaint the future Queen of Heaven, that her Son had not been unmindful of her prayer.‡

Before taking a final farewell of this perishable and transitory world, which she always considered a place of pilgrimage, Mary expressed a wish to see once more the sites of the redemption. St. John, who invariably considered her slight-

---

* The Abbe Rupert, in his first book on the *Canticle of Canticles*, informs us that the Blessed Virgin supplied, by her extraordinary lights, whatever the Holy Ghost—who was given according to measure to the Apostles—had not made known to them; and the holy fathers unanimously say, that it was from the Blessed Virgin St. Luke received his account of the many wonderful and particular circumstances of Jesus Christ's infancy.

† Apocalypse xxii., 1, 2.

‡ "There is a tradition that the Blessed Virgin received the news of her death through the ministry of an angel, who informed her of the particular day and hour."—*Nicephorus*, b. 2, c. 21.

est wishes in the light of commands, commenced preparations at once to lead her back to the scenes of her early years.

The Hebrew travellers embarked, not at Smyrna, being only a poor village since its destruction by the Lydians, but probably at Mileto, into the secure haven of which entered all the vessels of Europe and Asia, plying in those seas. During their passage through the Grecian Archipelago, the Virgin and the evangelist recognised the Isle of Chios, whose inhabitants, long in possession of the empire of the sea, introduced the degrading practice of slave dealing, a practice which the Gospel was gradually to abolish; then Lesbos, that country of lyric poets, where the hymn to the Immaculate Virgin was to succeed the burning odes of Sappho, and the more vigorous stanzas of Alcæus. On beholding the temple of Esculapius—its spire almost piercing the clouds—which attracted an immense concourse of strangers into the Isle of Cos, the mother of the Redeemer of men brought to mind the remembrance of her Divine Son, who alone, when on earth, had the power of saying to physical and moral sufferings, "depart," and to death, "let go your prey."* Delos, the cradle of Apollo, Rhodes, the cradle of Jupiter, rise up in succession out of the waters, with their verdant hills and antique temples crowded with gods, which were soon to be banished to the infernal regions by the God crucified on Golgotha. At some distance from Cyprus, they distinguished, in the region of the clouds, a dark murky spot clearly delineated against the blue vault of the heavens; it was the mound on which the prophet

---

* "The followers of Mahomet have preserved, by means of tradition, the recollection of the miracles of Jesus Christ. They pretend that the breathing of our Lord, called by them *bed Messih*, the breathing of the Messiah, not only raised the dead but could infuse life even into inanimate things."—*D'Herbelot Bibliothéque.*

Elias had erected, in the days of old, an altar to the future mother of Christ, and where his disciples were at that very time about placing themselves under her all-powerful patronage. Next day the galley, propelled by oars, entered a port of Syria, Sidon perhaps, a city which then carried on an extensive trade with Palestine, as the Sacred Scriptures remark.

Immediately on their arrival at Jerusalem, the Virgin retired to Mount Sion, situated a short distance from the crumbling palaces of the princes of her blood, and entered the house which had been rendered sacred by the descent of the Holy Ghost. St. John left her for a moment, in order to acquaint St. James, first bishop of Jerusalem, and the faithful composing his rapidly increasing church, that the Mother of Jesus returned to breathe her last among them.

The day, the hour had at last arrived. The holy of Jerusalem paid a visit to the daughter of David, and beheld her poor, humble, lovely as she had always been ; for it might well be said, that that delightful and blessed creature escaped the destructive action of time, and that predestined from her birth to a complete and glorious immortality, no perishable ingredient entered into the composition of her frame.* Serious, but not indisposed, she received the apostles and the disciples, reclining on a small couch of unpretending appearance, and in perfect keeping with the dress worn by her, a dress peculiar to women of humble descent—and one which she never laid aside. In her dignified yet modest bearing, there was something so solemn and affecting, that on looking at her, those assembled could not restrain their tears.

Mary alone remained unmoved in that spacious and lofty

* St. Dionysius, an eye-witness of the Blessed Virgin's death, mentions that even at that advanced period of her life, her countenance was strikingly lovely.

chamber, where a great many old disciples and new Christians, desirous of seeing her, were collected around her.

It was nightfall, and the lamps suspended by brazen chains from the ceiling were casting a flickering, lurid glare on that silent assembly, which imparted a new feature of solemnity to the scene. The apostles, deeply affected, were standing around the bed of death. St. Peter, who entertained such an affectionate love for the Son of God during life, was mournfully contemplating the Virgin, and his speaking look seemed to say to the bishop of Jerusalem: "What a strong resemblance between her and Jesus Christ!" The resemblance was indeed striking,* and the reclining position of Mary, recalling to mind that of the Redeemer during the Last Supper, rendered the likeness perfect. St. James, surnamed the *Just*, by the Jews themselves, endeavouring to master his feelings, drank the tears collected around his pupils. The prince of the apostles, a man of candour and impulse, was deeply affected, and made no exertion to conceal his emotion; St. John buried his face in the skirt of his Grecian robe, but his sobs betrayed him. Among all those there assembled, not a heart was there that was not broken, not an eye that was not moist. After a moment's recollection, Mary fixed her eyes on those faithful servants who were all united in love for Christ, and who were, in some time after, to give proofs of it in the midst of tortures. She spoke, and her musical voice assumed an expression so tender, so deeply affecting, and at the same time so consoling, that every feeling of sorrow was for the time suppressed. She told them that the filial attachment which they had shown her could alone cause her to regret

---

* "Jesus Christ's head was somewhat bent, and so he did not appear as tall as he really was; his countenance strongly resembled that of his mother, particularly the lower part of it."—*Niceph. Ch. His.*

life: that she had ardently looked forward to the day which should reunite her to her Son for an eternity; and that she was grateful to God for abridging the time of her mortal pilgrimage. After a promise that they should always receive aid and protection from her, and that, though surrounded by the splendours of the heavenly court, she would never forget that she had been a daughter of man, she gave them a sublunary view of the grandeurs of heaven, and her ideas became of a nature so elevated, and her reflections so sublime, that each and every one of them forgot, in his ravishing delights, that the swan was chanting her death note. But the eventful hour was at hand. Mary extends her protecting hands over those children which she was about leaving behind her as orphans, and raising her beautiful eyes towards the stars which were glittering without in serene majesty, she sees the heavens opened, and the Son of Man descending in a luminous cloud, to receive her at the confines of eternity. At this view a rosy tint overspreads her countenance; in her eyes is depicted everything which maternal love, ecstatic joy, infinite adoration, could express; and her soul, quitting, without effort, her mortal frame, drops sweetly into the bosom of God.*

* Some of the ancient fathers, and among others, St. Epipharius, had their doubts as to whether the Mother of God, really died, or had been taken up alive, body and soul into heaven; but the Church inclines to the opinion that the Blessed Virgin really died; and in the Oration of the Mass on the day of the Assumption, she plainly indicates such. The Blessed Virgin died on the eve of the 15th of August. The date of her death is very uncertain. Eusebius fixes it in the forty-third year of our era; and, so, Mary must have been sixty-eight years old. But Nicephorus, b. xi., chap. 21, expressly says, that she ended her days in the fifth year of the reign of Claudius, being the seven hundred and ninety-eighth year of Rome, or the forty-fifth of the vulgar era. In the supposition that she was sixteen years of age at the birth of our Lord, she must then be sixty-one years of age at the time of her death. Hippolytus of Thebes tells us in his Chronicle that the Blessed Virgin was sixteen years old at the time of Christ's birth, and that she survived him eleven years. Ac-

Mary was no more; but her countenance, which had assumed the appearance of a light and tranquil repose, presented such a lovely expression, that it might well be said that death hesitated to plant his banner on that trophy, the possession of which he could not secure even for one day.

The lamp of death was lighted; every window was opened, and the summer breeze, together with the pale rays of the stars, entered the apartment. It is said, that a miraculous light filled the chamber of death at the very instant that Mary had breathed forth her last sigh; the glory of God it might be, which encompassed the stainless soul of the predestined Virgin. When the death of Mary no longer admitted of doubt, deep sighs and sobs were heard on every side; then the canticles of death ascended on high during the silence of night; the angels sung out an accompaniment on their golden harps,* and the echoing tones of the crumbling palace of David were mournfully reverberated at the tombs of the kings of Juda.

On the day following the faithful brought in profusion the rarest perfumes and the finest linens, for the interment of the queen of virgins. She was embalmed according to the custom of her country; but her blessed remains exhaled a more savory odour than the perfumed cloths in which she had been wrapped. The funeral service being over, the Mother of God was laid on a portable bier filled with aromatics:† it was covered over by a gorgeous veil,

---

cording to the authors of *The Art of Verifying Dates*, the Virgin had been sixty-six years old at the time of her death.

* "All the heavenly host," says St. Jerome, "surrounded the Mother of God at the moment of her death, and chanted forth hymns and canticles, which were heard by every one present. Militiam cœlorum cum suis agminibus, festive obviam venisse Genitrici Dei, cum laudibus et canticis, eamque ingenti lumine circum fulsisse et usque ad tronum perduxisse."

† "The bier used by the Jews, at the time of Mary, was a sort of couch, so constructed that the body could be easily carried; this couch was filled with

and the apostles claimed the honour of bearing it on their shoulders to the garden of Gethsemane.* The Christians of Jerusalem, carrying lighted torches, and chanting hymns and psalms, walked (grief and sorrow depicted on every countenance) in the funeral procession of Mary.†

Having arrived at the place of interment, the funeral *cortége* halted. Through the careful attentions of the holy women of Jerusalem, the grave was stripped of everything that might have a repulsive aspect, and the sepulchral grotto presented the appearance of a bower of roses.‡ The apostles laid the bier gently down, and whilst doing so shed copious tears.

Of all the panegyrics pronounced on the occasion, that of Hierotheus was the most remarkable. St. Dionysius, the Areopagite, who as an eye-witness, gives an account of this scene, mentions, that in his eulogy on the Virgin, the orator spoke as if inspired.§

During three days the apostles and the faithful watched and prayed at her tomb, and the angelic choirs seemed to fling a charm over the last sleep of Mary.‖

aromatics. Josephus, in his description of the funeral of Herod the Great, says, ' that his body was carried upon a golden bier, embroidered with very precious stones of great variety, and covered over with purple; he had a diadem and a crown of gold upon his head; about the bier were his sons and funeral relations.' These honours were paid Mary with great magnificence: the rarest perfumes were scattered over her body, which was wrapped up in a magnificent shroud and laid on a bier, which the apostles themselves carried on their shoulders."—*Metaph. Greg. of Tours. Juv.*

* Gre. de Assump. Dam. Niceph., b. 1. chap., 2.
† Father Croiset, p. 143.
‡ Gre. Tours. Juve. Op. Eup., b. 3, chap. 4.
§ Book of Divine Names, chap. 3.
‖ Juvenal, patriarch of Jerusalem, who lived in the fifth century, writing to the Emperor Marcian and the Empress Pulcheria, said, that "the apostles, watching in turn, remained up day and night at the tomb of the Virgin, mingling their voices with those of the angels, who, during three days were heard pouring out the most celestial music."

An apostle, on his return from a distant country, and who had not been present at the death of Mary, arrived in the meantime at Gethsemane: it was Thomas, he who had put his finger into the wounded side of his Master after his resurrection. He hastened at once to take one last look of the cold remains of that privileged woman, who had borne in her chaste womb the Sovereign Master of nature. Prevailed on by his earnest solicitations and tears, the apostles removed aside the stone which closed up the entrance to the sepulchre; but, lo! they found only the yet scarcely withered flowers on which the body of Mary had reposed, together with the white shroud of fine Egyptian linen exhaling a celestial odour. The most pure body of the immaculate Virgin was not left a prey to the grave-worms. During her life, earth and heaven equally contributed to the formation of this noble creature: after death, heaven not content with a part, had taken her entire, and glorified her entire.*

* " Godescard makes a very judicious remark, which strongly confirms the doctrine of the Assumption: ' Neither the Latins, nor even the Greeks, a people fond of novelty, and so credulous in everything regarding relics, stories, and legends; no nation, not even a single city or church, have ever laid claim to the possession of the mortal remains of the Blessed Virgin, not even of the smallest particle of her body. Again, without prescribing the belief of the corporal assumption of Mary into heaven, the Church conceals not her leaning towards that belief.'—*Godescard*, vol. 14, p. 449. A beautiful church has been erected over the tomb of the Virgin. You enter it by a flight of fifty steps; the tomb of the Blessed Virgin is the eastern transept of the church; about the centre of the marble balustrade, you see on one side the monument of St. Joseph, and on the other that of St. Joachim, and that of St. Anne. This church is now in the hands of the Greek schismatics, who took it from the Latins."—*Annals of the Propagation of the Faith*, vol. 28, p. 519.

THE END.

www.ingramcontent.com/pod-product-compliance
Lightning Source LLC
Chambersburg PA
CBHW021356230426
43666CB00006B/543